SINGLE PARENTING THAT WORKS

Six keys to raising happy, healthy children in a single-parent home

DR. KEVIN LEMAN

Tyndale House Publishers, Inc., Carol Stream, Illinois

Visit Tyndale's exciting Web site at www.tyndale.com

TYNDALE is a registered trademark of Tyndale House Publishers, Inc.

Tyndale's quill logo is a trademark of Tyndale House Publishers, Inc.

Single Parenting That Works: Six Keys to Raising Happy, Healthy Children in a Single-Parent Home

Designed by Jennifer Lund

Edited by Ramona Cramer Tucker

To protect the privacy of those who have shared their stories with the author, some details and names have been changed.

Unless otherwise indicated, all Scripture quotations are taken from the *Holy Bible,* New International Version®. NIV®. Copyright © 1973, 1978, 1984 by International Bible Society. Used by permission of Zondervan. All rights reserved.

Scripture quotations marked NASB are taken from the *New American Standard Bible,* © 1960, 1962, 1963, 1968, 1971, 1972, 1973, 1975, 1977 by The Lockman Foundation. Used by permission.

Scripture marked "The Message" taken from *THE MESSAGE.* Copyright © 1993, 1994, 1995, 1996, 2000, 2001, 2002. Used by permission of NavPress Publishing Group.

Library of Congress Cataloging-in-Publication Data

Leman, Kevin.
   Single parenting that works : six keys to raising happy, healthy children in a single-parent home / Dr. Kevin Leman.
     p. cm.
   Includes bibliographical references and index.
   ISBN-13: 978-1-4143-0334-5 (hc : alk. paper)
   ISBN-10: 1-4143-0334-3 (hc : alk. paper)
   ISBN-13: 978-1-4143-0335-2 (sc : alk. paper)
   ISBN-10: 1-4143-0335-1 (sc : alk. paper)
   1. Single parents. 2. Single-parent families. 3. Children of single parents. 4. Parenting. 5. Parent and child. 6. Parenting—Religious aspects—Christianity. I. Title.
HQ759.915.L46 2006
649'.10243—dc22
                                        2005030822

Printed in the United States of America

12 11 10 09 08 07 06
7   6   5   4   3   2   1

This book is dedicated to you, single parent,
because of all the sacrifices you're making to raise your kids well.
You've got a tough job,
but you're making a difference.
The payoff someday is going to be great!

Contents

Acknowledgments

Move over, Anne Sullivan. I've found the real miracle worker—
my fantastic editor, Ramona Cramer Tucker. What a great job
and great insight you bring to every project we work on together.
If ever there was a person who could squeeze blood from a turnip,
Ramona, it's you. Thank you for everything.

Introduction
You *Can* Do It!

No one needs to tell you that single parenting is tough. After all, you're right in the trenches.

You're the one who has been up countless nights with babies and toddlers, with no one to spell off the diaper, bottle, or sippy-cup sessions. You've spent other sleepless nights wondering how you'll scrape together the money for rent this month.

You're the one who has wiped away tears when a first grader asks, "How come I don't have a daddy?"

You're the one who has been caught off guard when your fifth grader asks, "Why don't you and Mom love each other anymore? Will you stop loving me, too?"

You're the one who has stood, speechless and worried, watching your all-of-a-sudden teenage daughter getting ready for a date. As a dad, you've tried your best to explain the male side of things about sex and dating, but you wish she had a female to talk to. You wish her mother could have lived to see this moment.

You're the one who has felt like the odd shoe with no match in sight.

You're the one who has felt "different"—even ostracized—at church or by "religious folks," just because of your lack of a wedding ring. You wonder if others are eyeing you suspiciously or steering clear of you because they assume you're "out to get a spouse" (even if it means stealing theirs).

You're the one who has felt truly alone when your children are with your ex. Even if you've looked forward to a break from them—and the rejuvenation of having a minute to yourself—you can't wait until they come home to you again.

Does anyone else feel this way? you wonder.

Did you know

- there are currently 12 million single-parent family groups in the United States, and 10 million of those are maintained by women?[1]
- 20 million of all children in the United States under the age of eighteen live with only one parent?
- 84 percent of children who live with one parent live with their mother?[2]
- 32 percent of all births are to unmarried women?[3]
- the number of single mothers (9.8 million) has remained constant while the number of single fathers grew 25 percent in three years to 2.1 million in 1998? That means men now comprise one-sixth of the nation's single parents.[4]

Did you also know that, of children living with one parent,

- 38 percent live with a divorced parent?
- 35 percent live with a never-married parent?
- 19 percent live with a separated parent?
- 4 percent live with a widowed parent?
- 4 percent live with a parent whose spouse lives elsewhere because of business or some other reason?[5]

Clearly, you are not alone! Numerous single parents have walked this same road in the past, and many others are walking it with you right now. Let's say it up front: *All* parenting has its challenges—its twists, turns, and even a few roadblocks where you have to stop, think, and evaluate. And you already know that single parenting has some additional challenges. You're living through them right now, or you wouldn't have picked up this book.

But is single parenting doable? Certainly!

How do I know? Over nearly forty years, I have counseled and spoken to thousands of single parents and their children as they have made their journeys through life. So many come into my office with defeat written across their faces. They struggle to put one foot in front of the other, day after day. They are, simply, exhausted—not to mention financially, emotionally, and physically stressed.

Those single parents ask complex questions, and rightfully so. No doubt that they—and you—have significant challenges going it solo while raising children.

As the statistics show, and you know firsthand, there are many ways to become a single parent.

You may be divorced—and going through either the pain of a disinterested ex or an active battle with your ex.

You may always have been a single parent—through your child's birth or adoption.

Or you may have become a single parent when your spouse died.

No matter your "category" or whether you are female or male, it's up to *you* to decide what to do next. And it all starts with how you view your challenges on a day-to-day basis. Do they tend to depress you and incapacitate you, or do they make you even more determined to make it work?

If you want to succeed as a single parent, keep this in mind: Challenges are simply *challenges*, not insurmountable obstacles. And what any challenge requires is an extra dose of courage and determination, along with wisdom and advice for how to best approach it.

For years, I've seen single parents and their children not merely survive, but *thrive* together. They have developed loving, respectful relationships that take them over the puddles of life and through the deep waters. (In this book, you'll hear from some of them about their real-life challenges and what has happened to them long-term.) Although single parenting was not the choice for most of them, they have made single parenting work.

And you can, too.

I won't fool you by saying the path will be easy. After all, what parent's road is easy? And you already know better than that, so you'd know I was blowing smoke.

But just remember: Nothing that's truly valuable in life ever comes without cost.

There will be sweat. There will be tears. But with hard work and perseverance, you can do it. *Single Parenting That Works* provides six keys to help you unlock the door to a new and different way of living that will give you a balanced, healthy, loving environment where you and your children can move ahead with confidence.

KEY 1: CREATE A PLAN.

Nobody can do it all, but looking at the whole picture of your life—where you are right now and where you want to be—will give you great perspective to help you walk into the future.

KEY 2: KNOW YOURSELF, KNOW YOUR CHILD.

Do you long to be the best parent you can be? (Note that I didn't say "a perfect parent." If you're striving for perfection, you're fighting a losing battle. I should know—I've failed multiple times with my five children, yet they still love me.) Before you can figure out what makes your kid tick, you need to know what makes *you* tick. And there's a bonus, too—I'll reveal the three deadliest mistakes you can make as a single parent and show you how to sidestep them.

KEY 3: GATHER A TEAM.

When you're pressed for time and money and you need support, whom do you go to? Being a lone ranger can get lonely and exhausting, so don't be afraid to ask for help. (Surprisingly, you may just help others in the process!) Other adult role models—especially opposite-sex role models—are crucial to the well-being of your child. I'll explain why.

KEY 4: FOCUS ON THE ABCS.

Hopefully you learned them in preschool or kindergarten, so now we'll give them a new twist. All children long for Acceptance, Belonging, and Competence. We'll talk about how important this foundation is for every child, how to establish it in your home, and how to balance rules, love, and limits that will bring health to your child and to your home—and sanity to you.

KEY 5: KNOW WHAT TO SAY AND DO WHEN KIDS ASK . . .
Hard questions come up in every home—often at the most embarrassing or inopportune times. When they do, what should you say or do? This part will provide specific advice for those who are divorced, widowed, and never married, so read the chapter(s) that applies to you. (It's okay to sneak a peek at the others, too. You or a friend might find them helpful.)

KEY 6: REALIZE IT'S NOT ABOUT YOU,
IT'S ABOUT THE KIDS . . . FOR NOW.
Single parenting is a lonely job, with long hours and few breaks for "you" time. When you look at how many hours you have in the day, how do you want to spend them? Are you ready to launch out onto the dating scene? Do you wonder if the time has come to marry or marry again? What kind of parent do you want to be—in the long run? Now is the time to decide.

❈ ❈ ❈

Thousands of single parents have discovered that if they put these six keys into practice, they can meet any challenge that comes their way.

And so can you.

As a mom or dad, you are uniquely suited to make an indelible imprint on your child. But what will that imprint be?

In *Single Parenting That Works*, I'll ask you to reflect. I'll ask you to evaluate. I'll ask you to dream. I'll ask you to problem solve. And I'll encourage you to move ahead. At the end of each chapter you'll find three "Key Qs." You may want to think about these questions in private, use them as a topic of conversation over coffee with a friend, or use them as discussion starters in a single-parent group.

Although you can't see the future clearly today, I think someday you'll look back. You'll wonder at the children you've raised—children who are now confident adults, making their own way and their own impact on the world.

And you'll be amazed and humbled at how much has truly been

accomplished. How all the love, the time, the joy, and the tears over the years have culminated in a legacy you are proud to leave behind when you exit this world.

For what better legacy could you leave the world than a child who one day will in all sincerity tell others, "I wouldn't be where I am today without my mom/dad"?

You can do it.

One step at a time, with determination and courage.

I guarantee it.

❋ ❋ ❋

KEY Q̲s̲ . . .

- What's your biggest fear as a single parent?

- Do you believe the statement "Nothing that's truly valuable in life ever comes without cost"? Why or why not?

- If you could pick one character quality you'd want your child to have for a lifetime, what would it be? Explain.

KEY 1

CREATE A PLAN

If you want your kids to be happy
and healthy and successful,
the best place to start
is by looking at the whole picture
of your life and creating a plan.

CHAPTER 1

You Can't Do It All, but You Can Do What Matters Most

It's a typical Monday, and everything that could possibly become complicated in your life has done exactly that. Your new boss has asked you to put in overtime hours for the next week since another employee is on vacation. He wants you to start tomorrow. You're not sure how you're going to juggle the child care or getting everything else done at night with two hours less to do it in.

You've just picked up your two kids, who are five and eighteen months, from the sitter they really love. The problem is she's only available until 4:30 on weekdays, and your boss wants you to work until 6:30 for the next week. You didn't say no, but you didn't say yes either. Somehow between tonight and tomorrow you'll have to figure out how to keep everybody in your life happy.

You zoom home, feed the kids some leftover spaghetti—their favorite dinner—as you keep your eye on the clock. Thankfully, your son's 5:30 T-ball practice is just around the corner. You have enough time to pack up some Gatorade for him, put juice in a sippy cup for your daughter, and get them both tucked back into their car seats with a couple minutes to spare. You're feeling pretty proud of yourself for keeping to your schedule.

Then you smell something rotten. You've already changed little Tara's diaper once, before dinner. Now it looks like round two. You sigh, have your son start the process of tying his shoes, and go back to the bedroom to change the baby's diaper again.

As you're wiping her bottom clean of unmentionable goo, the phone rings. You grab it without thinking. "Hello?"

"Mrs. Williams?"

"Yes," you manage.

"This is Skye Jackson from KWOW Radio. You entered our contest back in February, and I'm happy to tell you that you've been selected for an all-expenses-paid trip for two to Hawaii!"

What's your first thought?

If you're like most single parents, before you imagine lounging in a hammock under palm trees and humming along to ukulele music, your first thought is probably, *What about the kids?!*

Whether you've just become a single parent, or whether you've been one for eleven years, this is the question that surfaces again and again: what about the kids?

When it's just you caring for them, how can you do the best with the resources you have? How can you manage to raise healthy kids? And how can you cope with a life that wasn't what you chose or what you thought it would be?

Great Expectations

Someone once said, "Life is a continuous process of getting used to what we hadn't expected." And certainly few turns in life are more unexpected than that of becoming a single parent.

Never in your wedding daydreams did you imagine that your walk together from the church altar down the aisle would one day continue on to the courthouse. As you were signing your marriage license, you weren't thinking, *Let's get one thing clear, sweetheart: In five years, you have your attorney call my attorney!*

You didn't expect your husband to walk out on you for another woman, or your wife of nine years to decide she needed to go off and "find herself."

You certainly didn't expect the visit from the police to tell you that your wife had died in a car accident while driving home from the grocery store.

You didn't expect to end up pregnant by your boyfriend, who now doesn't want anything to do with you or the child.

Losing a mate through divorce, death, or separation is one of the most heart-wrenching experiences a person can endure. You can sign up for marriage prep courses, but nothing can prepare you for these losses. One study showed that of life's most stressful experiences, the death of a spouse ranks highest, and few experiences in life rank more stressful than divorce.[1]

So if you're feeling stressed as a single parent, it's no wonder! All single parents wonder at one time or another, *Can I really do this? Are my kids going to be okay? Am I going to be okay? Life is just so different than I expected. . . .*

But just because your life has taken a different direction than you planned doesn't mean that you should throw in the towel. That you should give up on helping your kids be the healthiest they can be

> You've got something that no two-parent families have. And you can use it to the best of your advantage.

emotionally, physically, mentally, and spiritually. Instead, you'll need to focus your energies more intensely. If you look at the whole picture of your life and create a plan for where you want to go, individually and as a family, you have a great shot at fulfilling some great *new* expectations.

Yes, you'll have to work through some issues along the way. You may be sleep deprived since your seven-year-old daughter got the flu the night before your sales presentation. Your idea of a break may be downgraded from an hour of exercising at the local gym each morning to relishing a long stoplight or a few quiet minutes in the bathroom. If the technology to be two places at once is ever released, single parents will be the first in line to buy it.

But guess what? You've got something that no two-parent families have. And you can use it to your advantage.

Singled Out

I'll let you in on a secret. As a high schooler, I was always in trouble. Throwing water balloons in class and crawling out of the classroom on my hands and knees while the teacher was up at the board earned me a reputation among my fellow students as the class clown. Others knew me as a troublemaker for such outrageous pranks as tossing a lit match into the English classroom garbage can.

In my more "mature" moments, I'd pull everyone else into my acts. I once had the whole class bring in alarm clocks, set to go off at the same time. (Now there's a good way to frazzle a teacher!) I also organized students to crumple up newspaper and dump it in a huge pile in one of the school's corridors. That was only the start to my brazen creativity.

To slip by the administration's rule against water pistols at school, I once took a dictionary and, with a razor, cut a hollow out of the pages inside so I could carry mine wherever I went. I'd simply open the book, whip out the pistol, and squirt one of the teachers from across the hall. Then, before he or she knew what had hit, I'd swiftly hide the evidence. (Not that any of my teachers would have had a difficult time recognizing that Kevin Leman with a dictionary wasn't exactly the best of disguises.)

But my antics came with a high price academically. I was back in the same class because I failed for the third year in a row.

One day my geometry teacher, Miss Eleanor Wilson, pulled me aside. "Kevin, I've watched your antics. I know your family. It seems to me that if you applied yourself, you could really do something in life."

My jaw literally dropped.

It wasn't like someone had never challenged me to get serious. (There'd certainly been plenty of opportunities to do so.) In fact, I'd had a lot of people say to me, "Come on, Kevin. You better get your act together!" But Miss Wilson's challenge marked one of the first times I'd ever heard someone outside my family say, in essence, "Kevin, I believe you have the ability to do something significant with your life."

While others saw a big, red F written on my forehead, she saw a mind full of potential. She believed in me, and that belief made all the difference. Without her tutoring—on her own time, I will point out—I probably never would have graduated from high school.

I will always be grateful to this one woman who believed in me, even when everybody else thought I was a complete goof, a frustrating flunky, and a total clown.

When you were young, who believed in you? Who believed that you were capable of great things, even if you hadn't done them yet? even if you were doing the exact opposite to try to prove that person wrong?

Why did she (or he) make such an impact on you? Was it because she focused on your potential rather than your shortcomings?

Did you know that the most significant predictor of a child's development is not the opportunities you offer through education, material comforts, or even the number of hours you clock together as a family? *The most significant predictor of a child's successful development is the positive expectation you set for him or her. The belief that "you can do it," come what may.*

That puts a different spin on all the things you don't have or think you can't do, doesn't it? It means that you are in the driver's seat. And you have an even greater opportunity than two-parent families to have an impact on your child because you are *singled out* as the leader of your home.

The key to single parenting doesn't lie with your child's relationship with your own parents. You won't find it in your child's relationship with his schoolteachers, Sunday school teachers or youth leaders, coaches, or with his friends or siblings.

The answer lies with you, in *your* relationship with your son or daughter. No one matters more in the life of your child than you do. You are *singled out* to believe in

> No one matters more to your child than *you.*

your child. That puts you very high on the scale of importance! It is through your eyes, your behavior, your words, and your thoughts that your child learns about her self-esteem, her worth in the eyes of God, and how to relate to others. And all of those things affect not only her present, but her future . . . and the generations to come.

You bear an awesome and exciting responsibility. For if you believe in your child, you give him the power to believe in himself. And that belief will be crucial to everything he does for the rest of his life.

Single-Minded Clarity

You also have another advantage that dual-parent households don't have: single-minded clarity.

One of the threats to families today is all the extra baggage that goes along with modern life—the material possessions, the endless demands on our time and money—and dual-parent families are much more apt to attempt to juggle all these add-ons. But the clarity with which you see life will be more intense than most people because of your need to be focused and goal directed. After all, since most single parents are short on time and money, you have to figure out how to best use what you do have.

> If you believe in your child, you give him the power to believe in himself.

If you embrace that single-minded focus, you'll be amazed at how much more easily you're able to evaluate your priorities and choose what matters most from the long list of potential to-dos.

And that, over a child's lifetime, adds up to a kid who says, "My parent made all the difference in my life." Other parents may even look at your children and think, *Sarah has raised healthier kids by herself than we have with two of us.* And they'd be right!

My point is this: It's so easy to get lost in the rat race of what you think you should do, what others think you should do, etc. But if you have a single-minded perspective, life is simplified. All your choices come down to two key questions: *What is my ultimate priority,* and *Is this advancing that ultimate priority?*

An Olympic athlete trains twelve years for a ten-second race, but there's incredible focus that goes into those seconds. It's that single-minded purpose that enabled Lance Armstrong to come back so strongly from his bout with cancer to win the Tour de France seven times—more than any person in the history of the sport. It's that single-minded focus that enabled George Frideric Handel to compose one of the greatest musical masterpieces in human history, *Messiah,* in only three weeks.[2]

You, as a single parent, also have that single-minded focus. With it you can generate an energy that is like a laser, cutting through all the layers of "stuff" that surrounds you, vying for your attention, to get to the heart of what matters most. It's that single-minded purpose that gives you the tenacity to hang in there and the determination to be proactive in forming a plan for your own well-being as well as your family's.

The Thrive Plan

If you really want your family to thrive amidst all the challenges that come the way of any parent, and especially a single parent, here are some strategies that will help.

GET BACK TO BASICS.

I've heard of an old recipe for cooking rabbit that begins with this simple but necessary step: *First, catch the rabbit.* Whoever wrote that recipe knew that often the most basic steps are also the most crucial. No mathematician will get far if she forgets how to add and subtract. If a home run slugger forgets to keep his eye on the ball, pretty soon he won't be knocking any more baseballs into the outfield bleachers. And without first catching that rabbit, rabbit stew is reduced to a bunch of bland vegetables in a pot.

Likewise, if you're not taking care of yourself, how can you take care of your kids?

How available can you be to your kids if you aren't eating well enough to give you the energy to get through the day? or if all you eat is fast food? I sure learned my lesson after I ate too many hot dogs and chips and ended up with a trip to the ER— just ask me about it sometime.

> First, catch the rabbit.

And how can you expect to function if you aren't getting enough sleep? Sure, there will be times when you're up late to catch up on bills, dishes, a crash project at work, or to take care of a sick child. But if you have a late night every night (or an early morning every morning, for you early birds), you're going to crash sooner or later, and then you won't do anybody any good. The human body can only take so much before it says, "No more. I quit!"

Single mom Leanne had something else to add: "When I don't get enough sleep, I end up taking it out on my kids."

Enough said.

When it comes to exercise, I can already see you rolling your eyes. "Come on, Dr. Leman, I hardly have the energy to press the toilet lever down, let alone go pump iron over at the local gym." I'm not telling you to go join a gym. I'm not telling you that you should even do sit-ups every morning. One look at my belly, and you'll know I don't always get the exercise job done. (Well, it's either that or the whole pumpkin pie I ate, one tiny slice at a time, in the kitchen!)

The beauty of exercise is that it can be built into your life through the simple things. And you needn't go it alone. Include your child—it's a great way to get to know him or her and to spend time together without the ringing of phones or the chaos of carpooling or having to compete for attention with your child's peers.

If your child is very young, pop her in the stroller and go for a fast walk in the park. Point out the birds and the squirrels. Stop at the local 7-Eleven to get milk on the way home, so you accomplish an errand.

If your child is older, ride bikes together around the neighborhood. Shoot some hoops (who cares if the basketball ever actually goes *in* the net?) at a local church parking lot.

In other words, use your imagination, and you can come up with many creative ways to keep your body fit and give your energy a boost.

> Caring for yourself is not being selfish.

Geoff, now a single dad, used to work out at a gym three times a week after work. Now he comes home instead and gives his two children—six and eight—"rides" on his legs and arms for his workout. Not only does it keep his muscles in good working order, but it also provides a lot of emotional release and bonding time through laughter.

Often single parents feel "selfish" if they do anything for themselves. But caring for yourself is not being selfish. If you cut corners on your own health, both you and your children will suffer. If you look out for yourself, you're also looking out for your kids.

How are you doing taking care of yourself?

GAIN PERSPECTIVE.
Before you can figure out where you want to go, you have to know where you are right now. Although I know your time is very limited, I urge you to set aside fifteen minutes sometime this week, as you're reading this book, to reflect on the following questions and/or journal your thoughts:

- What are your greatest concerns right now? Are they financial? emotional? physical? a combination?
- When do things seem to be on an even keel in your life?
- What things (if any) do you specifically do to take care of yourself?
- When do you hit a level of exhaustion that is hard to overcome? (Pinpointing specific events or times helps.)
- When have you felt good about how you're doing as a parent? When have you felt as though you've failed in your mission?
- If you could do one thing to make your relationship with your child better, what would that be?

EVALUATE YOUR PRIORITIES.

If someone asked you right now what three things are at the top of your priority list, what would you say?

If you're like most of us, you'd start ticking off the hottest items on your to-do list—those things that seem to hang over your head until they're done—like, "Do the laundry so Katie has a shirt to wear to school tomorrow." Or, "Plan Jason's sixteenth birthday party since his birthday was last week."

But what I mean is something different. What are your top *life* priorities? When you look back on your life, what will you wish that you had done for yourself? for your kids?

It isn't until you decide those life priorities that you can choose among the many things you could do to arrive at what will matter most in the long run.

For example, let's say that you've been craving some time just for yourself, without the constant noise of the wee voices you love so much. After they are in bed, you debate with yourself. *It's the first time I've had to myself, without a sick kid or an intense project for weeks. Should I stay up to watch the late-night movie?*

You know you'll feel drowsy at the next morning's staff meeting, and you've got a big day ahead and multiple plans with the kids after work.

So is the late-night break tonight worth it? Or should you cash it in and just get some extra sleep?

If you know your life priorities, it's easier to decide what to do. If one of your priorities is to advance your career in order to gain a higher salary so you and the kids can move into your own home, you will decide that sleep is much more important than a late-night flick. Why? Because that meeting is your chance to show your supervisor that you're a good brainstormer—and then she may decide to consider you for the new position you've heard is in the works.

Let's take another example. You're asked to coordinate the end-of-the-year party for your son's class. It's at a time when all of your other commitments are very heavy, and you wonder if you should say no. But then you feel guilty. *It's important that I be involved at school,* you think. And there's that little twinge of embarrassment, too. *If I say no, they're going to think I'm not a good mom. That I don't care about my kid or what's happening at school.*

Should you say yes, or no? If one of the priorities that you've already set is to stay closely involved in your child's life, you're likely to say yes to coordinating the party. But if another one of your priorities is to carefully weigh how much of your time is being committed outside the home, then you're likely to offer this creative solution: "I'm sorry that I can't coordinate the party," you tell the head room-mom, "but I can clear my schedule to make special treats and come during the time of the party to help out." That way you and your son can make the treats together, getting a little mom/son time in the process, and you only have two hours and travel time invested in the party instead of a whole day of preplanning. Even better, you'll still have your sanity—and you'll be a much happier, relaxed mom, both at the party and at home.

TAKE ONE DAY AT A TIME.

Author Anne Lamott tells a poignant story about her older brother. One day when he was ten years old, he "was trying to get a report on birds written that he'd had three months to write, which was due the next day. We were out at our family cabin in Bolinas, and he was at the kitchen table close to tears, surrounded by binder paper and pencils and unopened books on birds, immobilized by the hugeness of the task ahead. Then my father sat down beside him, put his arm around my brother's shoulder, and said, 'Bird by bird, buddy. Just take it bird by bird.'"[3]

When you begin life as a single parent, the big picture can be incredibly daunting. You may make more adjustments than there are minutes in a day. But taking first things first, as President Eisenhower once said, "often reduces the most complex human problem to a manageable proportion."[4]

> "Just take it bird by bird."

So take it one day at a time. One hour at a time if you need to. Focus your energy on each challenge as it comes. Evaluate your decisions based on carefully thought-out life priorities.

At times single parenting will be rewarding; at other times it will be exhausting. When you feel overwhelmed by the immensity of the task, remember the reason you're doing what you're doing.

Your children.

They're worth it.

And they are what matters most, both now and in the long term.

❄ ❄ ❄

KEY Qs . . .

- What expectations did you have for your life? How have they been fulfilled or not fulfilled?

- What part of "The Thrive Plan" is the most tricky for you to carry out? Why?

    1. Get back to basics.
    2. Gain perspective.
    3. Evaluate your priorities.
    4. Take one day at a time.

- If someone asked you what your top three life priorities are, what would you say? In what ways do (or could) these priorities affect your daily decisions?

CHAPTER 2

You're More than a *Survivor*

When contestants for the reality TV show *Survivor* step off the boat onto the shores of Borneo or Thailand, ready or not to see who can outlast the others in the wild, life radically changes in a hurry. There's no fast-food drive-through for a bacon-double-cheeseburger, no motel to check into for a good night's rest, no drugstore to pick up some medicine for that nagging fever.

To put it bluntly, the situation looks dire. There seem to be very few resources for the teams to fall back on. They have to count on their wits and their creativity to even survive. Life simplifies down to what has to get done to live from day to day. Packs are stripped to the barest necessities. Luxuries are only dreamed of.

It's kind of like the character in the classic book *Robinson Crusoe,* who finds himself marooned on a desert island after a shipwreck. Alone without the prospect of rescue, he composes a list of the "evil" and the "good" that he is faced with as he surveys his situation:

> Evil: "I am singled out and separated, as it were, from all the world, to be miserable."
>
> Good: "But I am singled out, too, from all the ship's crew, to be spared from death; and He that miraculously saved me from death, can deliver me from this condition."[1]

Sometimes life as a single parent is going well for you. You're seeing the rewards of your decisions and feeling the hugs and affirmation from your kids. You can tell by their actions that they are confident of your love.

And then there are the times when you feel like Robinson Crusoe: marooned on a deserted island, with no other boat in sight to take you off that tiny piece of land. You truly feel "singled out and separated . . . to be miserable."

It's okay to admit when you feel like that. Even the most well-adjusted single parents have their moments (or days or months). And which of us doesn't play, at some time, the "if only" mind game?

- *If only we could have worked it out, then I wouldn't be in this mess. We wouldn't have had to move out of our home, and the kids could have stayed in the same school. Then they wouldn't have to find new friends. Everything in their lives wouldn't be changing all at once. What could I have done to try harder to make my marriage work? If only I hadn't . . . If only she hadn't . . .*
- *If only my husband hadn't died. I wish I could go back in time and keep that lady who hit him from talking on her cell phone. God, why didn't you stop her? And why did you allow her to be okay but not my husband? She didn't even have kids!*
- *If only I would have married that great guy instead of driving him away. I didn't know back then, in college, that great guys were so hard to find. Adam was that kind of guy. He loved kids, too. I could see him playing with Abigail even now. But I wasn't ready to settle down and get married, so I lost him. If only I could go back and change that decision, Abigail would have a daddy.*
- *If only I would have been stronger, I'd never have gotten pregnant. I knew the "facts of life," but somehow they disappeared in that one night of passion. I really thought I loved that guy, and he loved me. Even my mom thought he was a keeper. How wrong we both were. . . .*

You can play the "if only" game ad nauseam. But it doesn't really accomplish anything—other than to make you feel more miserable. And it does something else, too. It saps your laserlike energy and points your emotions and thoughts in myriad directions. It paralyzes you from evaluating where you are now, distracts you from dreaming where you'd like to be, and stops you from moving ahead to a healthier place.

A Tenacious Woman

If anybody had a reason to be down in the dumps, it was Sonya Carson. The year her son Ben turned eight, Sonya discovered that Ben's father already had a wife and five children across town. Sonya promptly kicked him out of the house.

A single mother in over her head, Sonya pleaded with God for wisdom on how to raise Ben and his older brother, Curtis, so they would not succumb to local gangs and drugs. But where should she start?

Sonya herself had had a difficult life as a child. She had been juggled from foster home to foster home and had only completed third grade. She had married by the time she was thirteen. Still, in spite of everything the Carson family had going against them, Sonya was determined that life for her boys would be different. She held resolutely to her belief that her boys could succeed, so she set out to do the best she could to raise them well.

From the beginning, the boys faced an uphill battle. *Dummy* was Ben's nickname, given to him by his classmates at his inner-city Detroit elementary school.

"I did not like school very much, and there was no reason why I should," Ben said. "What did I have to look forward to? The others laughed at me and made jokes about me every day. I really felt I was the stupidest kid in the fifth grade."[2]

As part of Sonya's resolution to help her boys, she limited their television watching to only two agreed-upon programs per week. She also required each boy to read two library books per week and turn in book reports to her on each one.

"If you can read, honey," she told Ben over and over, "you can learn just about anything you want to know. The doors of the world are open to people who can read."

"Several of Mother's friends criticized her strictness," Ben remembers.

"I heard one woman ask, 'What are you doing to those boys, making them study all the time? They're going to hate you.'

"'They can hate me,' she answered, cutting off the woman's criticism, 'but they're going to get a good education just the same!'"[3]

Now *that's* a determined single mother.

Sonya Carson refused to think of merely surviving because she wanted more than that for her children. Even when she couldn't see the end result, she didn't waver from her goal. She was single-minded in her pursuit of excellence for her boys. She didn't have much, but she was tenacious (and wonderfully opinionated, I might add) about getting the job done.

> Start from where you are now.

And you can be, too.

But it all starts with packing away the "if onlys" for good. Your life is what it is right now. Until you accept life *as it is*, there can be no moving ahead.

There will be parts of your new life that you like. For example, if you were in an abusive situation, your current home might be less chaotic and frazzled without your ex's caustic, volatile presence.

There will be parts of your new life that you don't like: climbing into bed alone at night, worrying about your child learning to read and having no one to share it with, dealing with your teenager's heightened emotion and anger because Mom is no longer in her life.

The important thing is to start from where you are now. Instead of thinking about what you don't have, take stock of what you do have.

It may be a lot more than you think.

Taking Stock

In the movie *Cast Away*, Tom Hanks's character, Chuck Noland, is marooned on an island after the plane he's on crashes into the ocean. At first he holds onto hope that he'll soon be rescued, so he dutifully collects the FedEx packages that the plane was carrying. But as the days wear on, he slowly gives up hope of ever being rescued. He begins to open the packages to take stock of all that he has to survive: a party dress made from tulle, a pair of ice skates, and a volleyball.

The items don't seem like much, do they? In fact, they seem ridiculously inadequate.

That may be how you feel as you look at your resources. The numbers in your savings account may look more like the numbers in your first-grade son's math homework than those in any investment portfolio you thought you might have at your age. Your wardrobe may be classic Value Village, and you may be on a first-name basis with the checkers at the local grocery outlet.

> Take stock of what you do have. It may be a lot more than you think.

But *Cast Away*'s Chuck Noland makes creative use of what he has: the tulle party dress for a fishing net, the pair of ice skates for a hatchet and to perform a rudimentary tooth extraction. One of the greatest surprises of the movie is that what seemed useless or inadequate got the job done after all.

So before we move on, I'd like you to take stock of all that you *do* have right now. Go ahead—take a few minutes to make a list. I'll wait right here while you do it. . . .

❉ ❉ ❉

What did you write down? Perhaps things like

- I have a cozy apartment. It's small but has the basics.
- There's mac and cheese on the table. (It's my kids' favorite!)
- I still have a job, even when so many people are losing theirs.
- My baby just said, "Mama!"
- I can see how my son has grown in patience with his sister this year since he's had to watch out for her more.
- This summer I was able to find some great clothes for my kids at resale stores. They're in style and in such great shape that my fifth grader isn't embarrassed to wear them.
- A friend just gave my kids her old computer to do their schoolwork.

- I was able to start a home day care business. It was a dream come true so I could be at home with my kids.
- I'm figuring out creatively, day by day, how to get things done. And I'm not feeling as guilty for what I can't get done or what I don't have to get done.
- My girls are healthy. We didn't have to pay for any doctor visits this year.
- I found a church my kids and I both love.
- My neighbor fixed my car. It's old, but it runs!
- My teenage son still wants me to come to his games.
- I'm managing to set aside $100 a month in a savings account. To most people, that wouldn't be much, but it's the first time I've been able to swing that, and it feels good.

Look over your list again. When you read these items, what emotions do you experience? Joy? A few tears? Relief? Gratefulness? Humbleness?

I've always found that when I step back to take stock of what I do have, my feelings of inadequacy and my anxiety fade to the background. I don't think about playing the "if only" game because I'm focused on the present and looking ahead to the future instead of wallowing around in the muck of the past. (After all, it's hard to get anywhere when you're slogging around in shoes weighed down with mud!)

Robinson Crusoe discovered the same thing. For a long while, he played the "if only" game and got himself depressed and discouraged. But as time went on, he began to take stock of what he did have. And then as he moved ahead to get creative, he realized, "From the experience of the most miserable of all conditions in the world . . . we may always find in it something to comfort ourselves from."[4]

Bluntly said, we will always have troubles in this world. But no matter how hard life may be at times, there is always something to be thankful for.

You know it, because you've experienced it through all the things you just listed.

The apostle Paul knew it, too. In his letter to the people at Philippi, he wrote, "I have learned to be content whatever the circumstances. I know what it is to be in need, and I know what it is to have plenty. I have learned the secret of being content in any and every situation, whether well fed or hungry, whether living in plenty or in want."[5]

That's a big statement coming from a man who endured beatings, multiple shipwrecks, a stoning, imprisonment, fatigue, hunger, thirst, cold, nakedness, and ridicule.[6]

But what did he mean by "being content"? Was he saying to slap a smiley face on, no matter how you feel? Or that you should gloss over your pain and grief with happy thoughts, such as, *And to think I get this deserted beach all to myself!* Or, *Goodie! Look how many challenges I get to solve now!*

That kind of a fake fix-it may work for a day or two, a week, even a month, but it's never a long-term solution.

Many people in our culture today interpret Paul's famous line "I can do everything through him who gives me strength"[7] as spiritual carte blanche—that with God's help they can do *anything* they wish: break records on the playing field, climb the highest mountains, or bench-press four hundred pounds. While God is certainly free to grant whatever he wishes, that's not the "secret" Paul was getting at, nor is it what we should expect. What Paul was saying was that whether we're living in plenty or in want, we can rest assured that almighty God has remembered us. And he has given us the strength to do what lies before us when it seems that everything—and perhaps everyone—has turned against us.

> "Adversity will make you bitter or better." Which has it been for you?

There's an old adage: "Adversity will make you bitter or better." Which has it been for you?

As for me, adversity has caused me to dig deeper into myself. To explore areas about my personality and my gifts that I may never have realized were there. Adversity has helped me figure out who I am and who I want to become. For none of us has "arrived" yet at who we are fully supposed to be. We're all meant to explore, to probe the depths of the water around our own individual island. And as we do so, our understanding grows. We mature.

Along the way, we uncover the *ahas*. We discover that we can do far more than we ever dreamed was possible. And so can our children.

You've just got to hear the rest of Sonya and Ben's story. . . .

So What Happened to Ben?

"Even though I was in the fifth grade," said Ben Carson, "I had never read a whole book in my life."[8]

Nevertheless, he and his brother dared not disobey their spunky mother, who insisted that they read. Each week Sonya faithfully collected the book reports that she insisted they do. (She is one smart mother—making *sure* her boys were not only telling her they were reading, but actually doing it, as well as comprehending and processing what they read). It was a decision that would change the boys' lives.

Soon Sonya's challenge began to make a difference.

"Up until the last few weeks of fifth grade, aside from math quizzes, our weekly spelling bees were the worst part of school for me," Ben explained. "I usually went down on the first word. But now, thirty years later, I still remember the word that really got me interested in learning how to spell.

"The last week of fifth grade we had a long spelling bee in which Mrs. Williamson made us go through every spelling word we were supposed to have learned that year. As everyone expected, Bobby Farmer won the spelling bee. But to my surprise, the final word he spelled correctly to win was *agriculture*.

"*I can spell that word,* I thought with excitement. I had learned it just the day before from my library book. As the winner sat down, a thrill swept through me—a yearning to achieve—more powerful than ever before. 'I can spell *agriculture*,' I said to myself, 'and I'll bet I can learn to spell any other word in the world. I'll bet I could learn to spell better than Bobby.'"[9]

At his mother's encouragement, Ben Carson began to study hard throughout the rest of his schooling. He entered Yale with a scholarship, then continued on to the University of Michigan Medical School, where he studied neurosurgery. Upon graduating, he joined the staff of Baltimore's Johns Hopkins Hospital, one of the world's leading medical institutions, where he ascended to the position of chief of pediatric neurosurgery at the incredibly young age of thirty-three.[10]

"Even though my nickname in school was *Dummy*," said Carson, "my mom gave me the confidence to believe that I could become whatever I desired. She had only a third-grade education, but she had a faith in God that more than compensated for what she'd been denied."

> Sonya Carson refused to think of merely surviving. She wanted better than that for her children.

Sonya Carson not only believed in her children, but she had the tenacity to encourage her children to succeed, even though she could barely read at the time she assigned her boys two book reports per week. She had everything going against her—a limited education, betrayal by her husband, health problems, and the demands of raising two boys by herself. Even so, Sonya refused to think of merely surviving. She wanted better than that for her children. She didn't have much, but after she took stock of what she did have, she was determined to use it. Because she exercised courage in the face of the unexpected turns in her life, Sonya made single parenting work through wisdom, perseverance, and the grace of almighty God. And as a result, her son Ben is one of the leading neurosurgeons in the nation.

If Sonya Carson could raise healthy children, *you* can, too. It all starts with taking stock of what you have.

Looking A-piece down the Road

An old Montana rancher once told me, "If you don't look a-piece down the road, toward that big, open sky, it's mighty hard to keep puttin' one boot ahead of another." How right that feisty guy was.

What do you want life to be like a year from now? five years from now? ten years from now? Unless you take a moment to look down the road, you won't know how to "keep puttin' one boot ahead of another." So now's the time to ask yourself three important questions. (You'll have the opportunity to reflect on them further at the end of this chapter.)

WHAT DO YOU WANT YOUR HOME ENVIRONMENT TO BE LIKE?

You may live in an apartment or a house, or you may share living space with parents or friends right now. But if you could choose your home environment, what would it look like?

Here's what some single parents said when I asked:

- "I want Trea to know that he's first priority . . . even if there are dust balls under my couch."
- "I want to make sure we eat dinner together four nights a week, even if it's just tacos."
- "I want to be there when my kids get home from school. That always meant a lot to me as a kid. My kids may not get homemade chocolate-chip cookies like my mom used to make me, but there's nothing wrong with Oreos, either."
- "My kid's going through a tough time right now. I want him to know that our home is a safe place for him, and that I'll still love him even when he gets mad."
- "I don't want to live my life 'on hold' just because I don't have a guy. I want my son to see that Mommy is okay, even if I do get sad and lonely sometimes."
- "I want home to be a place that's restful—a getaway from all the pressures that are hitting my kids from every direction the rest of the day. But I also want it to be a place where my kids know it's okay to ask any question. A place where they can voice their opinions, even if we don't always agree. A place where we learn to work things out *in love*."
- "When I became a single parent and had to go back to work full-time, I thought I'd given up my dream of being a 'neighborhood mom.' Instead, I found out I just had to be creative. Now my home's the busiest home in

> "I want my son to see that Mommy is okay, even if I do get sad and lonely sometimes."

the neighborhood—one day a week. And my kids love it. They know that every Saturday they can invite anybody and everybody over to play, and we make all sorts of fun snacks. It's the day they look forward to every week. It's amazing what I get done, too, even with a bunch of kids around. Like my laundry for the week."

What kind of home do you dream of having? What is most important to you?

These are key questions worth asking.

WHAT KIND OF PERSON DO YOU WANT TO BE?

When you take a long-range look at yourself, what characteristics or qualities would you want to have a year from now? five years from now? ten years from now?

- "I tend to worry about a lot of things," Sedra told me. "Sometimes I worry so much that I forget to enjoy what's happening in the present. A year from now I hope I'll be more comfortable just playing with my daughter on the playground . . . instead of sitting under the tree, worrying about what we'll have for dinner."

  When worry threatened to overwhelm Sedra, she and a friend brainstormed a creative solution. Sedra now carries a small "worry" notebook. Each time a worry comes to mind, she jots it down in the notebook. Then, without looking at any of the other words inside, she closes the notebook cover and tucks it away. She only looks at the worry notebook once a week, on Fridays, just before she meets with other single parents for a fifteen-minute coffee break between the beginning of the school day and work. "I'm amazed at how many of the worries end up solving themselves without my help." She chuckles. "Guess I ought to know better by now."

  Three months of keeping that worry notebook have

transformed the way Sedra thinks of the challenges in her life. No longer do worries incapacitate her.

- Jason told me, "My dad was the kind of guy who never quite listened. He was always busy doing something else. I want to be the kind of dad who puts down his paperwork, no matter what, when my daughter has something to tell me."

- Michael admitted, "I have a problem with anger. I always thought I was a 'nice guy' until my wife walked out. Adjusting to life as a single dad has been pretty tough. My son's fifteen, and I see my anger reflected in him. So we made a deal. We each have a 'safe person' to go to when we get ticked off with each other. Ethan goes to his room, and I go to mine. We take turns phoning our 'safe person' to talk it out so we don't take it out on each other. By the time we've talked to someone else, our anger cools off, and we're able to talk the problem through. We've done this for six months, and it really works. We're having fewer blowups all the time, and my son and I are growing closer. And that's my end goal."

- "I'm not a very organized person," Jacqueline said. "I'm kind of the artsy type. But as my girls grew older and began school, our house became even more chaotic because I didn't have a system for tracking anything. I'd forget to sign papers for field trips or would show up a day late for lunchroom duty. With a friend's prompting, I finally bought a pocket Day-Timer. Having all our activities, phone numbers, and dates in one place—rather than littered around the desk on Post-it notes—really helps. It's a simple thing, but organizing myself makes me less frazzled and our home less stressful. I know organization will never be my highest skill, but I hope that five years down the road, my kids will finally notice and say, 'Hey, Mom, you don't forget as much anymore!'"

- "I was never allowed to ask hard questions when I was growing up," Mandy explained. "My mom and dad would simply say, 'Do it because I told you so.' So when I became a teenager, I didn't know how to make good decisions, and I've dealt with that lack ever since. I want to be the kind of person who welcomes questions—whether I know the answer or not—from my kids. I want to be confident enough about myself that if the answers can be found, I'm not afraid to search them out."

- Keri was only seventeen when she became a single mom. "I never had the chance to finish high school, much less pursue college. I ended up pregnant and working at a coffee stand in the mall. When my daughter went to kindergarten, I decided it was time for me to pursue my dream. I always hated it when anyone found out I hadn't finished high school, so I worked hard in the couple hours she was in school to get my high school diploma. Now she's in second grade, and I'm pursuing my bachelor's degree online. I do the homework at night after Elizabeth is in bed. Some nights I'm really tired, and I don't feel like doing the work, but I push on. I'm determined to finish. I owe it to myself and to my daughter to build the best life possible for us."

> "I'm determined to finish. I owe it to myself, and to my daughter, to build the best life possible for us."

Keri's not the only single parent getting a bachelor's degree online. Online university work is becoming more and more commonplace (see p. 112 for more information). It has lots of benefits, too—easy access, the ability to do the work anytime (even in the wee hours of the night or morning) to pursue the degree in the amount of time that you have (there's often no set time in which you have to finish the degree, making this a great option for all working parents), and it's often more cost-effective than actually sitting in a college or university classroom.

> You can make great strides at becoming who you want to be. All it takes is a plan . . . and determination.

When you're the sole breadwinner for your family, it's tough to knock out a college degree. It requires tremendous sacrifice of your time and energies. But because you're a single parent, education is even more crucial to getting the kind of job that will support you and your family down the road. And, thankfully, online work is making this more doable for single parents.

So who do you want to be one year from now?

Five years from now?

Ten years from now?

Do you want to be more loving? less judgmental? more accepting of change? less of a worrywart? more organized? Do you wish you had more education so you'd have higher qualifications for higher-paying jobs?

Why not jot down some notes about who you'd like to be and refer to them once a week for fifteen minutes (as Sedra did with her "worry" notebook)? You'll be amazed at how much clearer your life path and future hopes will become when they're spelled out in black and white in front of you.

You can make great strides at becoming who you want to be. All it takes is a plan . . . and determination.

WHAT KIND OF PERSON DO YOU WANT YOUR CHILD TO BE?

If you want your child to live a balanced life and be a well-adjusted individual, you need to know who your child is (something we'll talk more about in the Key 2 section). What are her strengths? his weaknesses? And how can you best support your child?

Again, I asked those in the trenches, and here's what they said:

- "Katherine's a sweet, sensitive little girl who has a heart of gold for anyone who's hurting. She was so excited about starting kindergarten but then had a difficult time adjusting. She cried at school, after school, and often at home. When I asked her about her fears, she said she didn't want to be away from me. I finally realized that she was afraid that I would leave her and not come back—like her daddy had done. Because of her fears, I asked my boss if I could work an extra hour on Wednesday evenings so I could take an hour at lunch once a week to go to Katherine's school and be a 'lunchroom mom.' It really helped Katherine to see me there, and gradually her fears lessened. I can now see her growing more confident . . . something I really want to develop in her."

> "I can now see her growing more confident . . . something I really want to develop in her."

- "Jared is a social kid. Everybody loves him. But that great part of his personality has a downside, too. Because he's so social, schoolwork seems to be his last priority. When his report card came back with two "Incomplete" marks on it, I knew we had to have a talk. I explained that I wanted the best for him and that education was an important part of that. Since then I can tell he's trying much harder to succeed at school. It's still not going to be easy. Schoolwork will always be a struggle for him. But talking with him honestly about *why* I was so pushy about getting schoolwork done gave him some needed perspective."

- "Gianna is my adventuresome child. She's the kid who loves taking risks, like climbing the highest branch in the tree—and falling out. Now she's fifteen, she's still living life that way, and it scares me. She's just like I was—ready to fall in love with all the wrong guys. I'm

worried, because that's how I got into trouble.
I remember just how I was—outwardly cocky,
but inside desperate to know that some guy
accepted me.

"So I took a bold step. To say Gianna wasn't crazy
about it in the beginning is a major understatement.
(She slammed her bedroom door shut on me every
night for two weeks.) But I was determined. Four
months ago, I insisted she get involved in a Sunday
breakfast club for teens at our church. They break up
into groups of four, sit around a small table, and ask
any question they want of an adult special guest.

"For the first two meetings, Gianna sat in the
hallway and sulked. But then her curiosity took over,
and she decided to slink in the door. For the first two
months, she didn't tell me anything about what
happened there (she was still mad), but I gathered
information quietly from the adult sources.

"And then Gianna began to talk. Slowly at first,
but then more. 'Mom, everybody's pretty blunt there,'
she reported, 'but I like it. And they don't make you
feel stupid for asking any question.' Even though what
I did wasn't easy (who wants to put up with a furious
teen girl who thinks you're the worst and pushiest mom
in the world and treats you that way for weeks on
end?), Gianna's found three new friends to hang out
with. They don't go for life on the wild side, yet they
still have fun. I wish they'd been around when I was
a teen.

"Gianna has also met Lisa, who's twenty-five. They
now go out for lunch twice a month, with my blessing.
Lisa's beautiful, witty, outgoing, and smart—the kind of
woman Gianna wants to be. Even better, Lisa is blunt
about the mistakes she made as a teenager and what
those mistakes have cost her in her adult life."

I applaud each of these single parents. They've got a bead on their children's strengths and weaknesses and are doing their best to support their offspring creatively . . . while not letting them get by with any shenanigans, either.

In what areas does your child succeed? In what areas does he struggle? How can you best help her now, and in the long term?

As we discussed in chapter 1, you are "singled out" to believe in your child. No one knows your child better than you, so you are uniquely suited to help. Don't give up that role easily to someone else, but enlist help when you need it.

Above all, think of yourself as more than a *survivor.* If you're merely *surviving,* then you're taking the passive way out. By taking stock of what you do have, rather than focusing on what you don't, you're choosing an active role in your own and your family's welfare. You, too, like the other single parents in this chapter, can form a creative, tailored-to-you-and-your-children plan that will build confidence in the present and hope for the future. Then just watch your family thrive!

❖ ❖ ❖

KEY Q̲s̲ . . .

- What do you want your home environment to be like?

- What kind of person do you want to be?

- What kind of person do you want your child to be?

After you make your lists, do some brainstorming. What steps would you need to take to make your home into this kind of environment? to become that kind of person? to help your child develop in such a way?

This is a great time to enlist a friend or a counselor's help, too.

CHAPTER 3

Then . . . and Now

Congratulations! You've just slogged through a bunch of questions and self-reflection. All good stuff, but you're ready for a break.

That's what this chapter is about. You've heard the statements

- You can't do it all, but you can do what matters most.
- If you take stock of what you do have, you can form a creative, tailored-to-you-and-your-children plan that will build confidence in the present and hope for the future.

Sounds good, right? But does it work in real life?

Stories of Then . . .

Following are the stories of four single parents. Perhaps you'll recognize some of your own story within theirs.

NANCY, THEN . . .

Divorce wasn't something that Nancy—a devoted, compassionate Christian—ever expected to happen to her. Ever since she could remember, her dream had been to use her gift of caregiving in the nursing field. So she'd entered a local university to get her nursing degree. It was there, partway through her studies, that she met Steve.

Steve was Mr. Flashy, a handsome guy who on the surface seemed to be everything Nancy dreamed she might find in a man. Manipulated by his charms, she dropped out of school in her desire to please him. The two married shortly thereafter.

Within a few years they had two beautiful children.

But life was already unraveling. Steve bounced from job to job after routinely being fired for telling his bosses how to run their businesses. Then Nancy discovered that he was a womanizer. She was devastated. Even when confronted about his behavior, he chose not to change.

Five years later, they filed for divorce. Nancy and her children's lives were ripped apart as her ex seemed to go merrily on his own way.

TRINA, THEN . . .

Trina was in her senior year of high school when she fell for Darrick, another senior. Although her parents had given her all the lectures about sex, the warnings never hit home. The consequences were always "something that happened to other girls." She thought her parents were being a little too conservative for today's standards and figured she was old enough to handle sexual activity responsibly. So she and Darrick quickly became intimate.

One warm April day, right after prom, Trina discovered that she was pregnant. As she sat in the bathroom stall after school, staring at the truth of the pregnancy test, reality hit home. She was now one of those "other girls."

Trina waited three months—hoping the nightmare would all go away—before she told Darrick. The next day he left town, and she hasn't heard from him since. When her parents found out (she finally had to tell them because she kept throwing up), they were furious at her for being "so dumb" and told her the only solution was an abortion. They certainly weren't going to take care of the child, and she couldn't either, they insisted. They didn't want Trina's younger sisters to know about her pregnancy.

After checking out the possibility of abortion through a family planning clinic, Trina decided she just couldn't do it. "I knew—deep inside—that it just wasn't right," she told me. "But I didn't know why."

When she refused to have an abortion, her parents kicked her out. They insisted they would no longer house somebody who continued to make bad choices, since it would affect her sisters negatively. So at eighteen, Trina was homeless. She hit the streets with only a duffel bag of clothes and fifteen dollars in her pocket.

LAUREN, THEN . . .

"All my life I wanted to be a mother," Lauren, an only child, told me. "But there was no guy appearing on the horizon. So on my thirty-fifth birthday, I made a decision: I wanted to adopt a child from China." Lauren's decision was fully backed by both her parents, who were eager to become grandparents and very supportive in all areas of her life. Lauren spent eighteen months deep in paperwork before she received her referral. When she looked at the picture of the tiny face, she knew instantly that little Madelyn was the child intended for her.

When the time arrived for Lauren to meet her baby, she traveled with her mother to China. The first time Lauren saw Madelyn, tears of joy flowed down her cheeks. It was a long-held dream come true. Madelyn was fourteen months old, and Lauren had just turned thirty-seven. She was finally a mother.

That first night Lauren couldn't sleep, and it wasn't the jet lag from flying to the other side of the world. She couldn't stop herself from counting little fingers and toes and stroking Madelyn's baby-soft cheek.

Two days later—after dealing with Madelyn's numerous crying and coughing bouts and suffering some stomach ailment herself—Lauren wondered, *What have I gotten myself into? Can I really do this?*

Lauren had her mother with her those sixteen days in China. But she grew more and more anxious about what would happen when she got home. When it was just her and Madelyn.

Lauren couldn't help but think, *Was I crazy to believe I could do this alone?*

EVAN, THEN . . .

Evan and Terri had a storybook marriage. They'd met in college, married just after graduation, and soon had three beautiful blonde daughters, spaced two years apart. When the youngest child was two, the couple received some devastating news. Terri had a brain tumor. Everything was done to halt its development, and she even went through a radical surgery that caused her to lose partial control of her facial muscles, but Terri died nine months later.

Evan turned thirty the day after her death.

Understandably, he came to me as he was grappling with intense questions. "Why would a good God do this, Dr. Leman? And why Terri? And what about our girls? How can I explain to them that Mommy is never coming back? The oldest one understands a little, since our dog died a year ago. But the younger ones keep asking where Mommy is. They keep asking when she's coming home, and they run to our bedroom to check for her. What do I do without my wife? How can I raise our girls without their mommy?"

How indeed? And that would be only the beginning of the questions for Evan and for his girls.

※ ※ ※

It's no wonder that Nancy, Trina, Lauren, and Evan walked into my office looking exhausted.

Perhaps if you had a spare minute to look in a mirror, you'd see that's how you look, too.

These single parents were simply overwhelmed.

Much like you feel at times.

As we talked and I shared the six keys to making single parenting work, I first saw raised eyebrows.

Then chins began to lift in courage.

As plans formed, I saw smiles.

I even heard an occasional chuckle or two.

Each of these single parents walked out of my office, head held high, realizing that single parenting can and does work.

And Stories of Now . . .

Just look at what Nancy, Trina, Lauren, and Evan did as a result!

NANCY, NOW . . .

Nancy enlisted her parents' help as she made some tough but good long-term choices. She knew she needed to be able to sustain herself and her family in the future. So she moved herself and her kids, who were then five and three (not yet in school), from their apartment into her parents' home nearby. All understood it was a temporary situation and dependent on Nancy being in school.

While her parents helped with child care, Nancy returned to school to finish her nursing degree. "It wasn't an easy choice," Nancy admits today, "because my kids really needed me. They were as devastated as I was when Steve left. I felt so guilty leaving them even for a short time that I cried a lot at night over it. But I knew that unless I got my degree, I wouldn't be able to support my family in the years ahead. And because Steve went from job to job, I couldn't count on his help financially."

So, as difficult as it was emotionally, physically, and financially, Nancy stuck to her plan. Two and a half years later she received her degree. That was a happy day!

Six months after she got a full-time job in nursing, Nancy and her two children, who were both now in school, moved into their own home. She was able to juggle her hours so she could drop them off and pick them up at school, then finish up her paperwork in the evenings while they did homework.

Nancy had to endure many sleepless nights after her ex-husband repeatedly failed to send child support payments (yet was able, somehow, to buy a boat). But through her courageous decisions, hard work, and the wisdom and support of those around her, Nancy made single parenting work. Eventually she became a nursing instructor.

Today both of Nancy's children are experiencing what Nancy never had: a healthy marriage. They are well-adjusted, balanced individuals and a joy to be around.

I asked her kids, Lenya and Kurt, "What made the difference all those years when your dad wasn't involved in your life? Why do you think you turned out the way you did?"

They smiled. "Mom," they proclaimed boldly. "It was all Mom. She never gave up!"

Now there's a success story to make you smile (and choke up, too).

TRINA, NOW . . .

The day that Trina walked away from her parents' home and into the streets of the inner city, she was scared. More scared than she'd been in her life. Swallowing her pride, she headed to the only church she knew, which was five blocks away. Although she considered herself a tough girl, the tears started flowing as she began to explain her situation to the church secretary. Finally she took the fifteen dollars out of her pocket, placed them on the secretary's desk, and asked if she could sleep somewhere in the church that night.

The church secretary moved around her desk to hug Trina and gently tucked the fifteen dollars back into her jeans pocket. She got Trina a soda, then showed her to a comfortable waiting room.

That's when Trina got even more scared. She wondered if the nice lady was calling the cops. But out of desperation—she had nowhere else to go—Trina stayed in that room. Twenty minutes later, a man and woman entered the room and asked her to tell them her story. After she did, they smiled at each other and said, "Well, Trina, you have a new home now—with us—for as long as you and the baby need it."

That very afternoon Trina went home with the Wilsons. They weren't rich by any means, but this kind couple had a passion to help teen girls in need.

Tears shimmered in Trina's eyes as she told me about the series of miracles in her life. "Through the Wilsons, I found out why I couldn't make myself get an abortion. That my baby was really a baby, not a fetus, and that's why I felt that tug in my heart. I also didn't know back then that some churches have a hard time accepting single parents. I didn't know God at that time, but I'm convinced now that he led me to that exact church, where I could find unconditional love and help. If it wasn't for that church and the Wilsons, I may have given up and had that abortion, even late term. And then my little boy wouldn't be alive today. They were the ones who helped me, day by day, as my belly grew, to have the courage to choose life for my little boy."

When Trina made the difficult choice to keep her baby rather than give him up for adoption as many counseled her to, the Wilsons agreed to help. She continued to live at their home, and they cared for Basker, her baby boy, five evenings a week while she worked at a local grocery store. In exchange, she had dinner cooked and ready for them when they returned home from work three evenings a week. She also was responsible to keep her room and the baby's cleaned up and to clean the entire house once a month.

During the day, as she took care of the baby, Trina worked hard to further her schooling through an online course. Three years later, the Wilsons helped Trina and Basker move into their own apartment. Even more, they continued to care for the little boy for the next two years, until he was in kindergarten.

Because of a daring visit to a church and a secretary's kind heart, Trina and Basker have become an integral part of the Wilson family—very important to Trina since her own parents have never allowed her back into their home since the day she left. They also have never acknowledged her son, and they have allowed no contact with her younger sisters.

"I wish things could be different," Trina says sadly. "But Basker is growing up with a 'grandma' and 'grandpa' who really love him. . . ." And then she adds with a smile, "And they don't let him get away with anything, either!"

Basker is now seven. Trina knows he'll have lots of questions about his daddy. "I want to be honest with him about where he came from, but he's not ready to hear all the details yet. And when he does, I hope he will understand that although I didn't make a good choice, he is still a miracle. Most of all, I want him to know that the choices he makes will affect him the rest of his life. I'm a walking example of that, and so is Basker. I want to help him learn how to make good choices so that he'll have a different kind of life than I've had."

LAUREN, NOW . . .

Lauren would be the first to tell you she's no expert in raising kids. But if you saw her daughter today, you'd think she was. Maddie, now thirteen years old, and her mother have the kind of relationship that any mother would long to have with a teenage daughter. It is one of mutual respect. Of caring, listening, and talking.

Yes, they have gone through some rough spots. Like when Maddie was eight, and she kept trying to set Lauren up with any and every single male teacher in her school—and even the guys they met at the pool in the summer.

"Maddie was desperate to have a daddy," Lauren told me, "and she was so blunt, it was embarrassing. She'd walk up to total strangers and say, 'Are you married? Because if you're not, would you like to be my daddy?' I can't tell you how many times I winced, gave that 'oops' smile, and apologized.

"But as time went on, my relationship with Maddie grew even closer, I think, because there were only two of us. Sometimes Maddie asked tough questions, and I was always honest. When she'd say, 'I wish I had a daddy,' I'd tell her, 'Honey, I wish you had a daddy, too. But I don't want just any daddy. I want one who will love both of us for who we are.' I told her that Mommy was picky because she and I deserved that."

When Lauren chose single parenting, she fought critics who told her that she'd never get married if she chose to have a child first. That she was going against the Bible's model of one man and one woman as parents. That it would be a lot tougher to find a guy after she had a child in her life.

But criticism didn't stop Lauren. She had what she believed was a God-given passion to love a child from China and to take that child into her heart and home. Because being a part of that child's life was so important to Lauren, she decided that she was done waiting for the right guy to come along. If God was going to send a guy, she reasoned, then he could make it happen whether she was in her midthirties, forties, or fifties. If not, then that was okay, too. There were so many children who needed homes, and she certainly had the love to give. Wasn't one parent better than no parent at all? And, she reasoned, if she had to work that hard to find a guy who could love her *and* her child, then maybe marriage wasn't even the right thing for her.

So instead of focusing on dating or finding a guy, Lauren went ahead with her plans for adoption. And as soon as her child came home from China, she took my suggestion and went out of her way to make sure she had some solid, loving, male role models in her daughter's life (we'll talk more about why this is so important in chapter 9, "The Opposite-Sex Fix").

As a result, Maddie has had three consistent males—besides her grandfather—in her life for the past twelve years. One of them attends all of her band concerts and volleyball games, one has breakfast one Saturday a month with her, and the other pops in and out on a weekly basis to answer questions about boys, help with science projects, and even handle house or car repairs, as needed.

Maddie is one of those young teens who is beautiful both inside and out. Lauren has worked hard to establish with her child the kind of relationship that will weather a lifetime of change, even as this child becomes a young adult.

EVAN, NOW . . .

When Terri died, Evan had been in his sixth year as a traveling sales rep. But now his three girls needed him at home. So Evan made some tough decisions. He approached the president of the company with a plan for a restructured job that he could do from home, while he took care of the girls. His income dropped more than half within a month's time. He had to sell his three-bedroom, split-level home and buy a small, two-bedroom ranch in a lower-income part of town. The cramped living room, cluttered with toys, also became his office.

Evan, who had always prized a quiet environment in which to work, had to learn to work in the midst of chaos. He had to learn how to ask for help. "I had no clue how to shop for clothes for girls, how to play 'nurse' and 'doll,' or how to cook anything more than microwave meals. And that was only for starters!" he says with a chuckle. Then he grows sober. "What was even harder was dealing with my own feelings of loss and grief in the midst of my girls' questions and emotions."

Today Evan and Terri's three girls are twelve, fourteen, and sixteen. Evan will be the first to admit he gets all of the normal eye rolls that any other teens give their parents. But he works hard to have individual time with each daughter. "I can't get them the designer clothes their friends have or an iPod. We all share one aging computer, and none of the girls has a cell phone.

"For me, it was a decision between providing things for them or being available to them. I knew from the beginning what Terri would say. My girls needed me—even when they sometimes didn't want me around. Even though they're older now, I still want to be available. When you spend time together, questions arise. The kind of questions you want your kids to ask you first, before they ask anybody else. Sometimes I know the answer, sometimes I don't. But I'm smart enough to know that if I don't know the answer, I need to find somebody who does!"

If you enter their home, you'll still see lots of photos of the young girls with their mother. And they still celebrate Terri's birthday—complete with a slide show of photos of the girls when they were babies and a cake baked by Evan (a miracle in itself, he says). As each of the girls turns thirteen, he gives her a special journal, handpicked by their mother before her death, and also a letter from her. His third daughter can't wait to get hers.

❅ ❅ ❅

You see, with a gutsy courage that doesn't give up and some creative thinking, you, too, can make single parenting work.

Five years down the road, I can't wait to hear *your* story of then . . . and now.

———————————————— ❅ ❅ ❅ ————————————————

KEY Qs . . .

- Do any of these stories resemble events in your own life? Explain.

- Which aspects of these stories encouraged you? Why?

- One of the greatest gifts you can give a child is the story of your life. Why not take a few minutes a week to start writing your own story of then . . . and now? (To keep it current, you could even add a paragraph or two in upcoming years.)

KEY 2

KNOW YOURSELF, KNOW YOUR CHILD

Helping your child
means starting on yourself first.

CHAPTER 4

Got Guilt?

Remember that catchy commercial, "Got milk?" Some famous actor or actress was pictured with a big, frothy mustache from taking a swig of the white stuff.

I've got another catchy phrase for you: "Got guilt?"

Who on this earth doesn't? And you, most likely, have taken on far more than your share. Since most single parents operate on an income of less than fifteen thousand dollars a year, it's likely that your kids don't have all the material things other children from two-parent homes may have—the name-brand clothes, the iPods, the camera phones, the horse-riding lessons, etc. And as a result, many of you probably carry within you a nagging feeling of not quite measuring up.

You already know you can't do it all, but you still feel guilty because, underneath it all, you think you should. You don't want your kids to be different from other kids or to have fewer opportunities. But if you try to keep up with the Joneses and their dual-parent-powered lifestyle, you'll always feel the weight of never being able to do enough, of not being enough. And instead of being in the driver's seat, you'll find yourself a passenger in life, lurching around the turns as someone else drives your car.

So what's the answer?

Get to Know Yourself

This may seem like a strange answer to the above "Got Guilt?" question, but it's true. Before you can help your child, you need to know yourself and what makes you tick. Do you struggle with anger? disappointment?

sadness? bitterness? Dealing with what has happened in the past and how you feel about it isn't easy. But you can do it, and you *must* do it, for your sake and your child's.

You may have thought your life would go one way, but it has gone an entirely different way.

Perhaps after spending eight years in a bad marriage, you finally got the moxie to get out of it. But now when you have to be the big girl, you feel like a little kid. Lost, scared, and alone. You question your own ability to pull off the solo lifestyle, even though it was a move you had to make for your own safety and the safety of your kids. So you second-guess yourself. *Did I do the right thing?*

Or maybe you've just spent the last two years feeling bad because your kids don't have a dad. Should you go on a hunt to see whom you can find? Is any dad better than no dad?

Or maybe you've got a constant ache in your gut and you're wondering, *How am I ever going to support these two little kids on one year of college credit and a ten-bucks-an-hour part-time job?*

Now is the time to step back and get to know yourself, deep inside. If you want to make healthy, responsible decisions for yourself and your family in the future, you have to know what causes you to respond the way you do to life situations. You have to know what you are saying to yourself, even unconsciously.

THE POWER OF INTERNAL TALK

When you were fifteen, what did you dream that life would be like?

How much of that has come true for you now, whether you're twenty-two, thirty-two, forty-two, even fifty-two?

> No one receives all of their dreams.

Let's just say it bluntly. For all of us, there is a psychological distance between life as we once envisioned it and life as it has happened. No one receives all of their dreams. Everyone makes mistakes, has hard experiences, and even goes through times that seem like complete disasters.

For many single parents, this psychological distance is even greater. Once an integral part of your life, your dreams have been stripped away.

When a woman marries her prince and he turns out to be an ogre, everything she dreamed about—from the color of her bridesmaids' dresses to her hopes of a tender, loving life together—crumbles like a ruined castle before her eyes.

When a woman has a child outside of marriage, all her dreams of a career, a home of her own, and someone to share her life with can come to an abrupt halt.

And when a man or woman loses a spouse, the home environment that they have established together suddenly feels as if a puzzle piece has been removed, and there is no longer a "whole picture."

So it's natural to ask yourself questions, such as

- *How did this happen?*
- *Whose fault was it?*
- *Could I have avoided it?*
- *What did I do wrong?*
- *How can I ever move on?*

Your internal response at such a time—when the ground feels like it has dropped from under you—is crucial. For it's at this time that your "internal talk" starts to work overtime.

By "internal talk" I mean that little voice that whispers to your head and your heart things like

- *It's all your fault. If you hadn't . . .*
- *You're never going to make it.*
- *It was all her fault. If she hadn't . . .*
- *You can't do it alone. You'll fail.*

It's the sneaky voice of negativism that tells you all sorts of lies about yourself and others. Lies that are guaranteed to stop you in your tracks. If you're not careful, they will begin to rule over your life, making and changing present and future decisions for you.

Does that mean you should never evaluate what has happened or what you should have done differently so that you can make different choices in the future? Certainly not! In fact, put your cards on the table. Be honest with yourself about what happened, about your choices (whether wise or not), and about how they have affected your present and your potential future.

Why do I urge you to do this now? Because it isn't until you face what happened and realize any part that was your fault that you can move ahead and make proactive choices rather than reactive choices. Until you put your cards on the table, your internal talk will have a heyday, trying to snow you with negative emotions.

> The lies you tell yourself tell more than you think!

Think for a moment. What is your internal talk saying? Take a minute to jot a few thoughts down.

Here are what other single parents said they were hearing:

- *You can't do anything right, can you?*
- *If you hadn't gone on that trip, James wouldn't have had that affair. You left the door open.*
- *What are you thinking? How can you raise a kid when you couldn't even keep yourself out of trouble?*
- *Your life is a mess, so how are you going to tell Rachel not to mess around? You're such a hypocrite!*
- *You're going to spend the rest of your life alone. Nobody's going to want a woman who's got a kid already.*

Why did I make you relive such nasty thoughts? Because the lies you tell yourself tell more than you think! They reveal what you think about yourself. If you listen carefully to those inner conversations, you'll find out the message you're really delivering to yourself. You'll find out how you're really coping with any pain in your life.

For example, if you heap all kinds of abuse on yourself (*If only I had ____*, or *If only I hadn't ____*) the hurt you feel and your belief about its source—*you*—become a license for you to further beat up yourself and even your kids, both mentally and emotionally. If you tend to think the worst about yourself and your coping skills, if you exaggerate how bad it is (and internal talk is a pro at doing that!), you could end up wallowing in self-pity for a long time.

Your healing and self-confidence can also be stunted if your own parents shame you for your decisions and tell you in no uncertain terms how to run your life. If you're weak enough to listen to detractors, you'll spend your time circling back to the pain of the past rather than embracing hope and your future. Keep in mind that there will always be naysayers—even well-intentioned ones like a coworker, your girlfriend down the street, or your older sister—but *you* are the decision-maker now. You can listen to advice all you want, but *you* are the one who knows your life and your kids the best. *You* are the one who must choose how to live now.

So how's your internal talk? If you have just become a single parent, you may be living in crisis mode. You may need to take life one day at a time. There will be times

> You are the one who must choose how to live now.

when your psychological injury will seem so great that you won't know if you can ever trust anyone again. Or your fears will be so high that you're sure your kids are doomed to a "loser" kind of life.

But if you're aware of what your internal talk is saying, you can talk right back to it:

- *You know, things are hard right now. But one day at a time, they'll get better.*
- *Yes, some of it was my fault, but not all of it. I won't make that mistake again.*
- *You're just tired right now, or you wouldn't be telling yourself that.*
- *Just because I failed at my marriage doesn't mean my kids have to be a mess.*
- *Okay, you're right. Soloing isn't easy. But with God's help, I can do it.*

Your path is not written in stone. If you are a new single parent, as the days tick by you'll discover that life really does get better. The money in your bank account does somehow last through the month, then two months, then three. And six months from now, you'll feel much better about going it solo.

As you take stock of the resources at your disposal and become aware of your self-talk (and you talk back to it when needed), you'll begin to realize that you *can* do this. (In fact you are already doing it, right now!) You'll find new resolve because you realize that you are going to make it and your kids are going to make it. You see the light of hope over the horizon.

When you use the power of internal talk wisely, you won't be as likely to fall for the "nots," either.

ARE YOU TIED UP IN "NOTS"?

- *I'm* not *able to do that for my child.*
- *My child does* not *have what the Williamses' kids have.*
- *I'm* not *a good parent.*
- *I can*not *provide for my children what other parents have.*

The guilt of the "nots" is like a virus: unseen, contagious, and easily transmitted by those closest to you, especially the ones you most want to please—your family, friends, and those you live near and carpool with to your children's schools every day. But comparing yourself to families around you and basing your decisions on what others think of you can leave you tied in "nots." And those "nots" can incapacitate you, making you think you can't do anything right.

> If you're aware of what your internal talk is saying, you can talk right back to it.

But let me ask you this: If two parents are unable to keep up with our society's impossible standard of stuff and activities, how on earth can you, a single parent, possibly keep up? After all, you have only the twenty-four hours in a day of one parent instead of the forty-eight hours that two parents have. And during those twenty-four hours, you work, eat, parent, accomplish multiple to-dos, and hopefully get a little sleep!

It's crucial to be aware of the "not" messages in your life because they can really lead you astray. How? If you already feel bad for causing pain in your children's lives and for everything they lack (including a mommy or a daddy), you will try even harder to keep up with what everybody else has. And you'll exhaust yourself in the process.

That's why, in trying to make the best of a challenging situation, it's so easy for single parents, especially, to go overboard (it all goes back to the extra boatload of guilt you feel for being a single parent in the first place).

Carla, a single mom I know, has a hard time letting go of her daughter, who is now in first grade. She wants so badly to be known as "a good parent" that she's driving the school officials and Tyler's teacher crazy. Every day she walks her daughter into school, escorts her to her classroom, and later zooms back to school over her lunch hour from work so she can hand Tyler a take-out lunch every day. "The other kids in her class sometimes get a take-out lunch from their parents, but I want Tyler to feel special every day," Carla explained to me. She often shows up on the playground at recess time to make sure Tyler finds other children to play with, and she sits outside the first-grade classroom at the end of the day, waiting for Tyler to come out. Carla sacrificed getting her own hair cut so she could get Tyler the backpack and the type of gym shoes that everybody else was wearing.

"I don't want Tyler to feel or be or look different from other kids. I want her to have as much attention as any kid who has two parents," Carla told me. She's well-meaning, but in her desire to be a good mom, and in her desire to be seen as a good mom, Carla is undercutting her own daughter's social development. Sad to say, word on the playground is that Tyler is a spoiled brat.

Another single mother from Atlanta admitted in a *Newsweek* article that she bought her children brand-name clothes, top-of-the-line Nike sneakers, and a three-hundred-dollar electric scooter. Because they're well-behaved kids who make the grade at school, she reasoned, she wanted to buy them the toys that other kids have.[1]

But if you're like that woman, living on a custodian's salary, my guess is that you probably don't have the money to charter Santa's workshop. And even if you did—if you got a good job or won the lottery—*should* you provide all that for your children?

I'm convinced that *things* do not create healthy kids. Your loving, involved presence in their lives does. (And notice that I didn't say your *overinvolved, out-of-guilt* presence.)

How healthy your children are comes down to a basic question: How healthy are you? Are you tied up in "nots"?

WHAT DETERMINES YOUR WORTH?

Take a moment to answer these questions:

- *When do I feel good about myself?*
  Is it when others admire me?
  Is it when I'm the center of attention?
  Is it when I do something that makes my kids happy?
- *Do I determine my worth by what I have or by who I am?*

The last question is an especially critical one. If you determine your self-worth by what you have, then you're in particularly deep trouble as a single parent. Statistics across the board show that single-parent families have a much lower income than dual-parent families (whether one or both of the parents works). Most, as I've stated earlier, live on fifteen thousand dollars a year. That means you're far less likely than a dual-parent household to hold season tickets to any sports games or theaters. You're less likely to have your kid signed up for ballet or karate or band. You don't even drop money on a venti mocha at the local coffee shop. You simply don't have the time or the money.

So if your worth is based on what you have (your *net worth*, as those in the business world sometimes call it), then your life will probably revolve around guilt. You'll always be comparing yourself to your neighbors, who have more than you do. The glass of your family will always be half empty (and so will your thinking) because you can't fill it to the same level as those families with two people running the show. And then you'll fall prey to making all kinds of decisions for the wrong reasons.

> Misery may love company
> . . . but when the pity
> party's all over and
> everybody goes home,
> what are you left with?

You may fall into the "victim" trap. The kind of person who says, "I can't do anything right, so why do anything at all?" Another name for this is "throwing a pity party"! Misery may love company, and a lot of folks may be willing to come alongside you for a life-bashing (or an ex-bashing) party, but what do you really gain? When the pity party's all over and everybody goes home, what are you left with?

Or you might fall into the "overachiever" trap, because that's how you best get sympathy and admiration. Like Anita, who managed to bake two pies between her kids' soccer practice and her evening meeting. When a neighbor dropped by during that time and saw the flurry of activity in the kitchen, she asked Anita, "How do you do it? You have three children, you're working two jobs, you're a single parent, but you manage to make this house such a home and do all this, too!"

I see it a little differently. Anita is going to crash sometime, in a big way. Physically and psychologically. Underneath it all, she's nursing a martyr complex that feeds on her situation and the attention she receives from others when she overachieves (*I have no choice. I have to do it all myself. And if I don't do it, it'll never get done. Everybody else gets to play, but I never have time. It's all up to me. . . .*).

What is your worth based on? What you lost? What you don't have?

Or is it based on who you are—right now?

When your self-worth is based on who you are—not what you have done, can do, or will do—you will no longer be easy prey for negative self-talk, and you won't be tied up in "nots."

Gena grew up in a two-parent home. She was constantly criticized as a child for not doing things right. As a result, she began to think that she was not worth loving. When she was a teen, she figured, *Hey, I'm not good enough, and I'll never be good enough, so why try?* Such negative internal talk and "nots" set her on a rebellious path pursuing a wild lifestyle that continued until her sophomore year in college. Then she found out she was pregnant.

Gena's parents and the parents of David, the baby's father, joined into a force that pushed Gena and David together into a rushed marriage. But it wasn't a marriage that would last. "I married a bum," Gena admits. "Neither of us was ready to be a parent. And we weren't ready for marriage, either."

Five years later, Gena and David divorced. Gena was jobless, and little Nathan was four-and-a-half years old. In counseling, Gena finally made the connection to her self-talk. "I grew up telling myself I was never good enough. So I married a bum who wasn't good enough because I thought that's what I deserved. When we got divorced, I fig-ured, *You screwed up your life once, so you might as well screw it up again. It's the one thing you're good at.*"

It wasn't until Gena began to see herself as a person of worth that her life and her child's life began to turn around. She realized that she would probably never be wealthy. "I'll be lucky if I have an extra buck for ice cream," she says. "But I'm learning to give Nathan what I can. Time with me. And I'm learning how to talk to him in a different dialogue than I grew up with. I want him to know that he is my greatest treasure. And how much Mommy loves him, even if I can't get him the latest and greatest like his friends have."

> If you want your children to know their worth, realize your own.

If you want your children to know their worth, realize your own. Learn to treat yourself with respect. Fight the self-talk that says you're worthless, a loser. Take the "nots" out of your vocabulary.

Put Yourself in the Driver's Seat of Life!

Thriving in life means that you put yourself in the driver's seat. You're not waiting on anyone else to show you where to go, but you're making decisions for yourself and your family.

How can you best take control?

CONFRONT YOUR FEAR.

What is your biggest fear as a single parent? That you'll be alone all your life? That you will fail in raising the children you love? That you just won't be able to stand the pressure of doing everything solo?

If you're fearful, then good for you!

"What? Are you crazy, Dr. Leman? How can fear be good for you?" you're asking.

Let me explain it this way: A little dose of fear in anyone's life is healthy. Fear can be a motivating thing. It can push you to succeed and show you the direction you should go.

But it's important to identify the fear so that it's not some nameless thing hanging over your head. When you've got it pegged, I've got some advice for you. *Run* toward that sucker! No sashaying, waddling, creeping, meandering, or tiptoeing. *Run* toward that fear. If you approach your fear in such an aggressive manner, you're saying that you refuse to let that fear paralyze or control you any longer. You are taking charge. And rightfully so.

Cutting a path you've never traveled before will, understandably, generate some fear. Very few folks like to jump onto unfamiliar turf. It makes us uncomfortable. Well, I've got news for you. Different stages in your life will make you uncomfortable. Different stages in your children's lives (when he moves from baby to toddler or when she becomes an adolescent or when he moves from teen to young adult) will make you uncomfortable. And they will generate fear.

But that fear doesn't have to control your life. In the movie *What about Bob?* Bill Murray plays Bob, a psychiatric patient whose world is very small. He feels he can't "do life" without his psychologist, Dr. Marvin, played by Richard Dreyfuss. So when Dr. Marvin goes on vacation, Bob shows up at his lake house and pesters him relentlessly. He's determined to follow Marvin's book, *Baby Steps.*

You may not be ready for aggressive running. But I urge you to at least take baby steps (and no backward steps, either—at least not intentionally) to get yourself *moving* in the right direction. Once you become more comfortable with facing your fear, you can start walking . . . and then running.

> A little dose of fear in anyone's life is healthy.

The most important thing to remember is that, although it takes tens of thousands of baby steps to climb any mountain, if you keep putting one foot in front of the other, you'll eventually reach the summit. But you'll reach it faster if you take bigger steps.

At times you will still feel overwhelmed. You'll still get that ache in your gut that's the result of fear. But don't let that fear keep you from moving ahead. Continue to take life one day at a time, one step at a time. As you grow more confident, you can take bigger and bigger steps until you are running excitedly toward your goal of making single parenting work.

OWN UP TO YOUR PART.

"What is wrong with the world today?" the editor of a British newspaper asked in the early twentieth century.

Author G. K. Chesterton wrote this simple reply:

> Dear Sir:
>
> I am.
>
> Yours, G. K. Chesterton[2]

If you are divorced or separated, your immediate response may not be to admit, *Yes, I am what went wrong with our relationship*. It's so much easier (and, yes, satisfying) to point the finger of blame at someone other than yourself. But if you're honest with yourself and you carefully evaluate the past, you'll begin to see the part(s) you have played—however large or small—in the breakup.

Perhaps your desire for a house and a car that were nicer than you could afford contributed to your financial difficulties as a couple. (Material things often take priority over relationships, and before long, married couples find themselves out of touch with each other, their marriage left by the wayside.)

Or perhaps you realize that while your spouse was the one who ultimately blew up and hit you, you both regularly struggled for power in the relationship.

Almost certainly, neither you nor your spouse was the sole reason your relationship turned south. (Even those who have suffered extreme abuse at the hands of their spouse often realize that they saw hints of their spouse's unsettled state of mind before marriage, but they talked themselves into believing that their spouse would "settle down" after marriage. Or they saw hints of too much control but cast it in the light of "Oh, he loves me, so he wants to keep track of me every minute.") By acknowledging your part in the failure of your marriage, you become aware of your own shortcomings. You bring them into the light where you can study them and work on them.

No, it's not easy. In fact, you may feel more guilty as you examine your role(s) in how the past played out. But it's important that you heal from these critical issues in your life because they affect you and your family *right now*. What do I mean by that? If your controlling nature contributed to your divorce, imagine what effect your control might have on your children if you don't acknowledge it and open that wound so it can be healed. If you were uncommunicative with your spouse, which led to extreme distance between the two of you, imagine what effect your lack of communication might have on your children. Or if your expectations of your spouse were extremely high, do you think your children are going to live up to your expectations for them if you aren't willing to acknowledge what part that played in your relationship with your ex?

So toss the pity parties out the window and own up to your role(s). You're the one who decided to marry that person. You're the one who went through with the physical act and got pregnant. It's time for you to be the adult.

And it's time to make sure you aren't falling into the same bad patterns again.

STOP AND LISTEN.

When your mother-in-law launches into you, telling you how you should raise your kids differently, perhaps you're accustomed to simply nodding and taking everything in.

"Uh-huh," you blindly agree. "Okay."

Changing your life patterns isn't easy, especially when you're tempted to go on autopilot as you face certain situations. But it's important that you think about what you're doing before you react. Ask yourself, *What do I usually do? What do I usually tell myself? What am I going to do differently that's healthier for me and my family?*

Then listen to what you're telling yourself right now. You may already be a few sentences into beating yourself up with internal talk. If you are, you could say, "You know what? I just realized something. What I said isn't true, and it certainly isn't helping the situation. I hope you'll excuse me, but I think I just had a verbal pity party. Unfortunately, you were the one who had to hear it. So I'm going to take back everything I just said."

It's hard to change the way you respond to those around you or to moments of frustration or times of crisis. But by closing your mouth before it opens and listening to your internal talk before you respond, you're on your way to a much healthier way of living.

USE "I" RATHER THAN "YOU/HE/SHE."

"You make me so angry!"
"You never listen to me!"
"You men are all the same!"
"You only think of yourself—and never your family!
  Our family would be a lot better off if you thought
  about someone other than yourself for once."
"All you care about is *you!*"

What do these messages have in common? They're all about "you." There's a big difference between saying, "You make me angry" and "When that happens, I feel angry." Or between "What's wrong with you? You never even thought to invite me to the party!" and "I feel angry that I was not invited to the party. When that happens, I feel put down."

One points the finger of blame; the other simply describes how you feel without placing blame.

Using "I" instead of "you" messages works whether you're talking to someone face-to-face or whether you're talking to yourself in front of the mirror. If you can face the person who's making you angry in an adult way and talk civilly about how you feel, then take the high road and do so. If you tend to get emotional—your voice starts to quiver, your heart beats in anger the minute you spot that person—a vocal interaction could very well end up degenerating into a fight. So I suggest a different way of getting the "I" message across. Why not write out that "I" message instead? Send it in an e-mail or letter. Or if you're going to talk with the person face-to-face, have it written out in front of you so you can articulate it well.

You can't go through your entire life working out your anger toward your ex or the guy who decided never to marry you in the first place. Life has to go on. You have two choices: Either you hang on to your anger and become a victim, or you deal with it as best you can and become a survivor—and then after a survivor, a thriver!

BE GOOD AND ANGRY.

I may not remember many of the sermons I've heard at church, but I'll never forget one my pastor gave titled "How to Be Good and Angry." That title immediately caught my attention because it speaks to a misconception that many people have regarding anger. Being good and being angry aren't necessarily contradictory. We can be good (meaning that it's okay) and angry (due to real sin and wrongs) at the same time. The apostle Paul writes in his letter to the Ephesians, "In your anger do not sin,"[3] precisely because anger can either be righteous or can lead to sin.

Unfortunately, many of us assume that being angry is categorically bad. You may have told your child who expresses anger, "Now, don't you talk like that!" I understand why you wouldn't want your child to be angry, but the reality is that there are reasons for his or her anger—just as there are reasons for your anger.

I'd like you to try a little thought experiment. Close your eyes and imagine that every time you get angry, you take a deep breath and blow into a balloon. Before long, that balloon will be blown up too far. It will explode and snap back in your face.

Each of us has a kind of emotional balloon inside. As your emotions build and you become more and more angry, you can take the pressure only so long before you explode. But if you take that balloon filled with all your "hot air," pinch it at the neck, and let the air squeak out, you make that terrible squealing sound that used to annoy your brother or sister when you were a kid. Notice, however, what happens to the balloon. The pressure inside drops, and the probability of the balloon blowing up in your face is reduced to zilch.

What's my point? Holding in your anger won't help; in fact, it can hurt you emotionally, spiritually, and physically, as well as impede your relationships. Whether you're an NBA basketball player or a four-year-old—and especially if you're an NBA basketball player with the emotional maturity of a four-year-old!—learn to express your anger in positive ways. Talk it out with a trusted friend, journal it, or pray it to God.

You may have every right to be angry about the loss of your spouse to that drunk driver, about your spouse's affair, about the fact that you were left with the kids when your ex headed out to "go find herself," or about the fact that your weaselly boyfriend dumped you when he found out you were pregnant. And you'll find that the pain from these events may surface in unexpected ways throughout the years.

> Stay good and angry.

But if you stay good and angry, your anger won't be in charge of you. You'll be in charge of it.

REPLACE GUILT WITH GRACE.

Some moments in life, however mundane, have the power to transform our perspectives forever.

I remember one night, driving home from the airport over thirty years ago, listening to the radio. The program host was discussing Paul's letter to the Romans, in which he bemoans his inability to do what he wants to do and his propensity to do the things he doesn't want to do. At one point, in a fit of frustration with himself, Paul calls himself "a wretched man."[4]

"Wretched man"?! I thought. *Paul—one of the pillars of the Christian church, author of much of the New Testament, a man willing to die for the faith—thought he was a wretched man? If Paul thought he was wretched, what hope is there for you and me?*

Another Bible story came to mind—the story of David, Israel's king, who committed adultery with Bathsheba, the wife of one of his soldiers, and then had her husband killed in battle. Yet in spite of all that David did, in the words of Scripture he was still considered a man after God's own heart.[5]

I always thought that was inspiring news for the rest of us, because if King David committed adultery, conspired to murder his mistress's husband, and then carried out that dirty deed—yet *still* found himself within God's graces—then there is hope for all of us, no matter what we've done.

God's grace *always* trumps our worst circumstances and our worst actions.

As I listened to the radio host talk that night about God's grace in the life of the apostle Paul, it was as if a light went on inside me. *You know,* I thought, *in spite of the poor choices we make and the circumstances we find ourselves in, God loves us no matter what.*

One of the most important things you can do to promote your healing is to allow any guilt you feel for leading your children into a single-parent situation to be replaced with grace—grace toward others, grace for yourself, and most profoundly, God's grace for you.

Guilt will only serve to drag you back face-to-face with your past. If you realize that you married a creep, you may feel tremendous guilt that your child now suffers having only one parent around. If you got pregnant outside of marriage, your guilt

> God's grace *always* trumps our worst circumstances and our worst actions.

may take the form of, *How could I have been so dumb as to believe that creep?* If your wife died, you may feel tremendous guilt for any fights—uh, *loud discussions*—that you had.

Grace, on the other hand, frees you from the past and enables you to look forward in confidence and hope. But grace is tricky business, especially if much of your life has been based on rewards for what you've done (studying hard to make the grade in school, earning a paycheck, gaining sales commission) instead of for who you are. (In the Key 4 section, I'll talk about how you can develop healthy self-esteem in your child, starting right now.) That's why so many of us find the free gift of God's grace difficult to accept.

Grace doesn't mean that your past won't still hurt you at times. In fact, I can guarantee that events of your past may hurt worse for a time, as you work through them. It's kind of like ripping away a Band-Aid and cleansing the wound with an antibiotic. But the wound can never heal otherwise.

The question is, will you choose deep healing and its temporary pain, or will you merely endure—or even cling to—your familiar pain as a way of life for you and your children?

As you replace guilt with grace, hope becomes the driving force behind your decisions. It puts you back in the driver's seat of your life.

You still won't be able to see far ahead, around all of life's turns, but at least the road in front of you will be uncluttered with the garbage of guilt.

So why not toss out the guilt trips?

WHEN YOU GET STUCK, GET HELP!

During your healing process you may find yourself circling around again and again over the same problems you've dealt with a hundred times. Try as you may, you simply can't get yourself unstuck. If talking with trusted friends hasn't helped, it's time to find a counselor. Don't wait until you're totally overwhelmed.

> Toss out the guilt trips.

There's no shame in asking for help. And single dads, I'm talking specifically to you now. Single moms are far more likely than single dads to ask for help from a counselor. Perhaps it's because dads may feel the need to have it all together on their own and may feel like less of a man for needing to ask for help. But let me assure you—you are *more* of a man if you choose the brave route and get help for yourself and your children.

Look at it this way: Every one of us needs help from time to time, and this is simply your time. Asking for help from a counselor is not a sign of weakness any more than getting help from a plumber when you try to fix the bathroom pipes in your house without success. If you've tried your best by yourself and the situation still isn't fixed, you call the plumber. If you don't, you eventually end up with sewage backed up in your home. And who wants that?

A professional counselor is objective, has worked with others in situations similar to yours, and can offer ideas on how to get unstuck. Even though the bill may sting a bit, meeting with a counselor can help you get back on track again. And if there simply isn't any way you can afford to meet with one, look into professional counseling with social service agencies or a pastor at a local church.

When seeking a counselor, look for someone who encourages you and who offers practical suggestions on how to solve your problems at hand. Your counselor's job should be to work herself out of a position. Don't fall for the belief that you're chronically sick and need the good doctor for years or even for the rest of your life. Remember, you're still the one in the driver's seat. *You*, not your counselor. So you need to get behind the wheel and steer toward your family's destination.

GAIN PERSPECTIVE ON DISASTERS AND MISTAKES.

How do you feel, deep inside, about the mistakes you have made in your life? about the disastrous events that have happened to you? Have you allowed yourself to learn from them and move on? Or are they still dragging you down into the muck of feeling like a failure? like you'll always make mistakes?

Let me tell you a story that may help you put mistakes in perspective, like it did for me.

On the evening of December 9, 1914, fire blazed through the concrete building of Edison Industries, gutting the workplace of famous inventor Thomas Edison. The financial loss was estimated at more than two million dollars—an enormous sum even by today's standards and enough to make your head spin in the early 1900s. In those days, concrete buildings were thought to be fireproof, so Thomas Edison was insured for only $238. A lifetime of work by one of the world's great geniuses was lost in the fire!

The famous inventor, then sixty-seven years old, had lost everything.

Talk about a tragedy. A disaster. And Edison himself had contributed to it by making the mistake of only insuring his building for a small sum.

If you were Edison, what would you do? (I'd probably stare at the devastation in shock, kick myself around for a while, then get serious about figuring out what I should do next.)

The morning after the fire, as Edison stood among the ashes of his life's work, he said, "There is great value in disaster. All our mistakes are burned up. Thank God we can start anew."[6]

"There is great value in disaster." What a positive perspective in the face of profound loss! It takes great hope to survey the ashes around you and see value in them. If you're like most people, as you think back to your divorce, your unexpected pregnancy, or the death of your spouse,

your first thought probably isn't, *There is "great value" there. Look at everything I'm gonna learn!*

But stop for a moment and think back over your life. Consider the seasons when you really changed as a person, those moments of "great value" that altered your perspective. Did those times follow great success or great failure? If you're like most people, those significant moments probably followed great grief, failure, mistakes, or disasters.

Why is that?

Because difficult times are a stepping-stone to personal growth.

When I was assistant dean of students at the University of Arizona, part of my job was dealing with all the disciplinary action in that school of thirty-five thousand students—and trust me, thirty-five thousand students can get into an awful lot of trouble.

One day after I'd dished out a particularly heavy load of discipline, with more to come, I visited the office of the dean, my boss, to whine about the many problems facing me.

"Kevin," he said in his typically stoic manner, "be thankful for your problems. If it wasn't for your problems, I wouldn't have a need for you in this job, now would I?"

That whipped things back into perspective for this young pup!

"Thank you, Dean," I squeaked, and turned to go face my "problems."

I share that story because when we come across problems, we most often tend to see them as negatives rather than as challenges—even opportunities to make something new out of the stuff of our lives. But as you choose to head down that road, taking one step at a time in the dark, and then beginning to walk, then run as you start to see the light, you will build a track record of success. Your present crisis slips into the past, then becomes a memory, while the hopeful future you once thought seemed so distant becomes your present.

Edison was right—valuable lessons do come from the ashes of challenging experiences. And the famous inventor didn't just say that to sound good. He lived it. When one of his assistants once commented on the inventor's lack of results—fifty thousand failures as he endeavored to design a storage battery, for example—Edison had a great comeback.

"Results?" remarked Edison. "Why, man, I have gotten a lot of results. I know fifty thousand things that won't work."[7]

As you look back, you may be able to rattle off fifty thousand things that didn't work—and then add a few thousand more for good measure. But have you looked at it from the opposite perspective? Now that you know what doesn't work, you know more about what does work! Even more, you are already making single parenting work.

Thomas Edison could have given up after Edison Industries was leveled by fire. But three weeks after the blaze, he completed the first phonograph, one of his greatest inventions.

Thanks be to God that mistakes—our mistakes or others' mistakes—are "burned up" and that we can "start anew."

❄ ❄ ❄

KEY Qs . . .

- What is your internal talk saying to you right now? Do you hear any lies? any guilt? Identify the specific thoughts and emotions you are hearing and feeling.

- In what ways can you put yourself more in the driver's seat of your family's life? Explain.

- How have your difficult times been a stepping-stone to personal growth?

CHAPTER 5

Three Mistakes You Don't Want to Make

It's public knowledge that everybody makes mistakes. "To err," the saying goes, "is human."

I don't know about you, but I've certainly tested that age-old principle more times than I can count. I've fumbled my share of life balls.

One time in particular stands out. My kids and I were staying in western New York. I had volunteered to drive to the other side of Chautauqua Lake to pick up lunch for everyone at a local restaurant. (And to understand this story, you have to know that I'm the kind of thrifty guy who, on his first date, actually ordered one hamburger and split it into two.)

While I was standing there waiting for our food, the phone rang.

"Is there a Leman here?" an employee of the restaurant called out.

I held up my hand.

"Telephone." He held out the phone.

Telephone? I thought as I walked over and put the phone to my ear. *That's odd. Who knows I'm here?*

"Dad, Dad!" said my daughter Krissy on the other end. "Do you know where you're supposed to be *right now?*"

"Sure. I'm here getting everybody's food."

"No!" she said. "Dad, you're supposed to be at the Holiday Inn. A bunch of people are waiting for you to speak!"

It's during such times that you wish life had a computer's *Undo* function. I called the coordinator for my speaking engagement and nearly stumbled over myself in apology. He was gracious, saying that it happens to all of us.

Thankfully, many of our mistakes don't wind up nearly as bad as they could.

But sometimes the opposite is true. Sometimes our seemingly insignificant decisions carry *big* consequences. What may feel inconsequential or even helpful at the time—the decision to move to a different state following a divorce, for example, or slowly relinquishing responsibility to your parents to care for your family—can have detrimental effects on your children at a time when they need all the stability they can get.

When they especially need *you.*

And all this may come at a time when your own personal needs for help and for companionship are valid and at their very highest. It's no wonder that single parents often make some of their most damaging decisions while trying to set things *right.*

> Single parents often make some of their most damaging decisions while trying to set things *right.*

For example, you may justify your desire to date by telling yourself that you want to replace that missing parent "for your child's sake." But instead of falling in love, you're more likely "falling in *need.*" You're courting trouble by stumbling into a relationship that's far from fixing any perceived problems you may have. This new relationship only complicates them.

Or, with all good intentions for your children, you may be slowly relinquishing your parenting responsibilities to your own parents. But in the long run, what you're really doing is replacing yourself, little by little, with your parents as your children's primary authority.

Although you may strongly feel the urge to make major changes in your life, doing so now is a big mistake. The very urge you feel—to act quickly—may have been the very thing that led you to jump into marriage or into bed in the first place. And making quick decisions now can lead you into more trouble. It's the old "jumping out of the frying pan and into the fire" philosophy.

Single parents do it all the time in three areas.

Mistake #1: We're Going to Move . . . Now!

When change comes your way, you adapt. When you start a new job, for example, you acquire skills and establish a routine to fit in. When you begin a new exercise program, it takes your body awhile to get used to it—but you adjust.

> Change is fine—in moderation.

Change, however, sometimes leads to greater, excessive change. You change jobs, and suddenly you're not only acquiring new skills, you're out buying new clothes, rearranging your living room furniture, and leafing through magazines for new hairstyles. There's nothing wrong with repainting your plain white living room wall fire-engine red or getting that new hairstyle. Change is fine—in moderation.

But a peculiar thing happens following the sudden absence of a spouse. This is the time when many parents will suddenly uproot from all they know and strike off in a completely new direction. Instead of simply remodeling the living room, they're selling the entire place and moving three states away.

Let's say that you and your ex have lived in Maine's town of Old York since you married right out of college. It's your kids' home, and they don't know anything else. But following the divorce, you're tempted to pack your bags and the kids to move to New York to "start fresh," to do everything you can to distance yourself from that creep.

I strongly advise you, however, to avoid such major, trigger-happy decisions as moving when life knocks you squarely in the teeth with the loss of your spouse. When your family's foundation has been severely shaken by the emotional earthquake of divorce or death, that is not the time to yank out one of the load-bearing walls of your house. Or to leave that home behind.

Instead, if you stay put, you'll have the support of your own family, if they live nearby. You'll have your friends, your community of faith, your job if you have one, your child's friends and school, and familiarity with the community. You won't be spending precious time finding a new house or apartment and tracking down grocery stores and school possibilities.

And there's one key reason you may not have considered—your ex. Yup, the very person who got you thinking about fleeing for the hills. As much as you might want to completely leave that person behind and head for a more hospitable home—the windswept Mongolian highlands, for example—remember this: While your ex may have failed as a husband or wife, he or she is still your child's parent. Cutting your ex out of your child's life (unless he is causing physical, mental, or emotional harm to your child) is doomed to backfire because your child will begin propping up that irreplaceable relationship with an idealized parent who looks nothing like the real thing.

If you're trying to decide whether or not to move, consider this: *What kind of person is your ex?* If you have a four-year-old and a six-year-old, and their father holds a job that he can't transfer from, I'd opt to stay in that town *if* you feel that he will work at being the dad he should be to those kids. I'd do so even if your family lives three states away and is begging you to come live near them.

What I've just said may make you want to use this book as a doorstop as you pack the moving van. But give me a chance to explain. Maintaining that proximity to your children's involved father is worth it *if he is doing his best to succeed as a parent* (more on this in chapter 13).

If your child's father is choosing not to be involved or is not allowed to be involved (as in a court decision in the case of abuse), then you have another decision to make. Where will you find your best support in this situation? Where you are right now? Or with your family or close friends in another location? Even if you later do decide to move, I still encourage you, *for now*, to stay where you are for your children's sake. Until you can think through the options carefully and logically.

EXCEPTIONS TO THE RULE
But there are exceptions to this rule—circumstances under which it may be a good idea to consider moving.

If the town isn't big enough for both of you . . .
When you think of your ex, you may imagine yourself pacing down the dusty street of a Western town, your spurs chinking against the ground,

your hands hovering over the pistols at your side as the two of you face off. So I have to ask: Whether you live in downtown L.A. or rural Kansas, is your town big enough for the two of you?

You may want to head into the sunset without looking back at your hometown or your community of faith, where you keep running into your ex's friends, "the other woman," "the other man," or well-meaning acquaintances who naively ask what the two of you are up to these days. Maybe you can't help but run into *him* or *her* at every turn. And every time you see your ex, your stomach churns and you take out the stress on your kids.

> Is your town big enough for the two of you?

You don't need to be told, "Go west, young man (or young woman)," because emotionally your bags are already packed for the move! And I can't blame you. There's nothing like being slapped in the face with the pain of the past everywhere you turn. But do your best to work things out with your ex, if it's possible. Get careful counsel if you are considering moving.

If your spouse is absent (physically or emotionally) . . .

If your ex is scheduled to take the kids every other weekend, and in reality he shows up to take them every seventh or eighth weekend, I would advise you to move—if you can legally move. In other words, unless the courts have ordered you to stay, get out of there! Having that absent father drop in every now and then for a cameo appearance (I call that the "in-n-out" ex) does more damage to your children than it benefits them. Since he's not there on a regular basis anyway, and there's every indication that he's not committed to participating regularly in his kids' lives, I'd move if I had family in the next state asking me to come live near them.

If the people who surround you are toxic . . .

However, before you make that move, carefully evaluate your family members back home. Just as there's something inherently good about having healthy family around you, there's also something inherently destructive about having hypercritical family around you. Perhaps your family is toxic, tearing you down at every turn and driving you to beat yourself up and act out of obligation. As difficult as it may be, I'd opt for staying where you are. Or if you're living close to toxic family members, I'd suggest that you move away from them.

Wherever you live, you will need a support system, which makes moving to a completely new community particularly difficult. Plowing new ground in a new job, helping your children adjust to a new school, and developing all-new relationships—all at the same time—can be extremely taxing. But when it is necessary, in order to have a fresh start in a healthy environment, then you do need to move.

If your children have really suffered at school . . .

You might also consider moving if your kids have really suffered at school. Perhaps there was a period during which you and your ex were fighting—maybe the cops were even called in by your neighbors a couple of times. If that's the case, and your kids struggled in school as a result—acting out because of the pressure at home, tossing their schoolwork to the dog, enduring embarrassing comments about their parents and home life from their peers—a fresh start in a new school might be just the thing to help them get back on track.

If you do decide to move for any of these reasons, your next step is to figure out where to move. Now is the time to ask yourself, *What's the big picture? What do I cherish most? What's most beneficial for my children?*

If it's tranquillity and quiet, and you'd like your kids to be involved in 4-H, inner-city Chicago probably isn't the place for you. Maybe you were a small-town or country girl who ended up in the big city because of your husband's work. If you've never really liked the city or felt comfortable there, that might be a good reason to move back among your beloved corn stalks.

> This is a time to move slowly and deliberately—in wisdom rather than reaction.

Whatever your decisions, this is a time to move slowly and deliberately—in wisdom rather than reaction.

Mistake #2: Surrender the Parenting of Your Children to Your Parents

There's no doubt about it. Single parenting is hard work. Imagine pitching in a baseball game through a full nine innings and then being asked to put in a few more for good measure. Now it's the bottom of the twelfth and the bases are loaded for the other team with no outs. You've thrown more pitches than you can count, and you're exhausted. So when you see that relief pitcher, your own parent, trotting in across the field from the bull pen, fresh and with much more experience than you have, you're more than ready to hand over that game ball.

"Here," you say, "I've had enough. *You* finish this game!"

You may have disagreed with your parents' every move when you were a teenager. But now as you face the daunting responsibility of parenting by yourself, their every suggestion sounds inspired. (Funny how when we're thirteen, our parents can be very dumb. But then when we turn twenty-four or so, our parents get smart overnight.) While you seem to be a catalyst for war in your own home, your parents' solutions for handling your squabbling children seem worthy of the Nobel Peace Prize.

> You're exhausted and in desperate need of help. Who wouldn't be tempted to call Parent 911?

It's no wonder you're all too eager to hand over control to your parents—especially if you live in the same house. You're exhausted and in desperate need of help. Who wouldn't be tempted to call Parent 911?

Consequently, it's easy to slip into the trap of letting your parents take over your role as parent. And so many grandparents are willing to do just that. They want to take hold of the reigns for all kinds of reasons. They may be acting out of guilt because they feel bad about their own parenting or what has happened to you. They may miss parenting, and the work may satisfy an empty-nest syndrome. They may sweep in because they know how to get things done, and things certainly need doing! Upon seeing their child—you—floundering under the responsibility, their parenting instincts kick in again.

You, on the other hand, may wish, either consciously or subconsciously, that you could turn back the clock to be a child again. But is that what you really want in the long run? Do you want to give up control to your parents so that they once again become the parents, and you wind up more as an older sibling to your kids?

Remember this: While your parents may serve as wonderful coaches, you are still the pitcher on game day. And the pitcher can't turn the ball over to the coach in the middle of it all. It's much more important that you stay in the game, involved in the lives of your children.

Does this mean you can't ask for family to pitch in and help? Absolutely not. Our second oldest daughter, Krissy, who is now married with children, fell down the stairs one day. She broke her toe in more than one spot—and she was holding their ten-month-old baby when it happened. She could have been hurt worse. Miraculously, Conner wasn't hurt at all.

> Involvement becomes a problem when your parents' "help" renders you helpless.

"I'm so glad that we live close to each other," I told her in the hospital after we had visited with the doctor.

During that time of healing, with her husband gone all day, Krissy needed a little extra help at home—especially since Conner was at the age where he could get himself into a heap of trouble. And Sande and I, as Krissy's parents, were able to provide that.

It *is* good to have family near you. It's good for them to be *involved* in raising your children. In fact, grandparent involvement is often the very thing that helps hold single-parent families together. You do need the help of a team of people, which includes your family, to help you succeed as a single parent. More on that in chapter 7.

But involvement becomes a problem when your parents' "help" renders you helpless. Then even good intentions can be harmful—to you, to your parents, and especially to your kids.

What kind of "help" are you asking for?

Mistake #3: Just Jump from Lily Pad to Lily Pad

Gayle was in her late twenties when she filed for divorce. She'd discovered that Mike, her husband, was having an affair. But from time to time over the months that followed, they continued to talk on the phone. They would chat about the kids or how to exchange the kids on the weekends.

After a couple of years, Mike expressed an interest in making their relationship work again. Gayle was eager. She'd been on the "solo circuit" long enough to know that things were tough. There weren't very many eligible men in sight. *Maybe we could make a go of it again,* she thought.

So, in spite of her wounded trust, Gayle and Mike dove into "dating" again. Within a matter of weeks—after what seemed like such a wonderful time of reconnection, filling Gayle with hope for their relationship—they returned to a sexually intimate relationship. This, of course, happened after the kids were in bed, so they never knew. And Mike didn't move back home. Gayle insisted that the children not know unless it was going to work out for sure.

It wasn't long after that, however, when Gayle began feeling something strange happening to her body. When she began developing painful sores on her genitals, the first of her outbreaks with herpes simplex 2, she finally realized what a terrible mistake she'd made. Because she'd jumped back into a relationship with her ex instead of going slowly and asking questions about his lifestyle, she was the one who would suffer for years to come.

Now is the time to slow down. And when I say slow down, I mean slow *w-a-y* down. It's best to come to a complete stop. If you can, even back up a bit, because you can't see the whole forest when you're deep in the trees. You'll need to have others help you walk in wisdom during this time. Share openly with trusted friends; get the perspective of someone with more life experience. You don't want to jump back into a relationship with your ex or into the dating scene faster than your three-year-old whiz kid of a daughter can tie her shoes.

I call it leaping from lily pad to lily pad.

Life may look greener elsewhere in the

> When I say slow down, I mean slow *w-a-y* down.

pond—I can almost guarantee that. But a quick hop to the next lily pad will quickly complicate family matters, not simplify them. You are extremely vulnerable during this season of your life, and hopping from lily pad to lily pad in search of a kiss from your prince or princess isn't the best way to proceed. It will only confuse you and your kids. And it may turn a challenging situation into a nearly impossible one.

Jana knows about that. Four months after her husband died, she met Hank at a local restaurant. Since she was lonely and longing for love, things moved quickly in their relationship. Three months later, she found out she was pregnant—and Hank moved on. Imagine having to explain that to your ten-year-old.

"But Dr. Leman," you might ask, "what if I really *have* healed inside and I *do* meet a great guy?"

I'm not saying dating relationships that form at such times can't work out. Some do. But it is extremely difficult for you to gauge from within whether you've healed enough to date. (More on dating and how it affects you and your children in chapter 16.)

By plunging into another relationship during this period, you can get yourself into real trouble, and you can shake your child's world at a time when he needs it to be stable more than anything else.

Why Stability Is So Crucial

I'll share with you an important secret. Just when you may *feel* like running in a different direction—to a new home, to get help, or to a new relationship—you're better off following the advice of the White Rabbit in *Alice in Wonderland*: "Don't just do something. Stand there!"

> "Don't just do something. Stand there!"

If you "just do something" for the sake of distancing yourself from your present situation, you can easily compound the problem. That's why people who are down to their last dollar rack up twenty thousand dollars' worth of credit-card bills they know they'll never pay. That's why soldiers who panic in the heat of battle begin firing in any direction, sometimes killing their fellow soldiers. And that's why many single parents who feel the emotional void of a divorce or the death of their spouse "just do something" by plunging headlong into another relationship that, rather than helping, ends up hurting both them and their kids.

What your children need the most right now is stability, not change. They need to know that they are loved and that you are in control. They need to know that, even in a time of crisis, you are logical and levelheaded.

By making a plan for your family's present and future, you bring stability to what can often be a chaotic world. You focus your energy, your priorities, your time, and your money to do what is necessary at this time. Making the best of a difficult situation requires a level head, a firm grasp on priorities, and a healthy perspective on the big picture.

G. K. Chesterton, one of the great writers of the twentieth century, was once asked, "If you were marooned on a desert island and could have only one book with you, what book would you choose?" You might have expected the famous author to reply, "The Bible." After all, he was not only one of the greatest thinkers of his time, but he was also a devout Christian whose book *The Everlasting Man* helped persuade a young atheist named C. S. Lewis, who later wrote the beloved *Chronicles of Narnia*, to become a Christian.[1] But with characteristic wit, as Chesterton considered living out the rest of his days with only coconuts for company, he answered more matter-of-factly: "*Thomas' Guide to Practical Shipbuilding.*"[2]

The best solutions in difficult times are usually the most practical ones. If you're marooned on a desert island, build a ship. If your car is running on fumes, find a gas station. If you're in a building and someone yells, "Fire!" find the nearest exit rather than searching out the flames so you can run into them.

This is not the time for new beginnings—to move three states away or to look for personal enrichment. (After all, anyone who becomes a parent comes to realize, sooner or later, that part of parenting means you are choosing not to be selfish. You are choosing to put others first.)

If you maintain composure in the face of adversity, your children will notice. And your stability will set them on a healthy path for life. They will realize that, yes, bad things can happen. You can make mistakes. But those bad things and mistakes don't have to dictate the rest of your life.

If you proceed with thoughtful caution in your own decisions, your children will learn to do so, too.

And that's a legacy most parents want for their children.

✿ ✿ ✿

KEY Qs . . .

- Which of the three mistakes have you been most tempted to make? Explain.

  to move?
  to surrender your parenting to your parents?
  to jump from lily pad to lily pad?

- In what area of life do you need to "stand there" instead of doing something?

- How can you best provide stability for your children right now?

CHAPTER 6

What's Birth Order Got to Do with It?

I had been waiting nine months for our second child to be born, and nine months goes by unbearably slowly for Kevin Leman when a child's on the way. Because we'd already been through the birthing routine with our firstborn daughter, Holly, Sande and I were both familiar with what to expect when the day finally arrived.

But when the moment of the birth came, somehow it wasn't at all what I had expected.

My first thought as I looked at that little miracle who had just emerged wasn't an admiring *What a doll!*

Or a celebratory *Welcome to the world, kiddo!*

Or a more spiritual *Thank you, God, for the gift of this precious child.*

No, my very first thought as I looked at my second-born child entering the world was, *She doesn't look anything like Holly!*

With her little melon head, she looked about as un-Holly as she could possibly look.

In hindsight, I'm ashamed to admit my thoughts because they were incredibly disrespectful. Of course she didn't look like Holly—she's Krissy!

What did you expect, Leman? Holly, part 2? I ask myself now, shaking my head.

The birth of our second child was a big reminder of what I'd already known in theory but was seeing anew in the flesh—that God breaks the mold with each and every one of us.

Identical Twins?!

Every child has different gifts and abilities. Some have a knack for business and excel at charismatic leadership, while others go quietly about their creative endeavors behind the scenes. Some *are* social butterflies. Others would prefer to simply sit and *watch* butterflies.

I knew the moment Krissy was born that she was completely different from Holly—from the shape of her head to the shape of her heart—and the two of them are different even today.

Isn't it truly amazing that all of your cubs came out of the same den, yet are so different? Even identical twins, who physically appear to be the same person, are different in so many ways. Why did almighty God give them different fingerprints? To help the FBI? I don't think so. I think it's a small, tangible reminder that even children from the same family, who are alike in so many other respects, are still unique.

> Of course she didn't look like Holly—she's Krissy!

One of a kind.

But it's an easy thing for us parents to forget. You may assume that because your older son, John, is a star football quarterback in high school, his younger brother must at least have some athletic blood coursing through his body. But younger Peter is definitely not athletically inclined—unless you can call chess club athletic. He's too busy exercising his mind, reading books, and charting a course for himself academically to think about chasing a ball and running around outside in tights.

Interestingly enough, although each one of us is completely different, there are also some remarkable similarities among children, based on the order they were born in their family. It's called *birth order*. By knowing some of the basics about birth order, you can better anticipate potential conflicts that might arise in your home, as well as ways that you can help your children of different birth orders thrive.

The Birth Order Theory

I'm probably most well-known for one thing—and thankfully it isn't for setting that garbage can on fire in my high school English class. It's for my book titled *The Birth Order Book*. Birth order is simply this: whether you were born first, second, or later in your family. And my theory is that your birth order has a powerful influence on the kind of person you will be, the type of job you'll choose, the kind of person you'll marry, and even the kind of parent you'll be.

Everywhere I go, people ask me whether my birth order theory works.

It really does!

I won't go into all the nuances of birth order theory in this book—for that you can look to *The Birth Order Book* (see p. 273). But I do want to point out some crucial things that will affect the way you raise your children. The way your children will respond to each other. The way you and your individual child will relate to each other.

> Birth order has a powerful influence on the kind of person you will be, the type of job you'll choose, the kind of person you'll marry, and even the kind of parent you'll be.

Each place in the birth order has its built-in strengths as well as its weaknesses.

FIRSTBORNS

Of the first twenty-three astronauts in space, twenty-one of them were firstborns—and the other two were the only children in their families. That makes perfect sense, because firstborns tend to be decisive and make good leaders. And only-born children are like firstborns squared. They're mini-adults who think that coloring in the lines in preschool is good preparation for the SAT test. They're the kids who know the word *infinity* by the time they're four years old. (Ask a lastborn like me, and he'll say, "Huh?")

Firstborns (or only-borns) tend to be

- reliable
- perfectionistic
- conscientious
- list makers
- well organized
- serious
- scholarly.

Firstborns can get an awful lot done. (In fact, they're a little intimidating to lastborns like me.) They are usually very self-motivated (like the six-year-old only child who has practiced violin for two years by herself, without her mother's nudging). They are the ones you want on committees because you *know* they'll get the job done. They are natural leaders. They're the folks who always look put together.

> Firstborns can get an awful lot done.

But firstborns have their weaknesses, too. They can tend to

- be negative
- procrastinate (sometimes because they're afraid they can't do a job perfectly)
- find fault (with themselves and others). They can easily fall into flaw-picking, judgmental mode because they want everything to be perfect.

In short, they can be very tough on themselves.

MIDDLEBORNS

Middleborns might be the second born in a family of three or the second and third children born in a family of four.

Middleborns tend to be

- mediators
- ones who avoid conflict at all costs
- independent. After all, they had an older brother/sister busy doing activities and a younger sibling who needed his diaper changed!
- extremely loyal to a peer group (which is where they get most of their attention since home's a busy place) and have many friends. Friendship is the most important thing in a middleborn's life.

But middleborns have weaknesses, too. They tend to

- be introspective. It's hard to get them to share their hearts and lives around the family table.

- go outside the family for psychological strokes. A middle child isn't often noticed as much at home, so it's easy to see why he finds comfort in friendships rather than in family.

> Friendship is the most important thing in a middleborn's life.

And that's why you, as the parent of a middleborn, need to go out of your way to notice her and include her.

LASTBORNS

A lastborn is the baby of the family. They are

- outgoing
- "people persons" (they make great salespeople)
- charming
- show-offs and lovers of fun (if you've ever seen otters play at the zoo, you'll know what I mean)
- often seemingly fearless.

When you see kids "cutting up," it's more than likely that they're lastborns. Lastborns are the kids who spoil the annual family photo because they're unpredictable. They're the kids with the "I'll show 'em" attitude, and this often gets them in trouble.

Lastborns tend to

- seek attention negatively. In fact, many of them will demand that you pay attention to them because of their antics.
- love the spotlight. They'll do *anything* to stay in it.

> Lastborns are the kids who spoil the annual family photo.

- look for rewards. Like the seals at Sea World, lastborns look for a fish at every turn.

They're the kids who claim your attention because they're always up to something.

How You Can Help

Being aware of firstborn, middleborn, and lastborn characteristics—in both your children and yourself—has a host of benefits. You'll improve your relationships with your children, bring more stability to your home environment, and become more comfortable in making decisions for each individual child. It also helps to know what to expect *among* the different birth orders as your children interact.

How does this work? Again, let's take a look at each of the birth orders, with you and your family in mind.

FIRSTBORNS

Perfectionism is what I call slow suicide, and if there's one child you might have to coax away from the edge of perfectionism, it's your firstborn child. That's why I'll spend the most time in this chapter talking about firstborns.

You are in a perfect (no pun intended) position to help. Flaunting your own imperfections may not be the first thing you think of doing to help your child, especially if you're a firstborn or an only child yourself (you'd probably like to have it all together), but your firstborn needs to know that mom or dad fails, too, yet handles failure well. That's all part of your child's healthy development.

> If there's one child you might have to coax away from the edge of perfectionism, it's your firstborn child.

If your child is afraid of getting up in front of the class to give an oral report, for example, you might talk about the time in middle school that you were shaking so much you gave yourself a paper cut from the pages of your book report as you spoke. But now, as your child knows, you talk in front of thirty coworkers every day as you do computer training. In other words, you were able to overcome that fear, and now public speaking is no longer a scary thing.

If your child struggles with math, you might talk about the difficulty you sometimes have doing basic math yourself, like figuring out your checkbook or doing your taxes, or the difficulty you recently had doing year-end accounting at work.

Don't just slip in an "I messed up" every once in a while to your first-born. *Flaunt* your imperfections. Let your child know that you don't always have it all together (even if it sometimes looks that way to others). Then your child can reason, *It's okay if I don't have it all together. I can still go ahead and try, even if what I do isn't perfect.*

That may be particularly difficult for you to do if you are a firstborn or only child yourself. Why is that? Firstborn parents can spot a flaw at fifty paces, as I like to say, and they like to emphasize the perfections rather than the imperfections.

If you have a firstborn child who is always dragging his feet—and you are always pushing—most likely *you* are also a firstborn (and, no offense, a flaw-picking

> Firstborn parents can spot a flaw at fifty paces.

perfectionist). You need to know that one of the reasons your child will become adept at procrastination (if he isn't already) is to protect himself from your criticism, whether it's spoken or not. Your child's private logic (as illogical as it is) says that if he doesn't finish the job, whether it's staying in the lines when coloring his picture of Mickey Mouse or finishing his English term paper, then you can't criticize him.

The firstborn is apt to tell himself the lie that if he only had more time he could have done better, when the reality is that the firstborn lets time slide to avoid the pain of your criticism.

One of the best ways you can combat perfectionism is to tell your kids stories when you're tucking them into bed. Everyone loves a good story, but kids and stories go together like peanut butter and jelly. Tell stories about your life—not somebody else's life, but *your* life—and preferably stories with a moral. If there's a purpose served in telling your story in the third person, do so. "And then that girl got in trouble by . . ." But if possible, tell your story in the first person. "And then I got in trouble by . . ." That way your kids know the story is about you.

Amazing, isn't it, that of all the possible heroes—knights, adventurers, and astronauts rocketing to the moon—to your son or daughter, one of the most compelling characters in a story is *you*? They love to hear about your adventures, especially about the times you got in trouble.

"*You* did that, Mom?"

"Yes, I did."

"Dad! You threw snowballs at cars and got caught when you hit Aunt Gertrude's Cadillac with an ice ball?"

Kids absolutely love to hear about the times when you were in their shoes or got sent to your room because it breaks down their notion that you have it all together. They see that you're human, too!

The truth is, you, too, were a kid once. You made mistakes then, and you make mistakes now. We all make mistakes. Telling stories to your children is a great way to establish equality—that grand and wonderful idea that we're all in this thing called life together. As satisfying as being the "perfect parent" might be, it won't last. Don't think for a minute you'll get away with that deception, whether conscious or unconscious, forever. Children are the greatest sleuths on the planet. So the best thing you can do is tell the truth about your own life. Tell them when you make mistakes at work. When you've hurt someone's feelings and you need to apologize. Don't lead your kids to believe that somehow you've lived a life they can never live up to.

As five-year-old Mei told her mama, "Did you do that when you were a kid? Did you feel like that? I don't want to be the only one." Kids long for connection; they long to belong. And not just to anyone. To you. You can help them by being honest about your own imperfections.

When I taught at a university, I told my students to think of me as an old student. It was true. I was simply a former student who had graduated (thankfully!) and tucked a few more years' experience (and pounds!) under my belt.

Underneath it all, we're all flawed human beings, just trying our best. Sometimes we succeed. Sometimes we fail. But your kids—especially your firstborn—need to know that you are committed to walking alongside them and that your love is not based on how perfect they are.

There's another aspect regarding firstborns that is crucial for you to know.

Let's say it's evening, and you're paying bills at the kitchen table while your eight-year-old daughter does her math homework beside you.

"Oh, honey," you sigh as you finish writing checks, "sometimes I just don't know where the money's going to come from. Your father and I have really been at each other recently, and if he doesn't send that child support check in the next week, I don't know what's going to happen to us next month."

Stop right there. If you're sharing such thoughts and realities with your young firstborn, you're confiding too much in a child. And this is especially likely to happen between a father and a firstborn son, or a mother and a firstborn daughter.

Why is this? If you haven't cultivated deep, same-sex adult friendships, it's easy to treat your firstborn child as your intimate companion—the one with whom you share your innermost thoughts and feelings. It may feel as if the two of you are bonding when you share, but beware: You're actually loading your child with burdens too heavy for her at her age.

> Your firstborn might seem so grown up . . . but remember, she's still just a kid.

Your firstborn might seem so grown up—and compared to many kids her age, she probably is. But remember, she's still just a kid. Your firstborn is the one who has the most rules in her head and internalizes them. She is also the one most likely to have fears about losing you. She is the one of all your children who will tend to take charge. She is probably the one who has a home escape route planned for her younger brothers and sisters in case of fire, flood, or alien invasion. Of all your kids, your firstborn child is the one most likely to worry about what turns life might take if something happens to you, the sole parent.

So remember this: In your need for companionship, don't overstep your boundaries as your firstborn child's protector. Don't weigh her down with information that is just too heavy for her to bear. Instead, be the parent who builds her up, who nurtures her unique personality, birth order characteristics, and gifts, and who always sees the best in her.

If you are a firstborn yourself, most likely you have inherent organizational skills that you can use to help organize your family. Put your desire for order to work to help prioritize your activities and bring stability to your family. Recognize that your firstborn child may need more structure when returning from your ex's home (where the environment and routine may have been up for grabs—something particularly stressful for a firstborn or an only child). Also, look for ways of building up your firstborn, such as granting his "birthright" by letting him stay up later and earn a bigger allowance than his younger siblings.

Firstborns have tremendous potential to change the world. And how they see themselves is reflected through your eyes—and the way you treat them.

MIDDLEBORNS

When you were growing up, who was the rebel in your family? the one who did the kinds of things that put him behind the eight ball in life? the one who did what was unconventional—like wearing short hair when long hair was in vogue, or long hair when short hair was in vogue? the one who did things "just to be different"? the one who was the first to push the envelope in your family? the one who tended to do self-defeating things (like blowing off studying for a science exam to play b-ball with friends instead)? the one who rebelled the most against the standards of your family?

> When you were growing up, who was the rebel in your family?

Chances are very strong that the rebel in your family was a middleborn child. Rachel, a middleborn, is a beautiful blonde and a single mom. If you lived in her hometown, you'd often see her at baseball games, cheering her sons on. But here's her life story behind the scenes:

"I grew up feeling invisible in my family of five kids. When my parents did talk to me, they were always telling me what to do. I hated that. So when I was fifteen, I started steering clear of them. I hung out with my friends as much as I could and spent as little time at home as I could. I thought my parents' standards were ridiculous. When I was sixteen, I refused to go to church anymore. I went out of my way to show my dad, especially, that he couldn't be my boss.

"Well, now that I'm thirty-four, I realize how far I went out of my way to show them. If only I could have seen down the road what my rebellion would cost me. I desperately wanted attention, and believe me,

I found guys who would pay me attention. I was so naive, stupid, and immature that I fell for their lines.

"Now I have two kids by different men . . . and my boys have no relationship with their fathers. I had to quit college and start waitressing the first time I got pregnant, so I never finished school. Now I'm stuck in the same dead-end job, pouring coffee for all these guys who try to hit on me. It's weird. When I was a teen, my goal was to go my own way in life. To not let other people control my life or tell me what to do. Now I feel like everybody controls my life *but* me. I love my boys, and I wouldn't trade them for anything. I made mistakes, but *they* are not mistakes. But I'm worried. They're almost teenagers. I don't want them to fast-forward a few years and be replaying my life."

A middleborn is the most likely to feel excluded from her own family, perhaps because she's the kid stuck in the middle, who isn't noticed as much. She is used to adopting compromise as a way of life and is therefore the most likely to be overlooked. But she would make a great hostage negotiator from all those times of playing mediator between older and younger siblings!

> A middleborn is least likely to let you know how she really feels inside.

Since a middleborn is least likely to let you know how she really feels inside, you need to make a conscious effort to include her as a part of family activities. Go out of your way to pay her individual attention. Ask for her opinion. "Honey, what do *you* think we ought to do?" Give her an opportunity to give back to you and to realize that her opinion is important to you and to your family.

Since this is the child whose voice will tend to get drowned out by the dictating firstborn and the attention-loving lastborn, sometimes let your middleborn make choices that affect all of you. For instance, if you're heading out for an afternoon at one of the local parks, let your middleborn child choose which park she would like to visit. Put her first from time to time. Let her sit in the front seat of the car, if she's old enough to do so legally. Talk with her one-on-one. She will thrive with the attention she gets from you, which she might otherwise naturally relinquish because of her birth order.

If *you* are a middleborn child yourself, you might be tempted to go with the flow while raising your kids. You might naturally not want to rock the boat or cause any trouble by making decisions with which your children might disagree. You need to be careful that you're not allowing yourself to be walked on (especially by the lastborn child in your family), and you need to avoid making decisions out of guilt. Because middleborns thrive on other-than-family influences, it's crucial for you to find a friend or group of friends or a counselor you can trust. Run your decisions by them for a balanced, long-range perspective, and ask them to encourage you to not back down or compromise when faced with difficult situations.

LASTBORNS

If you were the baby of your family growing up, you've probably never met a stranger. And if worse came to worse, you'd be able to win people over so easily, you could sell dead rats for a living!

The baby of the family excels at anything where socialization pays off. He's the social butterfly of the school. The kid everybody knows. He's talkative and outgoing. He is much more likely than a firstborn or middleborn to tell you what's going on inside him. He's not afraid to step out and take risks, whether physical or emotional ones. He's the kid hanging upside down—by one leg—from the monkey bars. He has little or no fear of consequences because he's very good at getting himself out of them with his charms.

> Lastborns are like the seals at Sea World, looking for a fish at every turn.

Truly, lastborns are like the seals at Sea World, looking for a fish at every turn. They thrive on attention and reward and kick up their antics in high gear to remain in the spotlight. They need lots of strokes ("warm fuzzies," as some folks call them). And they're so charming that they tend to get a lot of attention.

But beware. Lastborns can also be demanding, powerful suckers (I ought to know. I'm a lastborn, and my antics kept my parents busy and scratching their heads for years). And if you give them attention when they're doing something negative, it only reinforces the "throwing them a fish" concept. They'll do something else negative to get another fish—the reward of your attention.

The best thing you can do with a lastborn is to reinforce any positive behavior. When your child does something good, praise him highly. Throw him a fish. But when he is doing something negative to get attention, don't offer him a fish. You may need to simply turn your attention elsewhere and ignore him for a minute. Or if the behavior is dangerous, you may need to hit the behavior head-on. "Michael, I will not tolerate that behavior. The next time you do that, you will lose your play time with your friends after school." And then you'd better follow through. Children have very good memories!

Because lastborns are so social, one of the worst punishments, in their view, is to be isolated from others. Or to have others not pay attention to them. This can work to your advantage—and your child's well-being in the long run—if you understand your lastborn and what makes him tick.

When You Lock Horns . . .

I'm convinced that knowing and understanding yours and your child's birth order are critical to the health of a family. That's why I recently undertook a project with my son, Kevin, to write books for children (and parents, too!) that would help them understand their birth order and how it affects them. There's also one for grandchildren and one for adopted children (see p. 273). I'm convinced that no age is too early to be aware of the traits of a firstborn, middleborn, or lastborn—and of the strengths and weaknesses that occur as a result.

> Which child loves to get your goat out and play with it?

Think for a minute about the child you lock horns with the most. Which child loves to get your goat out and play with it?

Which child in the family is most like you?

In all probability, you named the child with the same birth order as you!

You see, the child you tango with the most is most likely to share your birth order. If you are a firstborn, that child is probably a firstborn. If you're a middleborn, that child is probably a middleborn. If you're a lastborn, that child is probably a lastborn. It's no wonder, given the traits of your birth order, that you knock heads.

Look at it this way. Your powerful or strong-willed child didn't learn to be that way just out of thin air. She learned that interaction from a parent who was powerful and strong-willed. To put it simply, you deserve each other!

So what's going to happen next? That's up to you. When you and your child lock horns, someone has to lighten up or back off. You're the parent, the adult, so you need to make the choice not to walk into the midst of her shenanigans and start the horn locking in the first place. Don't allow yourself to fall into the trap of being the constant judge and jury of what she's doing. Otherwise, you'll only escalate the battle and end up in a huge fight that nobody can emerge from unscathed.

Sometimes the best thing you can do is retreat to your corner, do some thinking, and cool down. Then approach the subject at a later time with a more level head.

Yours and your child's birth order also affect how lenient or how tough you are on that particular child. For example, if you're the baby of the family, you may be much more sympathetic with what your lastborn son is going through with his two brothers. Although you may not realize it, you're taking his side emotionally. At the other extreme, if you're a firstborn, perfectionist mom, and you're always "should-ing" on your kids—as in, you *should* do this or you *should* do that—the child who will be affected most by that, and whom you will probably have the most conflict with, is your perfectionistic firstborn.

It all comes down to this: Each of your children is unique. And your interaction and the relationship you develop with each of them will be unique. If you are aware of the complexities of birth-order theory, you can do the least damage and the most good in your child's life. For you are the one that affects your child the most. You are the one who leaves a lasting, indelible imprint.

What do you want yours to be?

❁ ❁ ❁

KEY Qs . . .

- Are you a firstborn, middleborn, or lastborn child? Which strengths and weaknesses of that birth order do you see in yourself?

- Think about each of your children and which birth order they are. What "ahas" come to mind?

- Which child do you most lock horns with and why? What could you do to change that tendency?

KEY 3

GATHER A TEAM

Being a lone ranger can get
pretty lonely and exhausting.
You'd be surprised who might
be happy to help if you asked.
And your kids will benefit, too.

CHAPTER 7

Where's Your Support?

I'll never forget the single mom who approached me with tears in her eyes at Chicago's McCormick Place last year.

I had been conducting a parenting seminar and had just ended by encouraging parents with my firm belief that in spite of the challenges of parenting, anyone can succeed if he or she simply puts the time and energy into following the principles we had talked about.

After my talk, I stayed after to chat with those who had attended. The room had just about cleared when I noticed that a petite brunette was standing off to the side. She waited until everyone had left before she approached me. She introduced herself as Jani, then told me that simply getting away from her kids to attend the seminar was a real treat for her. She looked exhausted, and her lips trembled as she explained, "As a single mom, I'm working two eight-hour shifts. If it wasn't for my mother, who lives with me—she's on a limited income, too, and helps take care of my kids—none of us would make it."

My heart went out to her. I could see in her eyes her uncertainty and her unasked question: *How can I be a good parent with such a demanding schedule?*

"The very fact you're here," I told her, "shows how much you long to be a good parent. And that already makes you a good parent." I went on to affirm the help that she was receiving from her mom and to encourage her about all the things she already had going for her: a job that paid the bills, health that allowed her to work, and a willing mom to help her with her kids.

Jani and her mother are to each other what all single parents need most: support.

We *all* need help, whether it's medical help from a doctor, spiritual help from a pastor, or emotional help from a friend. And we especially need help when the task that lies before us is great (as all parenting is).

> You carry twice the load on your shoulders that a two-parent family does. So why do you feel so guilty asking for help?

If you're a single parent, you need even more help. I don't say that to be condescending at all. I say it because it's the truth. You carry twice the load on your shoulders that a two-parent family does.

So why do you feel so guilty asking for help?

Perhaps you feel sheepish about interrupting others' lives. It seems that wherever you turn, everyone is entrenched in carpools, soccer games, church events, and band concerts. And you may be tempted to think, *If people cared enough about me, they'd know that I need the help without me having to ask.*

Maybe you're giving others more credit for thoughtfulness than they deserve. No one can read your mind, and you can't expect them to. If you need help, you need to put aside any pride and embarrassment and *ask.* If you don't ask, people will most likely assume things are going just fine for you. They may be saying about you, *That guy is amazing. He does it all, even after his wife left him.* Or, *You should meet Laura sometime. She makes single parenting look so easy!*

But no one can do life solo. You are going to need support—a team of folks who can help you. But they're not going to collect like rainwater in a bucket on their own. You need to actively pursue forming your own support team.

So repeat after me: *Help!*

That one word surely ranks among the most difficult words to say because it requires admitting our insufficiency. But all single parents at one time or another need to ask—and should ask—this question: "Would you help me?"

Look at it this way: Suppose someone approached you and said, "I really could use your help. Would you help me?" How would you feel?

Honored, probably. Because someone thought enough of you to ask for your help. They saw you as a capable person who could provide something they could not.

And what would your response be? Most likely, if you're a caring individual, you would say, "I'm happy to do what I can!"

If that's the way *you* would respond, why not give others the chance to do the same thing for you?

There are all sorts of possibilities of places where you could go for support—to your family, friends, neighbors, coworkers, churches, youth groups. By asking for help, you're not saying, "I'm an incapable single parent who has totally fallen apart." Instead you're saying, "I'm a well-adjusted individual who knows she can't do everything herself. I need the support of others."

And that makes you no different, no more needy, than anyone else.

Back Home . . . on the Range

Jani, the woman I talked with at Chicago's McCormick Place, shared with me a wonderful example of a family that works together. While your parents should never supplant you as the one raising your children, as we discussed earlier, I can't emphasize enough how important the support of family members is to making single parenting work.

Trustworthy family members can be indispensable in helping watch the kids while you're at work or freeing up an evening so you can take an emotional break to spend by yourself or with friends. No one can keep working twenty-four hours a day for weeks, months, and years on end, so why should you expect yourself to? You need someone you can "trade" responsibilities with, if even for an hour or two. Then you will go back to your children more energized, focused, and ready to tackle any challenges. Family members can help you make ends meet and keep a long-range perspective.

> I can't emphasize enough how important the support of family members is to making single parenting work.

They can also provide a balanced view of men and women for your children where one or the other is lacking. For example, if you are a single mother, and your father provided a good male role model to you while you were growing up, he can also provide a positive role model for your children who have lost their father. If you are a single dad, and an older sister of yours was influential in your life as a great role model, see if your kids can spend some extra time with her. (And then offer to fix her computer, clean her car, or cook a meal in trade. Just because you're asking for help doesn't mean you can't give help in return.)

Of course, the support you receive from your parents or other family members is proportionate to the distance you live from them. In other words, if your family is a healthy one and not toxic to you or your children, the closer you live to them, the more realistic it is for them to offer you help. Living across the country, or even at opposite ends of the county, simply isn't the same as living nearby, within driving or shouting distance. So if your parents can provide a good support system, I recommend that you live in the same city (which might require a carefully thought-out move).

> No one can keep working twenty-four hours a day for weeks, months, and years on end, so why should you expect yourself to?

I also realize, however, that some of you may not *want* to turn to your parents, even to help ease the demands on your time and energy. Perhaps you wanted nothing more than to put as much distance as possible between you and your parents by getting out from under their roof, so you married against your parents' better judgment. At the time, it was a move that seemed like your salvation, but then that marriage began feeling worse than the prison you'd left. Perhaps you now see that the parental advice that you rebelled against was right on target and that you are where you are today because you chose, like Rachel in chapter 6, to live life your own way.

If there are wounds between you and your parents, *now* is the time to initiate reconciliation. If they are healthy individuals, you need them in your life. So do your children. Yes, it's difficult for anyone to admit that they need help, and going back to your parents may feel like a step backward, into childhood. But you are really taking a mature step forward by admitting you can't do it on your own. That you need their help.

Now is the time for you to be the adult—to realize and admit your own failures. To let go of any pride or embarrassment you have not only for *your* sake, but for your children's. Now is the time when they need a grandma and/or grandpa.

Some of you will be able to manage living near your family but can still maintain your own residence. Others of you may be forced to move back home, whether you're ready for that or not.

Living at home with your parents may be challenging because it's easy for you to slip into "child" mode and for them to slip into "parent" mode. But the pressure such a move can take off you financially can be just the thing to help you through a time when you need all the help you can get to make ends meet. If your parents generously let you stay with them for a time, you can be profoundly thankful for their help.

As we discussed already, one of the dangers of living at your parents' place is allowing them to usurp your authority. To let Grandpa and Grandma become the "Grand Pa" and "Grand Ma." As tempting as it may be to relinquish that responsibility to your parents, I recommend that while you are living at your parents' home, you make a conscious effort to remain in healthy authority over your own children and to ask that your parents remain in a healthy relationship with you.

If the lines begin to blur—for example, your mom starts telling you what your son should eat, wear to school, etc.—you should know how to respond to keep everybody in place. In this case, you could say something such as, "You know, Mom, I really appreciate your perspective. But I've got to tell you that I see this completely differently. Now that I'm an adult, I realize that I'm in charge of these kids and that I have to make these decisions. I value your opinion, but I need to tell you that's not the way we're going to proceed. Let me tell you why. . . ." Then give your reasons in a calm, confident manner, without pointing any fingers at your parent(s).

It may be extremely difficult the first time you have to do this. (After all, returning to your parents' home can make *you* feel, in many ways, like a child again.) But once you stand up to someone firmly and with direction, the chances that you'll stand up to that person the next time are much better.

Living at your parents' place should be, if at all possible, a transition to other living arrangements. That means during the period you're living with them, you should try to save as much money as possible. After all, if you were living on your own, you would be spending it on rent, food, transportation, babysitting, or whatever else your parents are helping contribute. This will take some discipline on your part to put money away, but I strongly encourage you to do so. Creating a nest egg will aid your transition down the road from living with your parents to greater independence.

> Living at your parents' place should be, if at all possible, a transition to other living arrangements.

Also, don't underestimate the importance of siblings you may have who are emotionally healthy and in good living situations, or other extended family members (such as a beloved aunt who's now an empty nester, or a brother who has recently retired from his job and would welcome the interaction and excitement of children in his home).

Creative Living Arrangements

It's a sign of the times when the majority of jobs are in the city, yet without paying an arm and a leg for rent, you can't afford to live there. But if you don't live in the city or commute ridiculous distances, you can't get a job. It's a cycle that leaves many people, including a lot of single parents, wondering what to do.

I know of one situation, for example, in which a mother and her female friend, both waitresses, are sharing an apartment. The mother's post-college daughter is living with them, and the mother's friend is raising two school-aged kids. Because it's the only place they can afford to live in the city, they have become a family of sorts. They take turns cooking and juggling housekeeping responsibilities.

This kind of arrangement can work out, but you can also find yourself in a situation reminiscent of that classic TV show *The Odd Couple*, where mismatched Felix and Oscar brought completely different ideas of cleanliness, boundaries, and lifestyle choices to their shared living arrangement. As someone once said, you only think you know someone until you begin living with them, so you wouldn't want to put yourself in a situation where you are legally locked in for a long period.

So if you're entering into this kind of arrangement—sharing housing with another single parent and kids—agree on a length of time for a trial run. Make sure that everyone clearly communicates their expectations and that together you decide what each person is going to contribute. How will you work out the differences in food and utilities

> Agree on a length of time for a trial run.

between the one mother and her two school-aged children and the other mother and her college-aged daughter, who is probably almost never there? There has to be an equitable way to make everybody happy for that arrangement to work, and those details should be spelled out from the beginning. You should also keep an eye open toward more independent housing.

As you work toward a better situation for your family, you may be faced with the question of how old your child should be before she can stay at home by herself. If your child is ten years old, that's pushing it in my book. Eleven years or older is preferable. There are, of course, all kinds of safeguards you can implement at your house for a child who is home alone: caller ID, for instance, so she will only answer the phone if family calls (or she won't answer the phone at all) and not letting anyone other than the folks who live there into the apartment or the house.

When putting together more creative living arrangements, the most important questions to ask yourself are always

- *Am I giving my children the help they need?*
- *Am I endeavoring to better my family's situation?*

Those two questions are what matter most to any family in the long run.

Pick 'em Carefully

For some of you, help from your parents, siblings, or extended family members may not be an option. If that's the case, you'll need to rely more heavily on friends, your community of faith, and community resources.

You don't pick your family, but you do pick your friends. So pick 'em carefully. This isn't always easy if you've been around people all your life who have been toxic to you. If your family was hypercritical, you may end up choosing friends who are like them—hypercritical of you and your parenting, just as your parents were of you.

> Take a good look at the friends you have now.

Take a good look at the friends you have now. Are they encouraging to you? Do they listen to what you're saying? Or do they seem to have their own agenda? Are they flaw pickers, telling you what you should do? telling you what's wrong with you or your child?

It is crucial that you pick supportive friends.

Do you have someone who listens, without judging? who asks questions to help you think through what you should do, rather than telling you what to do? If you do, that's a good friend. If that person does make a suggestion, you can rest assured that it is in your best interest.

If you find that kind of friend—someone you look up to who lives a balanced life as she raises her kids, give her a call when you need advice. Just be careful not to ask for help incessantly, because you don't want to impose on a friend, relative, or neighbor to be your caregiver. Friendships are like fires that need to be tended. But if you smother that fire with too many requests, that friend turns into a caregiver and full-time counselor. You may gain the help you need for a time, but you'll strain or lose a valuable friendship. Just remember that a healthy friendship has to go both ways. You need to be available to that friend, too, when that person is in need.

Keep an Eye Out for Surprises

Friendship and support can come from sources you may not immediately think of.

Take Megan, who discovered that the little old lady down the block just loved to bake and was thrilled when Megan asked if she'd be willing to provide an after-school snack for her kids once a week. "Lucilla even went a step further," Megan says. "She offered to walk down the block and pick up the girls from the bus stop on Mondays and Wednesdays and take them home with her for milk and cookies. So thanks to Lucilla, I'm able to work two extra hours those nights without feeling the guilt of not 'being there' for my girls. And Lucilla, who was feeling so lonely, has the delight of little-girl chatter twice a week. The girls just love her. She's become the grandma they've never had."

David had worked with the senior-high youth group at his church before his divorce and had developed a great relationship with the teens. One Sunday, two teens approached him with an idea. They offered to play with his two children—who were four and six at the time—for a couple hours after school. It would also help the teens' parents, who had to work until 5:00 and were having a tough time picking them up from school at 3:30. Since David's son's elementary school and the teens' high school were only two blocks apart, David picked up the two teens from school every Tuesday and Thursday and took them home with him. The teens played with his son and daughter, and later one of their parents picked them up from David's house. In the meanwhile, David had four uninterrupted hours a week in which to make phone calls for his landscaping business. It was an unusual situation, but it worked well for David, his children, and the teens and their parents.

So don't assume that the only folks who can help are your family and friends. That's limiting your options. Instead, take a look around. By keeping an eye out for creative solutions, you could not only receive support (as Megan and David did), but also give help to others, too (friendship to a lonely older woman; a "swap" arrangement with teens and their parents).

Don't Forget Your Greatest Support

All single parents feel somewhat alienated, somewhat overwhelmed. And these feelings can be especially intense if you've had to start over in a completely new community.

You'll always have a great responsibility—that's the nature of a single parent's life. So it's no wonder you may feel discouraged at times.

But you are not alone. There is another support source that is always around. Someone who has promised never to leave you, never to forsake you.

God.

"I believe in God," you might say. "But let's get realistic. What good is a guy in the sky when I need real help? I'm still the one who has no friends or family to speak of in the area, who has to work two jobs to make ends meet, and who has to juggle dropping off and picking up all three of my kids. God can't pick up groceries and fix dinner while I'm shuttling the kids around town, can he? Now that would be some help!"

If you're longing for help "with skin on"—as one little boy once told his mother—God might feel far away. But that doesn't make his help any less real.

Think of it this way. The next time you're walking through the local park, pick up a flower. Even a dandelion will do. Or when you're at the grocery store, pick up a flower from the florist aisle. You don't have to buy it, just pick it up and hold it. Inhale its fragrance and admire its beauty.

> God might feel far away. But that doesn't make his help any less real.

Do, in fact, what this writer suggests: "Walk out into the fields and look at the wildflowers. They never primp or shop, but have you ever seen color and design quite like it? The ten best-dressed men and women in the country look shabby alongside them. If God gives such attention to the appearance of wildflowers—most of which are never even seen—don't you think he'll attend to you, take pride in you, do his best for you? What I'm trying to do here is to get you to relax, to not be so preoccupied with *getting*, so you can respond to God's *giving*"[1] (emphasis mine).

You may feel that God's not good for much other than giving you a heap of trouble. You may be angry with him. Or you may be slowly drawing closer to him.

No matter your starting place, it's okay with God because he already knows exactly where you are. Just begin to interact with him. Open your heart to talk with him as you would with a best friend or the father you always wished you'd had.

"Lord, are you there?"

"Is that you again, Leman?" (You see, God's pretty used to this kind of a conversation.)

"Yeah, it's me," I say. "Could you help get me out of this mess?"

And so the conversation goes on, as I talk to God and lay the cards of my situation on the table in front of him.

"But Dr. Leman," you might say, "you don't know all that's gone on in my life. God and I aren't exactly on the best terms."

You're right. I don't exactly know what's gone on in your life.

But God does.

And if you're angry with him, he knows.

If you're embarrassed, he knows that, too.

So why not just talk to him?

Be honest.

You don't have to use Shakespearean-type language for him to listen, either: "Oh, Lord—dearest, heavenly Lord with sugar on top. Thou who dwelleth in the glory of glories, I beseech that thou wouldst grant my deepest longing."

Instead, just level with God. Tell him about things as they really are. Admit that you need help: "Lord, I don't see any way out of this situation. I'm scared, and I'm asking for your help. I really need you."

Prayer shouldn't be limited to only those things you'd talk about with Great Aunt Beatrice in the parlor over tea in a Jane Austen novel. God can handle your pain, your confusion, and your anger.

> God's not interested in your performance. He's interested in having a relationship with you.

God's not interested in your performance. He's interested in having a relationship with you. When you begin to pray from your real self, instead of trying to sound good or religious or acceptable to anybody who might be listening, God responds and begins to transform your life by his grace.

None of us can do life alone—whether it's parenting or anything else. God has created us to live in community. He didn't just create one person to live in the Garden of Eden and call it done.

That's why finding a healthy support team is crucial.

By asking others to get involved—family, friends, neighbors, coworkers, or youth group leaders—you give yourself a break, your kids a change, and those who help you receive a gift, too. They are encouraged by being a needed part of your life!

And in the process, you learn more about God's mercy and grace. He loves you just as you are. You don't have to get all dressed up before you talk to him.

❀ ❀ ❀

KEY Qs . . .

- Where do you go for support?

- How could you start—or increase—your support team?

- What "swap" type arrangements might you make for your own and others' benefit?

CHAPTER 8

Pressed for Time and Money?

Imagine for a moment that you have your own private servant. (Okay, so we're *really* imagining.)

You walk into your apartment or house after work. Your servant greets you at the door with a checked-off list of everything that has been accomplished that day.

Laundry? Done.

Bills? Paid.

Dinner? Hot on the table.

Everything else on your to-do list? Done.

And to make the day even better, an anonymous donor has just left a five-hundred-dollar bill under your door.

Now you really know you're dreaming, right? For you, there's no one to take over your to-do list. Your time is as tight as your finances.

But you can still spend them both wisely. And in doing so, you can stretch them further than you've ever dreamed possible.

Maximize Your Time and Money!

Singer Harry Connick Jr. told Oprah's *O* magazine this poignant story: "When my oldest daughter was two, I wanted to take her to the park. I was anxious to get her there as fast as I could because I only had a couple of hours to spare before I had to be somewhere. As I was hustling her to the car, she bent down and picked up a rock—you know how kids kind of squat so their tail end is almost touching the ground? I just kept telling her, 'Come on, we gotta go, we gotta go.' It didn't occur to me that she was discovering something right then."[1]

How easy it is for us to forget that, to kids, life is simple. What they want, more than anything else, is you. But when there is only one parent in the family, how can you stretch your time—and the few dollars you have—into an experience the kids will remember?

STOP AND SMELL THE ROSES.

Connie, a single mom, would get exasperated when her ex would buy expensive gifts for their twin girls because she knew her gifts could never measure up to his. She was always feeling guilty that she couldn't provide for them in the same way. Then one day she and her girls were walking by a park. The girls pointed to a picnic table where the three of them had had a picnic six months earlier. Both girls described and relived what they had to eat, how long they had stayed there, and the games their mom had played with them.

When Connie got home, she went and looked in the toy box. There, buried at the bottom, were all the toys her ex had sent the girls. Toys they hadn't played with for months.

> Cardboard refrigerator boxes will never go on sale at Toys "R" Us, but if they ever did, they would be a top seller.

Fun doesn't have to be expensive. Cardboard refrigerator boxes will never go on sale at Toys "R" Us, but if they ever did, they would be a top seller because kids so often choose cardboard boxes, old bedsheets, and living-room chairs over the latest tech toys (which, incidentally, cost hundreds of dollars). So don't get caught in the trap that in order for you to be a good parent, you have to somehow come up with a couple hundred bucks for an Xbox for your twelve-year-old son or sixty bucks for softball cleats for your daughter to participate in her sport of the month.

Instead, do the simple things. The things that matter most in the long run. Read a book together from the library. Build forts in your living room out of chairs and blankets. Walk in the park. Give your child a pile of scrap wood and let him build a tree fort in the backyard. Set an example in your neighborhood for being the creative parent, the one who does the fun things that don't cost much money. Making the most of time together at home with your family is so much more important than your child's collection of Xbox games to go with the plasma TV in his bedroom. When it comes down to it, all *things* disappear—but memories remain.

So remember that kids enjoy the simple things in life most. Simply said, stopping to smell the roses doesn't mean you have to buy them at forty bucks a dozen!

CONSIDER GOING PRIVATE.

Sending your child to a private school is probably the farthest thing from your mind, right? But consider this: Private schools aren't only for people whose children are picked up each day by the family butler, to be whisked off to the country club for tennis lessons. They can work well for single parents and their children, too, even if you are on a tight budget.

Many private schools offer all kinds of scholarships. If you are interested in having your child attend a private school, call and ask whether it has a scholarship available and whether you might qualify. You needn't feel funny about it, either. After all, you're only asking for help that's waiting to be used.

It's the same story with summer camps for your kids or church weekend retreats for you. If you see an opportunity that might benefit you or your kids, check it out more closely. Is financial aid available? If so, why not take advantage of it?

TRY SCHOOL ON FOR SIZE.

So many bright people start college, marry somewhere between Math 124 and 125, have kids—and never finish their degree. That may not necessarily have been a bad decision at the time, but if you're a single parent now, it may be tough to get by on just waiting tables. After all, when it comes to making ends meet, "green power" is where it's at. Those who have the ability to make money in our capitalistic society are going to be a step ahead of most.

How can you help your kids the most? If you don't have a college degree, start one. And if you quit college midstream, finish it. There are many online opportunities that allow you to do that in a short period of time, at your own pace, for probably half the cost of traditional campus programs (plus, there are often scholarships to further subsidize the tuition—grant money that you never have to pay back). I'm involved in teaching in one of these programs myself, through the Kevin Leman School of Applied Psychology at Phoenix's Grand Canyon University.[2] You can currently get a bachelor's degree in counseling online as well as online certificates in many areas that deal with the care of children.

Finishing a degree, of course, might mean night school or, at the very least, late nights studying. And it will mean some creative childcare options and ramping up your support network. But the results are worth it when you're the breadwinner for your family.

GIVE SOME AWAY?!

No matter how much time or money you have, give some away.

What? you may be thinking. *I have little enough of both, and you're asking me to give some away? I don't even have enough change left over to splurge on gumballs for the kids at the grocery store! And as for time, how can I give what I don't have?*

Yup, that's exactly what I'm suggesting. But hear me out.

I've always endeavored to live my life consistent with my words, as a model for my children. If I talk about how important it is to respond to the needs of others, trying to help them when we can, I want my actions to match up with what my children hear me saying. That means if I want my children to be caring individuals, giving what they can to others in need, I have to pattern that for them—no matter how much I have or don't have.

There are always those less fortunate than you. That extra can of green beans you pick up at the grocery store for the local food drive may not seem like much to you, but it accomplishes a lot. By giving that one can of green beans, you are nurturing in your children the perspective that giving to others is what you do as a family. That simple act sets an example. And it also helps to free you and your children from the victim mentality by reminding you of others' needs.

The victim mentality would have you believe that you are standing on the bottom rung of the social ladder with nothing left to give. *And why would someone want anything from you anyway?* this mentality says. *Nothing you have is good enough.*

But giving something away, even if only a few minutes of your time to go to the grocery store for the mom down the block whose kid has the flu, helps put your situation in perspective and empowers both you and your kids to become caring individuals. You might head to a local women's shelter together to help decorate the Christmas tree or help clean up after your church's missions luncheon. The ten minutes you spend listening to the neighbor in your apartment complex who is having family difficulties not only helps that neighbor but also reminds you that you and your children can still make a difference.

> There is always *something* that you can give.

There is always *something* that you can give. And such giving sets a healthy example for your children.

GET OUT OF THE DEN EVERY NOW AND THEN.

You probably love your kids as much as a mother bear loves wrestling and tumbling with her cubs in a sunny alpine meadow. You know that your primary mission is to take care of those little cubs, and they follow you everywhere, 24-7.

But even a mother bear needs to get out of the den every now and then for her own emotional well-being, or she's liable to feel the strain.

And mother bears aren't the only ones who need a break. In recent years, the business community has learned that employees who receive regular breaks make for more productive, happier, and healthier employees. They get sick less often and tend to stay with the company longer.

Taking some time to enjoy yourself, if done in moderation, is not only good for you, it's essential to your survival as a single parent. Recreation and renewal allow you to be a more present, attentive, and overall healthy parent.

It also sends a message to your children that as much as you love them, *you* are important, too. If you hover around your child as she grows up, then she may begin thinking that she needs or deserves that attention 24-7. She may begin to assume that either she can't handle life without you or that she's the center of the universe because you've made her the center of every waking (and sleeping) minute of your life. And that can cause multiple problems down the road for you and your child (not to mention her teachers, friends, and her supervisor at work someday).

So get out of the den every once in a while! Maybe you'd love to get your hair cut. Or you might choose to go for a walk or spend an hour or two at the local coffee shop with your best friend. It's important that you take a little time for yourself.

If you don't, you may find yourself taking out pent-up frustrations on your kids, or going on a spending spree you can't afford because you haven't been able to shop by yourself for three years.

"But Dr. Leman," you say, "when I'm barely making ends meet, how can I afford a babysitter or get child care in order to have some time for me?"

I have just the thing for you. And you might even get dinner in the bargain, too.

Try Co-oping

You can find strength in numbers by banding together with other parents (from single or dual families, so don't limit your options!) to help lessen everyone's load. By networking with others, you can build a mutually supportive base.

> By networking with others, you can build a mutually supportive base.

There are all sorts of co-op groups—from babysitting co-ops to exercise co-ops to vacation co-ops to cooking co-ops, to name a few.

The key lies in finding people with shared needs. People you can trust.

BABYSITTING CO-OPS

Most single parents have to work sometime—or a lot of the time. So what do you do when your children aren't yet in school or your work hours extend before or after school or you just need a break?

A babysitting co-op can be just the thing to allow you a low- to no-cost option for child care, shared among mothers in your community.

What is a babysitting co-op? It's a group of parents who get together to share babysitting duties. One parent may take every Monday afternoon; another may take Tuesday afternoons. Or you may switch off whole days, or even a few hours. The point is chipping in to make the task of caring for your children more manageable. Even a couple hours a week can give you time to take a class toward a degree, to go to a Bible study, or to attend a singles' function at your church.

However, how the babysitting co-op is set up is extremely important. You should never trust your child to strangers, so you should know the babysitters very well. In order for a babysitting co-op to work well, the parents sharing it must also hold similar values. The place where you leave your child should be, first of all, physically and emotionally safe. And second, your child has to enjoy the interaction with the other children who will be there.

For example, when five moms in Mandy's church decided to start a babysitting co-op, Mandy was highly tempted. It would mean that she'd be able to take a higher-paying job than the one she currently had typing law transcripts at home. But when she thought about all the angles, she realized that little Hanson was always getting pestered in the church nursery by one of the kids who would be in the group. The group wasn't a good match, personality-wise.

On the other hand, the same babysitting co-op was perfect for Kari. Her daughter, who was more comfortable in larger groups and could hold her own, couldn't wait for the two days a week she could spend with her friends.

> The key lies in finding people with shared needs. People you can trust.

If you do decide to pursue a babysitting co-op, ask around at your church. (That's the place you're more likely to find others who share your values. It isn't always the case, of course, but it generally provides a common denominator.). If you don't attend church, consider putting a notice in your child's school bulletin that goes home to parents. Ask for anyone who is interested to contact you, then set up a time to meet.

In that introductory meeting, explain your idea and how the co-op could work. Entertain others' ideas. Establish that it's important for everyone's trust factor to have an open-house policy so that parents can drop by at any time when their kids are there. It would also be good if you visited each member's home before starting the co-op. Breaking into smaller groups would also help to get to know others more intimately. Talk about your philosophy of child-raising and what you hope to accomplish with the co-op. Ultimately, each person should supply two or three recommendations from a pastor or clergy person, a friend or relative, or someone she works with, so there's some accountability. If someone isn't eager to supply a reference or doesn't understand why this is important, you probably wouldn't want your child under their care!

It's time-consuming to get to know other people, especially at a time when you have very little time to spare. You may be working two different jobs or six days a week just to make ends meet. And it might take hours at the local playground or a few Saturday mornings over coffee to get to know the people who will be watching your children. But investing the time now will help to safeguard your greatest treasures—your children.

If you are pursuing this option, here are some questions to ask yourself regarding the people in the co-op and the way they run the child care in their homes:

- Can I stop over at any time?
- Is the place clean? Is it safe for small children?
- Do our values match up?
- Does my child seem to enjoy this person and the other children? Are their personalities a match?
- Would *I* choose to stay there and spend time with this person?

If you answered no to any of these questions, why would you want your son or daughter staying there? The well-being of your children is priceless.

Yes, starting a co-op is a lot of work. Besides figuring out the answers to the above questions, you'll have a lot of other issues to decide, such as, How exactly are you going to swap child-care duties? An afternoon a week? A day a week? Five people each taking a different day a week, so you can work four days a week? Should there be a trial hour or two in each home to see how things go?

But take heart. Chances are, there may already be similar groups in your area, whether or not they are co-op groups. If you have preschool-aged kids, for example, look into the support group MOPS (Mothers of Preschoolers). Your local chapter can often be found through your church, and if you're not familiar with the church scene, you could go online to find a MOPS chapter near you.[3]

So ask around. You may find that the opportunities are already there for you to join. And the people involved may already have been screened.

As you get to know the people in the potential co-op group, you'll develop some close friendships that will allow you to find larger-scope support. For example, a mom you meet through the babysitting co-op may ask you to keep her two younger children while she goes on a missions trip to Mexico with her teenager. In return, she agrees to take your two children for the five days you have to be in the city for a seminar.

Or you may discover a group of people who enjoy exercising together. If you all have young children, you could pick one day a week that you stay with the children and the others do a fast two-mile jog. The next day, you jog with the others while another adult keeps all of your children. Perhaps on the final weekday, you do a stroller day, where you all speed-walk and talk while the kids get a stroll, too.

In other words, the sky is the limit to creative co-oping. You may start with a babysitting co-op and get much more in the bargain.

COOKING CO-OPS

"The thing I dislike the most," Muriel told me, "is trying to come up with what's for dinner."

I bet you can relate. After giving all your energy to getting your child out the door to school or child care, working all day, and then picking up your child after work, you arrive home exhausted. All you want to do is put up your feet on the coffee table for a few minutes, but the instant you do so, a little voice asks, "What's for dinner?"

Since fast food can get expensive, not to mention that all the fat and calories don't do you a favor in the long run, why not try some creative options?

Creating a cooking co-op with others from your neighborhood, church, or your child's school is a great way to save time and money and also meet people in your community.

I know of a couple ways that cooking co-ops have worked (but I bet you can come up with other ideas, too).

One way is for a group of adults to gather, with some rotating in and out of helping with child care in one room while the others prepare a variety of meals in the kitchen—say, thirty days of meals prepared in bulk, which can be divided among all the families, frozen, and then pulled out over the course of the upcoming month.

> What's for dinner?

It's a great idea for many reasons: First, it frees up time in your schedule. Once you have a freezer full of ready-to-go meals, you can pull one out a day or two ahead of time to thaw in the refrigerator, then pop it in the oven or microwave when you arrive home from work. Second, the preparation of the meals is a great time to meet others and simply enjoy talking together. Finally, as you get to know the others in your co-op and begin to build trust, those relationships may turn into good friendships and even other co-op ideas.

By forming a cooking co-op, you will gain insight into how those people work together, take directions, even work through conflicts—because when you get five people in the same kitchen, all with their own ideas on how pie crust should be made, you have the makings for a pretty good-sized brawl! That's not all bad, however, because it will give you the opportunity to figure out whether those people might make good partners in a babysitting co-op when the stakes are much higher than whether or not the pie crust was successful.

Here's another way a cooking co-op can work. Five single parents in Colorado decided to try something new. Each of them had an assignment: to make five of the same casseroles or main dishes once every two weeks. Then, every other Saturday morning, they would meet for a coffee hour at one of their houses or apartments, and they'd swap dishes. Because they were making five of the same thing, grocery shopping was easy, and putting together the dish was easy. And that meant each of them had five meals, ready-made, to use over the next two weeks. All they had to do was take them out of the fridge or the freezer and warm them up.

That Colorado group has been doing this for six months now, and all five of the cooking co-op members are enthusiastic.

"I just warm up one of the dishes every other night for a simple meal," Maralee said. "And then on the nights in between, I add a simple salad or some easy cheese-garlic bread that my kids love, and I have enough to make that dish from yesterday stretch for another meal. My kids think it's great, and I get a break on the weeknights, too, when our schedule is really crazy."

Dan, the one male member of the group, adds, "I'd never cooked anything other than boxed macaroni and cheese before I joined this co-op. Not only did it help feed my family in a creative way, it gave me the boost I needed to dive into some cooking books. My son, who's eleven, helps me, too. We take one Saturday morning a month and make ten casseroles, then stash 'em in our big freezer downstairs until we meet with the group. It gives Nate and me time to talk, too. It's incredible the things he shares with me now when all I used to get was a grunt. And being with the group for Saturday morning coffee is good for him, too. He doesn't mind playing with the younger kids. And he has a chance to talk with women I've come to trust—all at a time when he's really missing his mom."

> The sky's the limit to creative co-oping.

The sky's the limit for creative co-oping. So why not try a babysitting co-op, a cooking co-op, or something else altogether?

Above All, Be Creative!

There are so many ways to do life other than the norm. So why not be creative? Volunteer time with your kids at a soup kitchen. Widen your horizons by volunteering your family for free babysitting for married couples who want to go out on a date. If you focus your attention and help only on other single-parent families, your child doesn't have the opportunity to see how a man and woman can interact in a healthy way.

If you wish you had some cash to get a household project done, why not barter with a friend who can provide help on that project? Offer something that he might need in return.

Need your car fixed? Why not offer to do some office work for the mechanic down the block?

Barters work out beautifully, as these single parents found out.

"My little girl was longing to have a special doll that cost sixty dollars," Jason explained. "There was no way I could afford that. We're just scraping by. Then one day, when I talked with Susan, my new neighbor, I discovered her older daughter had a doll collection. I told her that I'd pick her daughter up from school one day a week if she'd let my daughter "borrow" one doll a week to play with. At first Susan was hesitant—probably because she wasn't sure how careful Emily would be with her daughter's dolls. But when she had Emily over to look at the doll collection, it was clear how much 'in awe' Emily was. Now Susan and her daughter let Emily freely borrow whatever doll she wants and even invite her over for a 'dolly tea'—something this dad forgets to think of!"

> Barters work out beautifully.

"My son had to have an animal costume for a school play," Tina told me. "And I had no idea how I was going to get that. I was bemoaning to my cooking co-op the fact I had to find one and I couldn't afford any at the local costume shop. All of a sudden my friend Marilyn, said, 'Hey, I've got a great leopard costume that might work.' Later that night I found out she needed a baseball glove for her son, and I had that. So we swapped. All it took for the costume to fit my son was a couple safety pins. It may seem like a little thing, but it was a big thing to me."

"I always hated pizza day at my kids' school," Gina said. "Because I have three kids, I can't afford the twenty-five bucks a semester per kid it costs for them to get a slice of cheese pizza once a week like their friends. Then my friend and I came up with an idea. We would attempt to make our own small cheese pizzas, in fun surprise shapes. After some effort—neither of us are real cooks—we found a dough recipe that worked and were able to buy bulk pizza sauce and cheese. We froze our creations. Each pizza day I took three out in the morning and popped them into the oven while the kids were eating breakfast. After they were baked, I wrapped them in a couple layers of aluminum foil and put them in an insulated bag in the kids' lunches.

"My second son, Keith, who's in second grade, thinks it's pretty cool that he gets his own special pizza. The other day one of the moms at school called to ask how I made them. 'My daughter just loves all the lunches Keith brings—especially on pizza day. Where do you get yours?' the mom asked. I had to laugh. She thought I paid something like five dollars a pizza at some specialty shop. That made me feel really good inside. My friend and I were able to make a semester's worth of pizzas for our five kids for about fifteen bucks of flour, sauce, and cheese."

So use your creativity. Enjoy the simple things in life with your kids. Don't try to keep up with the Joneses. Do life your own way. Give to others from what you have.

Never sell yourself—or your kids—short.

You always have something worthwhile to offer.

❄ ❄ ❄

KEY Qs . . .

- What's your favorite simple activity you do with your kids? Why?

- Do you ever "get out of the den"? Why or why not? What does "in moderation" mean to you, and how do you live that out?

- In what way(s) can you get creative and be giving with what you have right now?

CHAPTER 9

The Opposite-Sex Fix

There is a hole in your child's life. You feel it. Your child feels it.

And it doesn't take a PhD in psychology to figure out why. If you're a single mom, you can't be a dad. And if you're a single dad, you can't be a mom. You can never fully replace that other parent because each person has a unique connection with both of the people who brought him or her into this world.

You can't escape the reality that the influence of other adult role models—especially opposite-sex role models—on your child is inestimable. So what are you going to do about it?

An Alien Species?

If you're a single mom and you didn't grow up with brothers, boys may be a new species to you—probably even an alien species. You didn't know that they brought home grasshoppers and frogs in their pockets, that they beat up on each other for fun, and that it was possible for them to imagine that any stick was a gun. You didn't know that you'd hear their grunts, fire engine noises, and constant stomping for hours on end.

Likewise, if you're a single dad, you probably didn't know that anyone could take playing house so seriously, cry so much, enjoy talking on the phone or dressing up with such passion, or spend so much time e-mailing friends as your daughter does.

But while you're on your hands and knees looking in your son's bedroom closet for his pet garter snake, or while you're waiting for your daughter to get off the phone, I have good news for you. If I could choose the ideal parent-child combination for single parents, it would be a single mother with a boy (or boys) or a single father with a girl (or girls).

Does that surprise you?

If it does, it's probably because most of us have been duped into thinking that the most special relationship is between same-sex parents and children—between a father and his son or between a mother and her daughter. But the relationships carrying the real psychological punch are the father/daughter, mother/son relationships.

> The relationships carrying the real psychological punch are the father/daughter, mother/son relationships.

"Why?" you ask.

Mothers communicate to their sons what they see and admire in men, and those boys are going to learn all about females from guess who? Mom. If you discipline, love, and affirm those tykes (even when their noises and boy behavior are driving you crazy), then you're going to help those immature little boys grow into men someday—men you can be proud of, who will treat women right. (Unlike, perhaps, the way you've been treated.)

In the same way, Dad is the fundamental parent who is going to teach his daughters what men are all about. Your experience as a man allows you to tell your daughter what drives boys. (And that's why, for instance, there is a higher probability for girls to get pregnant out of wedlock when their dads are absent physically or emotionally from the home. The girls truly are looking for what boys are like because they haven't seen it modeled for them by their dad.) How you respond to pressure, to questions, and to emotions will reveal to your daughters how much you think they are worth. And a daughter's self-worth will impact everything she will do in her lifetime.

Because of this, here's my advice for custody decisions in certain cases. If you get along with your ex after the divorce, you live in close proximity to each other, your ex is a great father (even if he did fail as a husband), and you have one or more daughters and no sons, my vote would be that they live with Dad as the custodial parent. For most of you, that's not what you expected, right?

Likewise, if you have one or more sons and no daughters, I think they should live with Mom. But the same rules apply with moms as with dads. I suggest such an arrangement *only* in situations where the playing field is level and you're sure that the environment over at Dad's house or Mom's house is a good one for the kids.

Take Karen and Steve, for example. Both are good parents to their two children. They're just not a good match (*fireworks* is more like it) for each other. Since they live close—only a couple miles from each other—and they have two girls, together they made the tough choice for the girls to live with Steve, since Karen is currently going back to school. Karen misses the girls—who are now eight and ten—intensely during the week, but she has them every weekend. And that means that they can also stay in the same school. Steve, for his part, asked his boss to revamp his job (even though it meant a cut in salary) so he could drive the girls to school and pick them up every day.

However, in Mary's case, having her girls live with their dad would never work. Mary left Jake when she found out that he was sexually abusing their girls. She fought hard in court to win all custody rights and to get a written agreement that a third party has to be present if and when the girls see their dad.

When I suggest having boys stay with their mom and girls with their dad, though, I'm not talking about dividing up your sons and daughters between you and your ex. Siblings need to—if at all possible—stay together. One parent being absent is enough for a child to handle. Losing a brother or sister can be completely overwhelming to children at any age (as much as they may seem to war with each other).

I only suggest this opposite-sex arrangement when you have one child or your children are all the same sex and you and your ex live in close proximity. That way the kids will get to see the noncustodial parent regularly. Every daughter also needs a mother; every son also needs a dad. And the value of that can't be swept aside, either.

> A boy can give Mom a real run for her money.

One of the challenges with these mother/son and father/daughter arrangements, however, is that sons can manipulate their mothers pretty well, and daughters can manipulate their fathers with expertise. A boy can give Mom a real run for her money, especially in the teen years, and a girl can wiggle her way into her daddy's heart and wrap him around her finger even if he's six foot three. So if you are in that father/daughter or mother/son situation, you have to be even more aware that you aren't succumbing to decision-making based on guilt. (If you think you might be falling into that trap, reread chapter 4, "Got Guilt?")

> A girl can wiggle her way into her daddy's heart and wrap him around her finger even if he's six foot three.

Think Carefully If . . .

Opposite-sex custody may not be possible or shouldn't be considered if any of the following situations have occurred or are occurring in your family:

YOUR EX IS TOXIC.

If your ex is physically or sexually abusive, as in Mary's case, no way should he have custody of your children. And an emotionally abusive parent—one who yells constantly at your kids—can do enough damage to last a lifetime. If you can help it (and the courts haven't ruled other-wise), keep your children away from your ex as much as possible. Even better, *completely* away.

YOUR EX IS AN "IN-N-OUT" PARENT.

There's a great burger place called In-N-Out Burger. Even health-con-scious people love it because they simply can't resist. In-N-Out burgers are wonderful; in-n-out parents are horrible. You know the type. They show up at their whim—just to salve their own guilt—every nine months or so, hang out for a couple days, bring the kids lots of presents, and then take off again until another wave of guilt attacks them months down the road. Or they might live two hundred miles away and rarely talk to your children. They are parents in name only and not really a part of your children's lives.

Frankly, single Mom, if this is the case, your daughter would be better off without your ex. And single Dad, your son would be better off without your ex.

But even in such cases, be careful never to bad-mouth your ex. Although he or she doesn't have a positive influence on your child, keep your own nose clean. Don't launch into a litany of what's wrong with your ex (or the guy who never married you). The negative behavior of your ex (or your child's birth parent) will eventually become apparent to your child as she gets older and decides to develop a relationship with that person (or not).

> In-N-Out burgers are wonderful; in-n-out parents are horrible.

Bridging the Gap

If your ex falls into either of the categories above or if your spouse has died or if you have never been married, don't despair. There are *still* ways to help your child have the input that is lacking from the absent parent. You might think you have to be dating or remarried or married for the first time in order to bridge this gender gap, but such is not the case. All you have to do is be aware of that important influence, and then ask others to help.

Think for a moment. Who do you know who could be a surrogate parent to your child to "replace" the one who is missing? Who could enter your child's life immediately? If your child is missing a father, what about a grandpa? a brother of yours? a man you respect at church? If your child is missing a mother, what about a grandma? a sister of yours? a woman you respect at church?

> Who could enter your child's life immediately?

Grandparents especially can go a long way in filling that opposite-sex void. Look at it this way. You love your children. Deeply. But there are also times you want to string them up in the backyard. As the Billy Joel song says, "I love you just the way you are"—and that's how grandparents treat their grandchildren (probably because the children usually go home after a while). That's why a healthy grandparent can bring an element of unconditional love and acceptance that is sometimes difficult for you to give because you're on-duty 24-7 (and sometimes a little tired—rightfully so!). An opposite-sex grandparent's love can make your child feel especially prized.

"Isn't it important for a girl to feel prized by her grandmother?" you ask. "Or what about a boy by his grandfather?"

All love is important to a child, but love from the opposite sex makes an even bigger emotional impact on a child. And in today's world, that's easy to forget. Why else do you see announcements for upcoming mother-daughter banquets—not mother-son banquets? Or father-son weekends—not father-daughter weekends? It's much more common to find planned outings for the same sex parent and child.

> You love your children. Deeply. But there are also times you want to string them up in the backyard.

That's why I'm particularly happy to hear about a group of fathers who have started a "Purity Dance"—where the fathers take the daughters. As a dad of four daughters myself, I know the powerful connection between daddies and daughters. So I wholeheartedly applaud that group of fathers for their creativity.

In the same way, I applaud the group of moms who banded together two years ago to take their sons on two weekend camping trips a year. They rough it with only sleeping bags, canteens, and the bare necessities. The boys love it—cooking over an open fire, not having to take a shower—and the women put up with sleeping on tree roots. All for the purpose of getting to know their sons better.

When a Good Man Is Hard to Find . . .

If you're a single mother with a daughter (or daughters), I urge you to seek a healthy male influence in your daughter's life. If you don't, she may go seeking it in unhealthy ways later in life (perhaps as you yourself did). Although you can communicate to your daughter about men, if you had difficulty in your relationships with men yourself, you may have difficulty communicating exactly what a healthy man is. And seeing what a healthy man acts like is crucial to your daughter's development.

That positive influence might come from your brother, your own father, an uncle, or another male family member. But for some of you, a healthy male role model for your daughter may be completely nonexistent. Hertz doesn't have a "rent a dad," and you sure don't want to drag just any old guy off the street! Your daughter's male role model should be screened carefully.

What then can you do?

First, you can do what any parent can do, no matter how difficult the situation—be as loving and encouraging as you can, administering consistent discipline and believing in your daughter. Do that, and you'll have a good shot at raising a kid who can stand on her own two feet. That's as close as you can get to a guarantee in the parenting business!

> Hertz doesn't have a "rent a dad," and you sure don't want to drag just any old guy off the street!

But there's another thing you can do. Involve males who come naturally into your daughter's life whenever you can. If your daughter is six years old and just starting first grade, you could arrange to talk to the principal the summer before school starts and say, "I was wondering if you could help me with something. . . ."

If you're reasonable, rational, and you ask respectfully for help, not grabbing the principal by the pant leg and pleading with tears, most likely she will respond, "Of course. How can I help you?"

"I have a daughter who is six years old," you might say. "This is a new school for her, and she's doing fine in kindergarten. My real concern is that her father is absent. Her grandfather died a few years ago, and I don't have any brothers in my family, so she is essentially without male contact. I understand that there are a few male teachers at this school, and they are highly respected. I was wondering if it would be possible for my daughter to have male teachers for at least a couple of her years here at this elementary school?"

Or perhaps your daughter is gifted athletically and she wants to play in the bobby-socks softball league, where there are both male coaches and female coaches. If that's the case, my vote would be for you to try to arrange for her to play under a male coach.

Never try to force these relationships, because forcing doesn't work.

But if you find healthy male role models intersecting with your child's life in the form of a schoolteacher, coach, neighbor, babysitter, Sunday school teacher, church youth leader, or parent of your child's friend, see if you can gently encourage those relationships to provide the healthy male influence that is lacking in your daughter's life.

Single Dads Seeking Help

"I had no clue as to how to raise a child," recalls one father, a public relations executive in Ardmore, Pennsylvania. "My wife was a stay-at-home mom. As a guy, I was more focused on going to work to support us. Having to run everything—working, taking care of a child, doing the cleaning and laundry, and preparing the meals—was hard."[1]

Single fathers now account for one of every six single parents—that means there were two million single fathers in the United States in 2003—up from one in ten in 1970, or 393,000.[2] Like the single mother, unless the single father has a sister or sister-in-law that he's close to or a mother who lives in town, he doesn't have a lot of places to go for immediate help with the opposite-sex fix.

The collective knowledge of how to parent a child within the single man's social network is scant compared to a single woman's social network. It's difficult to imagine many men calling up their single buddies and asking, "Hey, Frank, instead of watching the L.A. Lakers' game over at your place, how about you come over and we take care of my kids together? You know, watch *Sesame Street* reruns, change a few diapers, trade recipes—that sort of thing?"

The good news for those of you who are single fathers is that, in general, over the course of your son's life, he is probably more likely to naturally run across female role models than your daughter is to run across male role models. Elementary schools have a much higher average of female teachers than male teachers, for instance. And the majority of Sunday school teachers for younger ages are females.

But you, too, can benefit your son's development by going out of your way to provide additional female role models. If your child is young, look into the option of a local babysitting co-op (see chapter 8). As your son gets older, look into extracurricular activities where he might get that female input, such as swimming lessons or tutoring help with school. And, as always, some of the best female input your child can have, apart from that of his mom, of course—unless she's toxic or uninvolved in his life—is that of his extended family: your mother, sisters, sisters-in-law, and nieces.

The Opposite-Sex Fix: How Did They Do It?

Opposite-sex influence is indeed crucial to your child's healthy development and the choices he or she will make down the road. Here are how some other single parents handled it—and their results.

PAULA'S STORY

"When my daughter turned fifteen and was begging to go on a date, I set her up on a date—with a father from my church whom I trusted. He also has a daughter, so he knew how high the stakes were to me in talking about dating. During that date, he treated her the way a respectful date should. He knocked on our door, greeted me first, told me what time he'd have her home and what they would be doing, then asked if she was ready to go. After escorting her out the door of our home, he opened the car door for her. When they arrived at the restaurant, he pulled out her chair for her. In all ways, he treated her with respect. He showed interest in her life and asked her questions.

"By the time Mika got home, she had a different view of dating than when she'd left a few hours earlier. 'Mom, I felt like a princess,' she told me. Later I heard her talking on the phone with a friend. After she raved about the date, she added, 'I can't see Darren treating me like that, though. Maybe he isn't as great as I thought he was. . . .'

"And inside I smiled."

TIA'S STORY

"When my daughter was five, she really wanted to learn how to swim. I'd never taken her to swimming lessons because I'm scared of the water. Kinda dumb, I know, but that's the truth. I was talking about that one day at my office, and Chuck, one of the guys I've worked with for five years, said, 'Hey, I need to teach my son how to swim, too. Why don't you guys come on over this weekend, and we'll try out our new kiddy pool?'

"That's exactly what we did. Not only did Anna get her first taste of swimming—without me passing on my fear of the water to her—but Anna also got to see how Chuck played with his son, John. How they had fun together—laughing and wrestling. And Chuck and his wife, Karen, invited us to stay for a simple dinner of corn on the cob, burgers, and ice cream. We had a great time. I was so glad Anna got to see how a healthy family acts around each other. She hasn't had much of that in her life."

ANDREW'S STORY

"Jamie was eight when his mother died. I'd often find him down in our basement, flipping through memory albums that his mom had put together. He'd stare at the photos of him with his mom when he was younger, and he'd spend hours looking at the drawings of his that she'd saved in that book. Jamie loved to draw. Before, when I would come home from work, I'd often find Jamie and my wife together on the porch step, looking at a drawing of his.

"When Natalie died, Jamie stopped drawing. It was like he didn't have the heart to do it anymore. I'd encourage him, but he didn't seem interested. One day I saw a flyer in his backpack about Artist Adventures—a new group the art teacher at school was starting to develop. She was going to invite local artists from around the area to come in and teach techniques to any students who wanted to come to the group.

"I brought up the flyer to Jamie. At first he didn't seem interested. But a couple days later he told me he'd like to do it. Every Wednesday for the past four months, he has spent an extra hour after school in the Artist Adventures group. And through that group he has met a woman—a local artist—who has become like a surrogate aunt to him. She now goes to the group every week, checks out Jamie's drawings, and even calls him sometimes during the week to see what he's up to and what he's been drawing. I'm so grateful to that group for providing what I never could, and to Judy, his new 'aunt,' for showing such interest in him when he's missing his mom."

Paula, Tia, and Andrew all came up with creative ways to introduce the opposite-sex fix in their kids' lives. How about you?

❋ ❋ ❋

KEY Qs . . .

- What is your own view of the opposite sex? Is it positive? negative? both?

- How has your experience with the opposite sex affected your child? Explain.

- What is one creative way you could introduce an opposite-sex role model into your child's life?

KEY 4

FOCUS ON THE ABCs

Want to nurture your
child's self-esteem—for a lifetime?
You don't have to be a superparent.
It's all about knowing your kids,
nurturing and encouraging
each child's unique gifts,
and incorporating them into family life,
all the while remembering
that you are the parent,
and your child is a *child*.

CHAPTER 10

The ABCs, Inside Out

"You're the greatest kid in the whole world. I love you, and God loves you, too!"

Sounds great, doesn't it? Most of us think that by saying things like this to our child, we're building his self-esteem. But as nice as that message is, and as crucial as it is for your child to know that you love him, such a comment has little to do with how your child develops self-esteem.

Sure, telling your daughter that she's the prettiest girl in her new dress or telling your son that he's got a golden arm on the field will give your child a fleeting buzz. And if they hear the same message repeated frequently enough, they'll begin to believe it about themselves. But what happens when your daughter reaches puberty and doesn't feel that she's the prettiest girl? What happens when your elementary school-age son finds out that others throw much better than he does?

Much more significantly, what happens in adolescence when your child doesn't feel at all like "the greatest kid in the world"? She wonders whether her father really loves her (since he left the family) and doubts that God exists at all, let alone that he loves her.

What, then, is the foundation of your child's self-esteem, and how *do* you nurture that self-esteem?

Building Self-Esteem, One ABC at a Time

If you want your child to have healthy self-esteem that lasts for a lifetime—through successes as well as failures, through easy times as well as hard times—you need to build your child up from the inside out, rather than from the outside in.

That means you help your child grow through what I call the ABCs for nurturing true self-esteem:

- Acceptance: your affirmation of who your child is, with all his unique traits
- Belonging: your child's understanding that he is an indispensable part of your family because of how he pitches in
- Competence: your child's experience that he can make a difference in the world by exercising his unique gifts

For children of single-parent families, the ABCs are particularly important because those children, at least on a subconscious level, may be battling rejection, abandonment, and a fear of incompetence. Every child deals with these fears to some extent, but the child of a single parent will certainly deal with them more, *especially* if the father or mother chose to walk out on the family.

Nurturing your child's self-esteem may be particularly difficult when your own self-esteem may be shot through with holes. You may still feel the pain and the betrayal of your ex walking out on you. You may still be experiencing grief over the death of your spouse. You may still be angry because "that guy" chose not to stick it out and marry you. Or you may wonder if you're not good enough for any guy, since nobody seemed interested in marrying you.

Let me assure you. You don't have to be a perfect parent or a superparent to make single parenting work. Being a good parent—one who cares about her children but allows herself plenty of grace to make mistakes, freedom to cry, and room to get angry—is all that's needed. By knowing your children, nurturing and encouraging their unique gifts, and incorporating them into family life, your children can thrive in your home.

Here's how you can incorporate the ABCs into your family's life.

REPLACE REJECTION WITH ACCEPTANCE.

Everyone knows the classic Christmas story *Rudolph the Red-Nosed Reindeer*, and it's a great one to share with your kids. I'll tell you why.

Rudolph is that lovable leader of Santa's team of reindeer who lights the way on Christmas Eve. But if you remember the story's beginning, not everyone is initially thrilled with Rudolph's famous red nose, including his father, Donner. Even Santa, jolly old man that he is, speaks disparagingly of Rudolph's nose.

It's not the loving, accepting family a reindeer might hope for.

Meanwhile, over in Santa's workshop, Hermey the elf isn't faring much better in finding acceptance for his aspirations. While all the other elves are busy making toys, Hermey is dead set on becoming a dentist, to the great frustration of the head elf. (Heaven knows they need at least one dentist up at the North Pole with all that candy, but apparently the elves didn't see it that way.) And so, rejected by their family and peers, Hermey and Rudolph set off to make a life of their own.

It's a sad start to a great story about how each person, having unique traits, can find acceptance and make a difference in the world. And as it is with reindeer and elves, so it is with children. Every one of them is different, vulnerable to others' rejection, and in search of acceptance.

"One of the deepest feelings a child experiences in a solo-parent situation is rejection," writes Pastor Clyde Besson in his book *Picking Up the Pieces*. "Whether the parent has left by death or by divorce, the child still experiences a sense of rejection."[1] In time, if you as a single parent make your children a priority, they will most likely one day realize and appreciate how much you gave in raising them. But at times, growing up in a single-parent family, your child may mistakenly experience your lack of presence for rejection. Because of your situation, you may be the only parent cheering your daughter on at after-school sporting events or the only parent there at your son's orchestra performance. Sometimes, because of your shortage of time and energy, you may not be able to be there at all. Or your second job, which you had to take to make ends meet, may preclude your being there.

> Children have a healthy appetite for your attention.

If you are regularly still at work when your child arrives home from school, your absence can be a great challenge to your child's self-esteem.

But the way you help combat your child's fears of rejection is to accept her for who she is.

That sure sounds like something a shrink would say, doesn't it? But it's true. Your kids need to know that your occasional absence does not mean your rejection and that you accept them for who they are.

It's no secret that children have a healthy appetite for your attention. They want your full attention when they take their first steps. They want you to listen patiently as they learn to read. And as much as they may say otherwise, they really want you behind them at their volleyball games in junior high school (at least emotionally, if not with your physical presence so they can spot you).

So when you can't be there, don't despair. Your absence is sometimes unavoidable. But with the time that you do have together, encourage your child's gifts. Watch your child carefully to see what motivates her. Encourage her interests.

> Buying your children stuff will never replace your presence.

By encouraging interests, I'm not talking about buying stuff. "Oh, she likes My Little Pony. Maybe I should go buy her a new one because I missed her ballet recital." (That's guilt talking again, my friend.) Buying your children stuff will never replace your presence. What your children need is for you to be encouraging and actively participating with them in their interests. If you miss a ballet performance, perhaps you could set up a special performance time at home, where your daughter can be the "star of the show" for your family, and you can create a special treat afterward. Maybe you could even twirl together around the living room (if it doesn't make you dizzy). Participating with your children in their interests shows them that you accept them just the way they are.

Praise and *encouragement* may sound synonymous, but there's a distinct difference between the two. Praise focuses on a child's performance, appearance, or accomplishments. Encouragement, however, focuses on the character qualities that went into an activity.

So rather than praising your son by saying, "If you keep that up on the football field, you'll have talent scouts banging on our door," encourage him by saying, "I've been noticing how hard you practice, and that's really making a difference in your games, isn't it?" One comment focuses on the performance (and, quite honestly, piles on the pressure). The other focuses on the child's perseverance, which could have application in any area of life—whether or not the talent scouts ever show up on your doorstep.

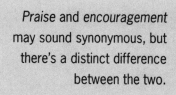

Praise and *encouragement* may sound synonymous, but there's a distinct difference between the two.

By accepting your child's unique traits, encouraging the good you see in him, and not trying to get him to conform to others, you help fight your child's fears of rejection and you nurture self-esteem.

Even good old Rudolph found out in the long run that what had once been rejected about him—his big, bright, red nose—was accepted after all.

REPLACE ABANDONMENT WITH BELONGING.

One single dad I know is raising five daughters by himself. *Five daughters!* Just imagine! He makes that old TV show *My Three Sons* sound like a warm-up for the real thing. In his family, everyone pitches in. The older daughters help prepare dinner and wash the dishes, and the younger ones set the table and pick up toys each night without prompting. Each child has specific tasks that make her feel like a necessary part of the family, as indeed she is!

If you love your children, it's tempting to want to hand life to them on a silver platter (especially if your guilt is working overtime for not providing a mother or a father for them). But don't do it! It won't help your children, you, or anyone your children are around in the future to do so. Instead, give your kids opportunities to pick up the platter themselves and serve others around them.

I often say it this way: You are running a home, not a hotel. If you do everything for your children, you're setting them up for failure. That may sound harsh, but it's true. Your children will never learn how to get by in life without doing things for themselves and others. And without pitching in to do their part, they'll also never learn that their contributions to the family are not only valued, but *essential.*

Healthy self-esteem is nurtured in your children when they feel that they belong to your family. I've mentioned this point in other books, but it's such an important one that it bears repeating: When kids feel that they belong to your family, they have little reason, from a psychological standpoint, to engage in any aberrant behavior whatsoever. Kids join gangs because they are trying to replace that lost sense of belonging.

> You are running a home, not a hotel.

By having your children give back to your family, you help foster that need for belonging. You also do it when you listen to them, when you talk with them, when you ask them questions about their interests, and when you give them an active role in family activities and chores around the house, such as helping prepare dinner, watching a younger sibling when you are studying for a night class, or helping research family travel plans online.

"We can't afford to fly to Grandpa and Grandma's for Christmas, so we're going to have to drive," you tell your teenage son.

"But that's a day and a half of driving," he begins to complain.

"Exactly. So would you please go online and figure out how far we can reasonably drive on that first day, then find the least expensive motel for us to stay at in that town?"

That's one way to put your son's computer expertise and innate curiosity to constructive use!

When you involve your child with family activities and responsibilities, you're communicating to him, "You are important in my life and indispensable to the life of this family."

You can involve your older kids with your home finances. Have your twelve-year-old help you write checks to pay family bills. Not only will you be teaching her financial responsibility, she'll see a portion of the family responsibilities that have to be met on time—responsibilities that she may otherwise be unaware of.

In any single-parent family, having your kids pitch in is particularly important because you *can't* handle everything yourself. As much as you may like to. As much as you may try. So why not get some help from the very people living with you?

Your family may be fractured, but your children need to belong to your single-parent household *now more than ever*. When you experience pain or loss in a relationship, your child will feel it, too.

Why didn't my mom stick around? your son may wonder.

Why did that guy get my mom pregnant and then leave? Didn't he care about us? your daughter may think.

Why did my dad have to die and leave us behind?

Why does everybody else have a dad, and I don't? What's wrong with my mom and me that nobody wants us?

Because part of your family has been lost, your child will feel some abandonment. And her psyche will work overtime to make sense of what happened. She will wonder if she did anything to cause your current situation. *Is it my fault that Dad died? If I hadn't gotten mad at him for missing my game and told him off on his cell phone, would he have paid more attention to the road?*

Subconsciously, your child may take some of the responsibility for the failure of your relationship: *If I were a better kid,* he might think, *maybe Dad and Mom wouldn't have gotten into so many fights. They might even still be together.* The message that many people—parents and children alike—feel following a divorce is, *If only I had been different, things might have turned out differently.*

How can you help? To help combat your children's fears of abandonment, let them know you're committed to them forever.

By allowing your child to play a major role in your family and receive equal social standing with other family members, you build his self-esteem. And don't allow any child in the family to play a minor role, regardless of age. Everyone should have major roles (age appropriate, of course).

> To help combat your children's fears of abandonment, let them know you're committed to them forever.

Emphasize the team concept in your home. That means every single member of your family should keep the family as a whole his most important priority. No individual member's priorities or schedules—even *yours*, as the parent—are more important than someone else's. That means your career, for example, while important to providing for your family, shouldn't intrinsically be more important than your daughter's growth or education.

Your kids need to know—and to see this concept played out daily—that together, your family can accomplish more than you can apart from each other. Values are always caught, not taught. And of all the people in the world, your kids will be the first to sniff out any inconsistencies between what you say and do.

> Values are always caught, not taught.

When my daughter Lauren and I were walking together through downtown Tucson, we came across a homeless man selling newspapers. This was one time when, through my best powers of observation, I felt that this was an honest man, trying to make the best of a bad situation. He wasn't just sitting there, asking for a handout. He had taken the little money he did have and was trying to make a living for himself through the few dollars he earned. So I stopped, handed the man a ten-dollar bill for my paper, and waved away the change.

Lauren saw that. After all, like most children, she's continually taking psychological notes on me, her favorite subject.

Later that evening, Lauren disappeared. I found her in her room, busily putting together a care package for a classmate who had been out of school for a couple of weeks with bad asthma. After she had finished collecting her gifts, she put it all in a manila envelope and decorated it with her drawings and the words "Asthma Care Package."

I smiled. That ten-dollar bill had been a little thing, but Lauren had "caught" my values. She was living out her heart through my positive example, and it gave me such joy. (I only wish my example was always so positive.)

Be assured that a child will always take note of what you do with what you have—whether you have a little or a lot. That's why I emphasized giving of what you have in chapter 8, even when you're pressed for time and money. As your family works together and your children watch you, they'll pick up your values. They'll learn what is most important to you in life.

What are you teaching your kids by what you do?

REPLACE INCOMPETENCE WITH COMPETENCE.
The only thing worse than being the last one picked for the team is being left off altogether. Everyone needs to feel that he can do something well in life—and that includes contributing to family, friendships, work, school, etc. But when life hands you more than you can handle and you're beginning to drop the ball left and right because you're so overwhelmed, it's easy to begin thinking that you can't do *anything* right.

The same is true for your child, who may feel incompetent because of the loss in his family relationships. Because self-perception is tied to what we do, if we *feel* competent in life, then we're more apt to *see ourselves* in a positive light. The competency that people develop from working hard at school, in friendships, and around the house begins to make a difference not only in what they accomplish, but also in their character, in who they are.

> If we *feel* competent in life, then we're more apt to *see ourselves* in a positive light.

I was waiting for a flight when I came across a guy who was so large I knew he either played football or wrestled bulls for relaxation.

"Are you a football player?" I asked. (It was probably a dumb question.)

He said yes and told me who he was.

Well, I recognized his name and remembered that he had graduated the previous spring. "Oh, number ten!" I said.

He lit right up. *Wow,* he must have been thinking, *this guy recognizes my name and jersey number.*

The more we talked, the more impressed I was with how he carried himself. So out of curiosity I asked him, "Would you list a few characteristics that describe yourself?"

He could have mentioned his number of tackles or how fast he could run the hundred-yard dash. Fact is, this guy was very competent. I'd seen him play on TV. But rather than talking about what he had accomplished on the football field, he talked about the kind of person he was—kind, social, helpful, and honest. Because this guy felt competent, he saw himself in a positive light and treated himself accordingly.

It's back, once again, to the difference between praise and encouragement.

When your son goes four for four in his Little League baseball game, including three stolen bases and two RBIs, you shouldn't praise him by saying, "You're going to be in the big leagues someday—you wait and see!" Instead, encourage him by saying, "I saw you really hustling out there on the field, and that seems to be paying off, doesn't it?"

If your daughter is a whiz at math, let her know you admire the hard work she puts into studying to make that happen. If your child is chosen to play trumpet in the all-state band, for example, or earns a blue ribbon at the local fair for his science project, that gives him a sense of accomplishment that will build his self-esteem in a healthy way.

If you focus on real encouragement rather than praise (which can be false or can disappear if the child fails in the same area in the future), your child will begin to move full esteem ahead.

All children long for Acceptance, Belonging, and Competence—the three ABCs that are the foundation of self-esteem. But the child of a single parent needs it even more. You can provide the ABCs, from the inside out. It's a gift that will keep on giving!

KEY Qs . . .

- How do you think your child is doing, self-esteem-wise? What factors do you see contributing to your child's perspective about who he/she is?

- What, to you, is the difference between *praise* and *encouragement*? Which do you tend to use more with your child, and why?

- Of the three ABCs—Acceptance, Belonging, Competence—which is most crucial to develop in your child's life right now? Explain.

CHAPTER 11

It's the Relationship, Not the Rules

CHEN-LI'S STORY

"I'll never forget my little boy's first week at school. Chun had loved kindergarten and was so excited about going to first grade and seeing his friends again. But when the time came for him to walk through that door, his feet started to drag. His head started to droop. Tears started to flow. I pulled him aside, under a nearby tree and out of the flow of traffic.

"'Honey, what's wrong?' I asked him.

"He wiped tears off his face and met my eyes. 'Mom, I'm going to miss *you*.'

"That nearly did me in. I could have cried on the spot, too. After all, it's just Chun and me at home. Instead, I assured him that I would miss him, too, but that I was excited for him in this new adventure. I gave him a hug and told him that we would do something special after school. 'How about if I make some of those special almond cookies you love, and we have a little picnic right here under this tree after school?'

"Chun's eyes grew wide. 'Really? But Mom, you always say, "No sweets before dinner." Is that okay?'

"I smiled and told him that we'd make a special exception because this was a special day."

Wanted: You!

I just have to say, *that* mom is one smart cookie. (And she makes great almond cookies, by the way.)

She knew what her kid really wanted—and needed—most in his life.

Her.

Not a trip to the store for more stuff.

Not an elaborate system of play dates so he'd get to know all the other boys in school the first month.

He simply needed his mommy to be there.

He needed to know their relationship was still intact—even in times of change.

And, for once, he needed his well-ordered, firstborn-personality mommy to break a rule for the greater good of their relationship.

> No one can replace you in your child's life.

Want to know what your kids really want and need the most?

A generous piece of *you!*

You see, kids just want what comes naturally to them: the desire to have a relationship with you. No one else can replace you in your child's life.

Your love and your example are more important to them than anything else. Yet there may be subtle ways that you're sabotaging your relationship without even knowing it.

Rules . . . or Relationship?

While attending a fundraising event, humorist and author Mark Twain decided the cause was a good one after listening to the speaker for a while. He made a mental note to donate a hundred dollars. As the speaker continued, however, Twain grew restless and cut his donation in half. With no end in sight to the speaker's talk, he again cut his donation, this time to ten dollars.

When the speaker finally finished and a basket was passed around for contributions, Twain reached in and pulled out a one-dollar bill for himself and passed the basket on![1]

He'd heard so much from the speaker, over and over, ad nauseam, that he was sick and tired of hearing it. By the end, he figured *he* should be paid, just for listening!

Do you think your kids ever feel the same way about your rules?

You may have had good intentions making your rules—to have well-behaved children who sit at attention on the living room sofa like birds on a telephone wire, or who use the correct fork for their salad and say all the appropriate things, as prescribed by Emily Post, to those who visit for dinner.

But in spite of your best intentions, sometimes your rules will get in the way of your relationship with your children. They will hamper your communication and shut down your children emotionally (not to mention shutting down their ears, as in Twain's case). Sometimes rules will make your kids want to do *exactly the opposite* of what you say.

> Sometimes rules will make your kids want to do *exactly the opposite* of what you say.

How does this happen? If your parenting plan is high on structure and short on heart, it will eventually cave in. After all, there isn't a strong enough relationship with your children—an understanding of them and who they are from your time spent together—to back up your rules.

Josh McDowell has said a lot of great things throughout his life, but one of my favorite one-liners of his is this: "Rules without relationship leads to rebellion."

You can't get any more succinct than that in communicating the importance of your *involved* love in your child's life. If you focus on rules and neglect the relationship, you're setting your child up for failure. In essence, you're then communicating that your child's performance— what he *does*—is more important than who he *is*. The child who lives by rules without relationship lives in constant fear that he or she may never quite measure up.

Andrea was continually telling her son, "Stop wiggling in your chair!" It embarrassed her that he could never sit still—no matter how much she asked him to do so. Her other children had never been like that, so what was his problem?

What Andrea didn't realize is that Johnny, who was four, was doing what was age appropriate for a little boy after sitting still for twenty minutes. Wiggling! She was measuring him against the standards of the two other children in her family—both quiet, introverted girls who loved to read. Johnny was a go-for-the-gusto kind of boy. And every time he broke his mother's rule about wiggling, he was being told subconsciously,

What is the matter with you? Why can't you sit still? What's wrong with you? You're not as good as your sisters. . . .

When Andrea realized what she was really saying to her son, she was shocked. She admitted that she needed to make some adjustments in her life. One was setting up a playtime for Johnny at a friend's house while the two girls had their piano lessons so he didn't have to sit quietly for an hour every Wednesday afternoon. And she realized something else, too—how much the girls were like her and how much Johnny was like her ex. She was taking out her anger toward her ex on Johnny in setting rules for him that were physically impossible for him to keep.

"But, Dr. Leman," you might say, "my child *needs* rules."

I agree. Every child needs the boundaries that rules provide. I'm not saying you shouldn't have rules in your family. Rules keep everyone safe. They keep a level of respect between you and your kids, and between your kids and their siblings.

But rules are worthless without relationship. If you run your household like a military establishment, making sure your kids hop to it and keep all the rules, you may have a well-run house and good behavior from your kids . . . for a while. But eventually the rules will break down because there is no relationship. If you don't spend time with your kids and they aren't assured of your love and support, they will not have the internal motivation to please you, which means they will not consider it a priority to obey your rules anymore. And they certainly won't be learning to make independent, healthy decisions if they are just "told" what to do, rather than thinking through consequences themselves.

Rules may start kids on the straight and narrow, but kids need a relationship—an encouraging companion—along the way to keep them on that path. And the companion they care about the most is you.

If you have that kind of relationship with a child, you are saying, by your presence and your actions, "I love you just the way you are, and I believe you can make it in life." Such belief is like rocket fuel, propelling your child to succeed.

So instead of a rigid blueprint for behavior, what your children need

> Belief is like rocket fuel, propelling your child to succeed.

to succeed is your involved love and healthy example as you relate to them.

And, interestingly enough, if you make your relationship with your children a priority over their behavior (and the rules you have to make as a result), you won't have to worry so much about rules!

To make anything a priority, you have to give it time (something we'll talk more about in chapter 17), and you also have to develop a healthy communication style.

How to *Really* Talk

- "I wish I knew what she was thinking. She never talks to me anymore."
- "I feel bad that I can't be there when he gets home from school. That's the time he used to tell me the most about his day."
- "Lately Stephanie's been crying a lot. But when I ask her what's wrong, she just shakes her head and goes to her room and shuts the door."
- "Todd has been so angry since his dad left, and he's taking it out on his sister and me. It's not our fault Frank left, but Todd makes us feel like it."

Whether you and your kids have had major crises or minor skirmishes or no skirmishes at all, now is the time to learn how to communicate in a healthy way with them, no matter their age. Here are some principles that will help:

ACKNOWLEDGE YOUR CHILD'S HURTS.

Do you remember the day you learned how to ride a bicycle? It's a wonderfully exhilarating experience—that thrill of *finally* figuring out how to balance as you weave down the driveway or the neighborhood sidewalk. When you fell and skinned your elbow, did your mother or father kiss your owie? And if so, wasn't it magical how the pain stopped almost immediately, just because someone cared?

That's exactly the kind of magic I want you to work right now. Talking with your child is keenly important. Ask him how he's feeling about your divorce or the death of your spouse. Ask her how she feels when other kids at school talk about their daddies, since she doesn't have one.

> Think before you open your mouth to respond.

Encourage your child to share what's going on inside. And when he does, think before you open your mouth to respond. Judging a child when he shares with you will only shut him down. Instead, when your child opens up, give him a hug. Say things such as, "Honey, thanks for sharing that. I know that was tough to do. It never feels good, does it, to have to say things like that? But I really think it's better to get it out like you just did than to hold it in." Or perhaps you empathize with your child: "You know, I've felt that, too, since Dad died."

If your child has retreated into himself and doesn't talk with you outright about how he's feeling, don't assume that everything is fine and that you only need to discuss things as they crop up. Children and teens *always* have a lot going on inside their minds and hearts!

You can never force a child to open up, but you can encourage him by leading through your own example of opening up. You could say, "You know, honey, sometimes I get lonely. Have you ever felt that way?"

Eventually, as your child sees you talking about how you feel inside, he will probably come around and begin sharing what's going on inside him as well. And he will do so even more if he doesn't fear your judgment—whether through a verbal onslaught ("How could you even think that? After all I've done for you!") or giving him the cold shoulder as punishment.

If you talk openly about the hurts your family feels, you are communicating a very important message: "We are all in the journey of life together. We're going to help each other. And with each other's help and God's help, we're all going to be okay."

HELP YOUR CHILD DEAL WITH ANGER.

Let's face it. All of us get angry sometimes, and children are people, too.

They may just show their anger differently and in ways you find unacceptable.

But here's what's really going on.

A young child may not yet have developed the skills to articulate his feelings well, but what he lacks in verbal ability he can certainly make up for in body language. Your two-year-old may bang his head repeatedly on his high chair tray and fuss. Your eight-year-old may toss his book bag on the floor with a loud *thud.* Your twelve-year-old may slam doors, knowing he gets center stage to show you how angry he really is by his dramatic performance. Your sixteen-year-old may take a more minor role in the drama, simply brooding over on stage left.

However your child responds—whether with aggressive or passive behavior—it usually isn't difficult to read the cue cards your child is holding that read "Anger! Anger!"

When such situations occur in your family, those are *your* cues to acknowledge your child's anger and help him learn to

> All of us get angry sometimes, and children are people, too.

deal with it in an appropriate way. You could start by simply saying, "Hey, I see you've had a bad day." Or, "You seem bothered by something." Or, "Whew. By the look on your face I can tell it's been one of those days."

Those comments are open invitations for your child to respond and allow the emotional balloon inside to deflate as soon as he opens his mouth. Many times, however, a kid will respond with a no. If he does, let it go.

Then, perhaps after dinner (it's amazing how a full tummy can help in opening a child's mouth), go back to him and say, "You know, bud, you were pretty mad today when you came home from school. Now that you've had some time to unwind, do you want to tell me what happened?" Sometimes a kid will still say, "No, it's no big deal." But if you show sincere interest without pestering your child, most likely he'll eventually open up to you (whether it's that day, the next day, or even a week down the road). Some children just need to process their thoughts before they can verbalize them.

Keep in mind that your kids want you to affirm them. That may sound contrary to what you might believe about them (especially teenagers!), but they really do want you to connect with them. Often a child whose family is going through the difficulty of a divorce, a separation, or a death can begin feeling unwanted at school, alienated from his friends and classmates. If a parent is missing, he may feel as if he failed or is failing at life—even if he isn't—and that only makes his life more miserable.

But what a difference it makes if that child can open up and tell his mom or dad what's really going on in his life at home and school, and that parent in turn affirms him by saying something such as, "You know, honey, I'd be angry, too. But it seems you're handling it about as well as a ten-year-old could handle it." Such words tell your son (or daughter) that he is making great choices. That you're proud of him—not simply what he does, but who he is, at his core. And that means the world to your child.

So how do you respond when your child is angry? What do you say to her? Your words and actions are important; they open up your child's self-esteem bank, and either make a deposit or a withdrawal.

GIVE YOUR CHILD PERMISSION TO TALK
ABOUT THE ONE WHO'S MISSING.

You've probably found yourself in a situation at work or your place of worship where everyone tiptoes around your divorce or your spouse's death or your lack of a spouse in the first place. They avoid the subject like the plague, while inside you are screaming, *Would someone please bring this subject up so I can talk about all that's going on inside?!*

If someone does break the ice with you, asking in a quiet moment, "Hey, how are you doing?" you know what a comfort it can be. You know firsthand that people need to be able to talk about their loss and grief, and that it's still best for those around you to say *something* rather than nothing at all.

The truth is that a lot of kids *don't* feel permission to talk about their missing parent.

If you've got an ex, your interaction may be rocky, and children know that Mommy and Daddy don't get along very well. Well, I've got news for you. Your ex may be partly or completely missing in action, but he or she still exists in your child's mind. And if you don't allow your child to talk about your ex (as mad as you might be at him or her), your child can place that parent on a pedestal. After all, it's easy to paint people you don't see every day with rosy colors and to uphold them as "the perfect dad" or "the perfect mom."

So, trying to keep your child away from your ex or telling your child not to listen to him won't do you or your child any favors. That's why it's important (unless, as I stated earlier, your ex is toxic or an "in-n-out" ex) to allow your child guilt-free access to your ex. Even if your ex hurt you badly and is now living with another partner and you don't agree with his lifestyle, your child needs to know that he can call Dad anytime he wants, without you hanging over his shoulder and listening.

This is one of the toughest choices you'll ever make as a single parent. After all, you've been hurt by your ex, and you don't want your kid to be hurt. But remember this (again, unless safety issues are involved): You are not responsible for your ex's relationship with your child, and vice versa. You are only responsible for *your* relationship with your child.

So, when you can, allow your child free access to her other parent. It's hard to do, but you can do it. Open the door for your children to have that same kind of open relationship with your ex that *you* desire to have with your children.

If your spouse has died, allow your child to talk about that parent without the fear of making you sad or uncomfortable. Relive memories of times you had together. Look through photo albums. Giggle about the time your child and your spouse made a boat for the cardboard regatta in the park . . . and it sank three minutes after it hit the water in the lake.

Find ways to include someone of the same sex as your missing spouse, a person your child really likes and identifies with.

> Relive memories of times you had together.

When you go to a ball game and your child feels sad because her mommy can't be there, you might want to say, "Oh, honey, Mommy would have loved this, don't you think? She would have loved watching you get dressed up in your new uniform. She'd be your greatest fan in the stands. She'd want this first game to be really special. So guess what?

Since Mom can't be here, I've asked Aunt Andee to come. And she's going to join us for vanilla shakes afterward, too!"

Just wait and see what smiles that will bring. No, your wife can't be there. But Andee, your wife's sister, can. And that will make all the difference in the world to your child.

And if you've never been married, allow your child to ask questions about his missing daddy or mommy.

- "What was he like?"
- "Do I look like her?"
- "Did she like to ice skate, too?"
- "Did he ever know he was a daddy?"
- "Do you ever see her? Do you think I'll ever see her?"
- "Would he be proud of me?"

Let your child know that *any* question is okay to ask. Some questions you may be able to answer (always age appropriately, of course). Other answers you may not know. But answer those you can, and admit when you don't know. If you are honest, you will only improve your relationship with your child—and solidify the bond of trust between you.

> Let your child know that *any* question is okay to ask.

Certain subjects are never easy to talk about. When was the last time you sat down to enjoy an evening talk with your pubescent son about sex, or to chat around the dinner table about the growing frustrations you sense in your children about their new neighborhood? Talking about your divorce or the loss of your spouse to death or separation is inherently painful—it's much easier to switch on the TV or for everyone to retreat to their respective rooms. Kids may not want to talk about the divorce because they don't want to rock the boat any more than it's already been rocked. Or perhaps they feel partly responsible for the breakup.

But do you realize the tremendous pressure you take off your children by letting them know that they don't have to play games? that any question is okay to ask? that the only way you can have a healthy, growing relationship is by talking?

And that's why this next point is so crucial to any family.

SET UP A REGULAR FAMILY MEETING.

Whenever there's significant loss or missing pieces in a family (or when you're blending families), there's bound to be the possibility for significant anger. And when it is not dealt with, anger hardens, growing into bitterness. There's a reason why Scripture wisely says, "Do not let the sun go down while you are still angry."[2]

What will help your family most in such times is having regularly established family meetings. Some folks prefer to call them "communication meetings." Whatever you decide to call them—one family calls them "The Turner Talks"—it's important that these meetings happen regularly. One of the best formats is to have them once a week as you sit around the table after dinner. That way it's less likely that a significant problem will build up and not be addressed.

> Share the "pows" and the "wows."

As you talk informally, share the things that stressed you out about the week as well as the things you enjoyed. I call them the "pows" and the "wows." You, as the parent, must discern what to talk about in each meeting. You'll have to take the lead most of the time in order to get the conversation flowing.

For instance, you could bring up that your boss has been demanding and that the pressure from the home office for higher sales has made it a rough week. But you could mention, "So our Friday night movie night was just what I needed. A quiet and fun time on the couch with just you guys and some popcorn." And then you go on to say, "What was your week like, Nate? . . . What about you, Carlee?"

If you only get the silent treatment, rolled eyes, or sighs, you might prompt further, "I take it from your expression that you're not crazy about sharing. But you're an important member of this family, and I want to know what you're thinking and feeling. Is anything bugging you these days? making you unhappy or angry?"

As you take the lead, your kids can follow, opening up about their own experiences. "Hey, Mom, I got news for you," one might then feel free to say. "Life down at the junior high school isn't a piece of cake, either."

Sometimes your kids will be mad at others outside the family, sometimes they'll be mad at their siblings, and sometimes they'll be mad at you. But no matter who they're mad at, the same rule applies: Hear them out, because they may have good reason to be angry.

With all the emotions flying around any house, you'd have to be a saint not to mess up every now and then. When you do (notice I said *when*, not *if*), don't be slow to admit that you're sorry. Admitting that you are wrong is not a sign of weakness. In fact, you never look bigger in the eyes of your child than when you step down off the throne of Almighty Parent and say in all humility to your child, "I'm sorry, I shouldn't have said that. Will you forgive me?"

I want to note here, however, that a family communication meeting should never become a free-for-all. For example, you as the parent need to be especially careful about the specifics you share. If you announce to your kids how angry you are at your ex because he blew off the kids, you're not helping matters any for them. And you're feeding your own emotional fires. If you just found out that your ex is cheating on the woman he left you for, for example, you may have the emotional energy (and satisfaction) of a nuke. But don't detonate it at the next communication meeting. You need to protect your kids. They're more fragile than they may look, at any age.

> Admitting that you are wrong is not a sign of weakness.

And here's another good rule to enforce during a family meeting: Have you ever been deep in conversation with someone, getting ready to make a really important point, when someone else interrupted you and you lost your train of thought? Frustrating, isn't it? So when one member of the family has the floor at the family meeting, make sure he or she is allowed to speak, *with no interruptions from anyone else.* Otherwise, you'll shut down any attempts at conversation because your child will assume, *Nobody listens to me anyway, so why try?*

Make this communication meeting a priority. It may be the only time in a twenty-four-hour period (or even within a week's time) when you're all together to sit down and talk, so don't give it second billing and jump up from the table to answer the phone. Let your kids see that they are your top priority. And that means listening to them should come before telemarketers selling long-distance service.

Yes, sometimes your conversations will begin in an emotionally charged way. But the conversation that follows can be especially healing for your family.

Because every person in the family will view things through a different psychological lens, it's important to have these meetings regularly— even if there is no outward sign of anger. Your job is to raise the questions. If there's anything to talk about, fine. If not, fine. You don't have to dredge up anger if there's none there; that isn't the point. The point is to open channels for communication so that if there *is* something to talk about, it doesn't go unresolved for weeks or months or years on end, compounding itself within your family relationships and growing into bitterness.

The Top Three Don'ts for Any Single Parent

Because you are the head of your family, you face some unique temptations. Becoming aware of them will go a long way toward smoothing the communication in your household. Even more, you'll be establishing a relationship of honesty and trust with your kids that will reap rewards for a lifetime.

DON'T TRY TO BE MOM AND DAD.

You're either a mom or a dad, but you can't be both—no matter how much guilt you feel because your child is missing a parent.

The realities are what they are. Since you now set three places at the dinner table instead of four, you can bet, Mom, that it won't be long before your children start missing those after-work wrestling matches on the living room floor with Dad. Or you can bet, Dad, that your Saturday morning blueberry waffles won't turn out the same way Mom's did, even if you follow her recipe.

It's hard for any caring mother to watch her deflated children flop in front of the TV when you know they'd much rather be out throwing the football around with Dad. And it's hard for any caring father to know what to do on that first Mother's Day when Mom is no longer around.

So no wonder it's tempting to salve their wounds by trying to be both Dad *and* Mom to your kids, especially if your ex is an in-n-out parent who was absent before but even more so now. You may soon find yourself trying to lessen the sting for your kids by trying your ex's shoes on for size. But getting out in the backyard and throwing the football around with the boys yourself, like Dad used to do, isn't going to help, Mom. And trying to create the same breakfast Mom did won't help, Dad.

Even if you develop the throwing arm of an NFL quarterback, your boys are still going to miss that time with Dad. It's not the act of tossing the football around that they miss, or being mock body-slammed into the sofa cushions, so much as it is the *time* with Dad, talking together as they tossed the football. It's not the heavenly taste of Mom's blueberry waffles they miss so much as *being* with Mom as together they mixed the blueberries into the batter and then you all sat down as a family on Saturday morning to a meal everyone helped make.

> By trying to fill the missing parent's shoes, you're trying to replace a relationship, which simply can't be done.

That's why you *cannot* replace that absent parent. If you try to, you will only frustrate yourself and your children. For by trying to fill the missing parent's shoes, you're trying to replace a relationship, which simply can't be done. Sure, there will be tasks to do that you didn't do before—getting the kids' lunches ready for school, for example, or picking them up from after-school baseball practice or playing tooth inspector after they brush before bed. But you can never replace that missing parent. Nor should you try to.

Instead, empathize with them for their loss: "Boy, I wish I could make waffles like Mom does," or, "I can tell you miss your wrestling time with Dad, don't you?" That opens the opportunity for them to share their hearts with you, and for you to connect with them.

That relationship with your child is worth its weight in gold.

DON'T BE FAKE.

"If you could choose one thing—and only one thing—to suggest to parents about raising their kids, what would it be?" I once asked my friend Chuck Swindoll.

He didn't hesitate. "'Be authentic," he said boldly.

Simple words, but they pack a wallop of profound insight on how parents can put a relationship with their children above rules. But what does that mean for you, specifically, as a single parent?

Imagine this: you're driving to the nearest grocery outlet with your child to pick up groceries for the week, and you happen to pause by a stoplight in front of the corner restaurant where you and your ex-husband had your first date so many years ago. Memories of your mutual interest, the kind words, and that evening filled with giddy excitement all rush back and a wave of grief hits. You pull away from the corner, but tears begin to well up.

"Mommy, why are you crying?" your son asks from the back seat as a tear slips down your face.

What do you say?

Many parents will brush off these emotions by saying, "Oh, it's okay, honey," or, "I'll be all right."

But do that, and you miss a wonderful opportunity to communicate your heart and build that relationship with your child as you help each other navigate through the emotions that come with being a single-parent family. What could be healthier for your children than to see that Mom is upset from time to time? that the divorce affects her just as it affects everyone else in the family?

"Mommy's feeling sad," you might tell him.

"Why?" he asks again. It's a typical three-year-old's question that suddenly now seems so reasonable, even profound in its straightforward simplicity.

"Mommy is sad that Daddy's gone."

As much as you may want to hide those tears from your children, you cannot schedule your emotions any more than you can schedule the weather. By hiding those moments, you may miss an opportunity for

> You cannot schedule your emotions any more than you can schedule the weather.

your child to appropriately love and nurture *you*. That doesn't mean, of course, that you should look to your child to "parent" you in all the ways you wish you could be loved and taken care of. That's far too big a responsibility for any child. But just because you're in healthy authority over your child doesn't mean that he or she can't comfort you, too. If you allow your child to do so occasionally, you develop in your child a gentle, nurturing heart and an awareness of those who are hurting.

"It's okay, Mommy," your child might say, "I love you," which at that moment may be the most nourishing words you can hear, words that might not have been spoken if you had tried to "keep it all together."

And by voicing your emotions, you are effectively modeling to your child how to describe his emotions to you when he is hurting.

So share your life with your child—its ups and downs. Your laughter and your tears.

So don't fake it. Be authentic. Be real.

DON'T SPILL IT ALL.

When I tell you to share your life with your child, I'm not talking about spilling every detail of your life. There are, of course, things that you would be better off not sharing with your child.

Such as all the details of your past sins. You've probably made decisions that you regret. Don't tell your four-year-old daughter, for example, that when you were sixteen, you experimented with sex, got pregnant with her, and then had to get married. Leave that conversation for your best friend, your counselor, or your diary.

You can't inundate your kid with all of your financial and relational pressures. He is just trying to get through school, and frankly he cares more about being liked by other kids and not forgetting his locker combination. Your job is to be judicious in how much to tell him.

If you find yourself confiding in your children too much, check yourself: Do you have another outlet to share those intimate details of your life? Do you have a friend with whom you can share what's going on in your life, or are you relying too heavily on your kids for companionship that can only be found through another adult?

A Simple Thing

I'll never forget one special Father's Day celebration at our house. My children had worked hard to surprise me. They'd even found and set up around the table photos of me as a kid.

But what touched me the most was a folded three-by-five card on the chair next to mine. On it were these words scrawled in Magic Marker: "Reserved for Lauren Leman."

"Why," you ask, "was that so important?" You see, Lauren is the youngest of five siblings. She was staking her place at the dinner table so she wouldn't be elbowed out of the action that evening. The most important thing to her was being right next to me.

Some kids will wait by the computer to secure online tickets for the hottest concert to pull into town. Others will wait endlessly in line on opening night for a movie they've been talking about for weeks. But blessed is the parent whose child makes sure she's secured her place next to her mommy or daddy.

When it comes down to it, what children want is simple.

They long for a generous piece of *you*.

❖ ❖ ❖

KEY Qs . . .

- Which do you tend to emphasize in your home—rules or relationship? Give an example.

- If you asked your children the same question, what would they say? Would there be a discrepancy between your answer and theirs? If so, why? What one thing could you do this week to help you and your children see more eye to eye?

- If you already have regular family meetings, what works—and doesn't work—about it? If you haven't yet tried a family meeting, why not start one this week? (If your kids are older, expect the initial groans, but put your plan into action anyway.)

CHAPTER 12

Love . . . and Limits

"I just love my child so much," Karen told me. "We're a team, the two of us, and we do everything together. I never have to worry what Libby is thinking because she always tells me."

Sounds good, doesn't it? What parent wouldn't want that kind of relationship with their child?

But there's more. Listen to what else Karen said. "I've never once had to discipline Libby in any way. I couldn't. We're pals. You wouldn't spank your best friend, would you? So I'd never spank Libby."

But I can tell you what's going on behind the scenes, folks, and if there's ever been a child who *needed* to be spanked, it's Libby. She's a mouthy, bossy kid who's always telling everybody else what's wrong with them and pushing smaller kids around on the playground. All because, frankly, she has a mom who has decided to be her *friend* instead of her mother.

But loving someone doesn't mean you don't have limits. Or discipline. You can't have one without the other, or you get a child like Libby, who's constantly out of control. The kind of kid nobody wants to play with. The kind of young woman no one wants to hire. The kind of woman nobody wants to marry.

Weed Control

There's a story often told about the English poet Samuel Taylor Coleridge, who was talking one day with a man about raising children. The man was adamant that children should not be given formal religious direction of any kind, so that when they came of age, they could decide what path *they* wanted to choose, free from external influence.

Coleridge listened politely.

Some time later he invited the man back to his house and took him outside on a walk through his garden, which had become overgrown due to Coleridge's neglect.

"Do you call this a garden?" exclaimed the man. "There's nothing but weeds here!"

> Just because your child is growing like a weed doesn't mean you should raise him like one!

"Well, you see," replied Coleridge, "I did not wish to infringe upon the liberty of the garden in any way. I was just giving the garden a chance to express itself and to choose its own production."[1]

Just because your child is growing like a weed doesn't mean you should raise him like one! A beautiful child, like a garden, doesn't grow by himself. He requires the cultivation of values, the nurturing of a relationship, and pruning through discipline. Though your child may never say it, he needs you to be in healthy authority over him.

The apostle Paul reveals this important concept clearly in his letter to the Ephesians: "Children, obey your parents; this is the right thing to do because God has placed them in authority over you."[2] But Paul doesn't just give the rule; he gives the reason. "Which is the first commandment with a promise—'that it may go well with you and that you may enjoy long life on the earth.'" Now there's a great reason to discipline your kids! To make sure they're not wayward weeds, growing in every which direction and not doing anybody any good.

Today's world is a laissez-faire one. Live and let live, some say. Let people do what they want to because everyone has rights, some insist. So many parents let their children grow like weeds, unchecked. The parents neglect their authority—and their *responsibility*, I might add—over their children.

Then there's the parent at the other end of the spectrum—the authoritarian parent. The guy or gal who will go through the garden three times a day, spraying chemicals to manage every moment of growth. That's the kind of parent who will say things such as, "You shape up, or I'll shape you up!"

The truth is that kids will rebel against either extreme. If you're a pushover, live-and-let-live parent, they'll eventually push you over since firm guidelines aren't present. If you're a pushy parent, you'll eventually find your children pushing back because your boundaries are too rigid. The key is to strive for the middle ground, exercising healthy authority with love in your discipline.

Every child must learn proper respect for authority, but it may be particularly important for children who have been through their parents' divorce. These kids need to learn respect because of the issues that often precipitate a breakup. Perhaps now your daughter receives one set of messages from you regarding authority and an entirely different set of messages from your ex—or she may have seen her father disrespecting her mother's authority (or vice versa). There may be conflict in your child's mind regarding what exactly authority is and how one responds properly to it. (More on this later in the chapter.)

You may not feel that you're the kind of parent whose presence inspires much respect, but a friend of mine, who is a wonderful parent himself, once made a comment to me about a parent's inherent authority: "You know we hold all the aces, don't you?"

What did he mean by that? That if your son says defiantly that he isn't going to help fix dinner, when he knows quite well it's his job, where is his own meal coming from that night? If your daughter says she never wants to see you again and then storms out of the

> Strive for the middle ground, exercising healthy authority with love in your discipline.

house, where's she going to sleep that evening? As much as your kids may try to wrestle control away from you, there is little they can do without you. In the game of parental poker, as I call it, you hold the winning hand. And you'd better not give it up by offering to run to McDonald's for your son when he gets hungry around 10 p.m. or by allowing your daughter to enter your home and stomp back to her room without talking to you. From time to time it is your job to lovingly show your child those four aces, which is your healthy authority as you exercise discipline.

You can't love your child without disciplining him; the two are inseparable. Scripture says that "the LORD disciplines those he loves, as a father the son he delights in."[3] Discipline isn't a package option that you add onto parenting, like supersizing your fries and soft drink with your double cheeseburger. It's not something you do only if you have the time. Discipline is fundamental to getting your child through the elementary years, the hormone-laden years, and the adolescent years.

> Discipline isn't a package option that you add onto parenting, like supersizing your fries and soft drink with your double cheeseburger.

Your children won't always like what you do, but they'll learn to respect your discipline. And one day, as far away as it may seem now, they may even thank you for it!

But how can you do it?

LET REALITY TALK.

You've worked all day, threaded your way through rush hour traffic, picked up the kids from after-school soccer, and swung by the grocery store to pick up the evening's dinner. By the time you arrive home, you're well past exhausted. You notice that your older daughter, Amy, hasn't set the table for dinner, as she's supposed to. So what do you do?

Would you simply sigh and decide, *Guess I'll have to do her chore myself. Disciplining her just isn't worth the hassle. I'm beat?*

Fatigue, lack of time and support, and guilt can all conspire to keep you from following through on discipline. Any time you're under pressure, which for the single parent is about eight days out of seven each week, you tend to revert back to previously learned behaviors, such as lashing out in anger, or avoiding confrontation and simply doing the job yourself.

But look at the situation this way. If you discipline your children, you won't always be liked, but you'll be respected for your authority. And this is a key element, especially for a boy whose father didn't respect his mother. Discipline is tough to carry out, especially when you're beat, but it's one of those good tough decisions. If you follow through on it, you can raise kids who will one day say, "If it wasn't for my parent's love and discipline, I wouldn't be where I am today." If your child learns respect, he will become responsible, reliable, and resourceful—the kind of person you'd love to be around someday!

Does disciplining your children mean playing the role of hardened judge, dropping the gavel on them? No, that's not what I mean. You simply have to introduce your children to the reality of their actions. For example, if your daughter didn't set the table as you asked, then you set the table that one time. But here's the catch: You don't set a place for her. So when she goes to sit down at the table for dinner, she has no plate, spoon, fork, knife, cup, and maybe even no chair. You see, she needs to realize that by deciding she didn't want to do her assigned job, as part of your family, she was choosing not to be part of your family. And the consequence of that is not eating dinner that night.

If you're shocked and think I'm being harsh, just consider the long-term view. Will Amy think twice next time before she blows off setting the table? You'd better believe it!

For me, discipline all comes down to something called *reality therapy*—a term coined by Dr. Bill Glasser, whom I was honored to study under. Much of my early thinking on what I call "reality discipline," which I wrote about extensively in my book *Making Children Mind without Losing Yours*, was formed by Dr. Glasser's theory and research, Dr. Alfred Adler's individual psychology, and Dr. Rudolph Dreikurs' application of Adler's individual psychology, combined with the wisdom of the apostle Paul. Reality discipline is the practice of letting natural consequences, or reality, be your child's teacher when it comes to discipline.

Let me give you another example. I heard about one boy (I'm not making this up!), who bought three baby pigs, without his mother's permission, from a neighboring farm for about twenty bucks apiece. The problem was, he and his mom lived in an apartment, and pets were not allowed (not to mention the fact that pigs can be . . . well, a little smelly . . . and aren't intended to live indoors). As soon as the boy's mom arrived home and found out, she promptly took those little porkers to market. In less than twenty-four hours, she had sold those porkers— and at a great loss to her son's initial investment because he hadn't bothered to clear the purchase with her.

"But, Mom," he pleaded, "I thought you would say it was okay."

"You may have thought that," the mother replied, "but you didn't ask." And that's why she sold the farm, so to speak.

That's reality discipline in action. Even though your child may want to say (or may actually say), "What you're doing to me is unfair. You're such a terrible parent," the reality is that your child's failure to do what he was supposed to do is what got him into trouble.

So the next time your teen lollygags and doesn't get his term paper done for English, don't rescue him by helping him write it at midnight. Let his teacher do the talking. The lower grade and the lecture—some reality therapy—will do far more for his long-term perspective. The next time your eight-year-old leaves his baseball mitt in the yard, don't go bring it in out of the rain. Let a little soggy reality therapy do the talking when he needs it the next day for baseball practice.

In other words, don't rescue your kids from reality, or they may end up in an alternate universe where they believe that they're the sun around which everybody else has to revolve.

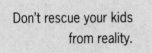

Don't rescue your kids from reality.

Reality discipline is not the easy road for you as a parent. It's always easier to lose your temper and strike out at your children or to ignore the behavior and fix it yourself. When you're totally exhausted, disciplining your children always takes more thoughtfulness, restraint, and discipline on your part, so that you're *training* your children rather than simply *punishing* them.

But with devotion to your children, a love that graciously refuses to let them continue in bad patterns, and a belief in the best that is in them, they can develop into adults who not only know the consequences of their actions but make responsible decisions from the inside out.

DON'T GO ALONG FOR THE RIDE.

You've been shopping for three hours straight for items you absolutely have to have but seem impossible to find. You're tired enough to curl up on the restroom's fold-down changing table for a nap, and you only have a few minutes for lunch in the mall food court before it's time to shuttle your son to his doctor's appointment. Because the line is too long at McDonald's, you step up to order teriyaki instead. Your three-year-old son, however, *really* wants a Happy Meal.

"Mommy, I want an Action Guy figure," he whines.

"I'm sorry, honey," you try to reason with him. "I wish we could, but not today." You glance over at the long line of parents waiting to get their children Happy Meals with Action Guy figures.

"But Mommy, you said I could get an Action Guy."

"I did, but remember I said that we could get it this weekend?"

"But Mommy, I want it *n-o-w!*" yells your child, who then drops to the food court floor and flails like a beetle stuck on its back.

Is there a method to your child's madness?

As strange as it may seem, there is.

The goals of your child's misbehavior are described by Adlerian individual psychology, which is simply a fancy term for psychologists Alfred Adler and Rudolph Dreikurs' conclusion that your child's behavior—from sneaking down the stairs an hour after his bedtime to throwing that tantrum for the Action Guy figure at the mall—serves a specific purpose in his life as described by Dreikurs' phases of manipulative behavior.

There isn't a kid around who doesn't fit Dreikurs' first phase: attention getting. All kids at times say by way of their behavior, "I only count in life when people pay attention to me." That's the kind of behavior that causes your toddler son to always want "up" and your three-year-old daughter to slip pieces of paper under your home-office door while you're working in hopes of distracting you.

As a child gets discouraged in life, however, he moves from attention-getting to power-driven behavior, and the power-driven child says by way of his behavior, "I only count in life when I dominate the situation." He still has the skills to get attention, but now he can *make* people pay attention to him. So when you tell him to sit down, he might do so, but he might add some colorful commentary under his breath.

A few kids will move into Dreikurs' next level: revenge. This child says, "I feel hurt by life, so I have a right to strike out at you because I feel you've hurt me." You'll see this type of behavior from children and adults who have been abused or who have been beaten down in life in other ways.

Since the vast majority of kids will pass through the first two categories of manipulative behavior—attention-getting and power-driven—
we'll focus on those two areas. When faced with such behavior, the
temptation for any parent is to respond, "You're not going to get away
with *that!*" But when you respond that way, you walk right into the
power struggle. And when the rope goes taut as the tug-of-war begins,
guess who loses?

I'll give you one guess, and the answer isn't your child.

You lose because you have more at stake than your child does. Do you
think your three-year-old son cares a lick whether or not he makes a fool
out of the two of you in the mall food court? Do you think your two-
year-old daughter cares what other shoppers think about her Academy
Award–winning performance in the checkout aisle over whether or not
you're going to buy her favorite candy? But *you* care, don't you?

All of these manipulative behaviors arise from what I call your
child's "private logic," which is your child's worldview, or the way he or
she uses cause and effect to get the love and attention that she wants. If
your child knows that by slipping pieces of paper under your door she
can get you to stop work and spend thirty seconds with her—even if it's
thirty seconds of reprimand—she understands the cause and effect for
getting the attention she wants. *If I slip pieces of paper under Daddy's office
door, I get to see Daddy.*

But here's a fascinating key to unlocking your child's behavior: The
power trip's no fun if no one's along for the ride. Simple, huh? If your
child is trying to manipulate you, don't play the game.

For instance, if your son is flailing on his back, you can just say quietly, "Okay, Trent, I can see that you've decided not to be happy with
what we're able to do today." And then you walk away (keeping that
child, of course, within visual range). Try
this with any three-year-old, and chances
are that within two seconds, the child will
get a little panicky, realizing that you are
walking away, that he's surrounded by
strangers, whom he now realizes are watching him, and suddenly his
beetle behavior will quickly turn into a scampering squirrel to catch up

> The power trip's no fun if no one's along for the ride.

with you. Even better, embedded in his little psyche is now the knowledge, *Hey, she didn't play the game. I didn't win. Maybe I shouldn't try that next time.*

But along with this reality is also another question you need to ask yourself. Is your child getting your attention through mostly negative ways or mostly positive ways? How you respond is vastly important.

If your child is always doing stupid, attention-getting things, what is he saying? *I don't get enough attention! Please, give me attention!* You certainly don't want to reward your child with attention for his negative behavior, but make a note that your child is short on attention. Perhaps he's trying to elbow in on the limelight that his brothers and sisters have been taking up recently. If so, go out of your way to give him positive attention in appropriate ways. When you see your son helping his younger sister with her homework, tell him how much you appreciate that. When you see your daughter sharing her candy, compliment her.

> "Give them an inch," as the saying goes, "and they'll take a mile."

Your positive affirmation helps feed your child's need for attention, which he might otherwise try to get in negative ways.

STICK WITH IT.

If any of us in Mr. Schmidt's junior high class ever wanted to derail the day's science lesson, we all knew how: Get him talking about the army. If we could get him talking about his days in the army, before we knew it, class would be over!

Kids are adept at finding our weaknesses and manipulating them to the full extent. "Give them an inch," as the saying goes, "and they'll take a mile." Consequently, while many parents will start off with a great plan for discipline, because of their kids' manipulation, they'll soon soften up and begin to buckle. And single parents in particular will give in because they feel guilty about their child's missing parent. They'll give in even more if *they* are the ones who brought pain into their child's life, whether through a rebellious spirit that led to pregnancy outside of marriage, or a premature or unwise marriage.

If you have gone through a divorce, your children will be even more likely to exploit this weakness of yours. They may lash out at you, using four-letter words, giving you the finger, even striking at you, which would have been unheard of decades ago. Needless to say, when a family breaks up, there's enough anger to go around for everyone to have seconds and thirds.

How, then, do you handle such behavior, sticking with the program for reality discipline?

Imagine, for example, that your four-year-old lashes out at you. "I *hate* you!" he says, echoing comments he's heard tossed back and forth between you and your ex. Now, as a compassionate parent, you probably recognize that the comment came from the pain your child feels from the divorce. If you feel guilty for bringing that pain upon your child, you might just absorb his abuse and overlook the incident.

But don't. Rather than caving in, stick to your plan for consistent discipline. Don't overreact, but since he screamed, "I hate you!" that's an appropriate time to respond. Take a breath to calm yourself so that you don't react in anger. Then, taking an open hand, give him a little *whop* on the tail. Then explain to him why you did it. Don't worry; it's not going to damage his psyche for life. But it will show him that you are in healthy authority over him and that you are not going to allow him to be out of control.

Then wait for your teachable moment to come later, because you can always put off reality discipline's teachable moment until the time is right. Twenty minutes later, perhaps, when you and your child are at the bakery where you both usually get a free donut hole, he might ask you, "Mommy, can I have my donut hole?"

I advise you to turn your back on your child and keep on walking.

"Dr. Leman," you say, "surely you don't mean *that*. You don't mean that I should turn my back on my child."

Yes, I do. You see, your child does not want you upset with his behavior—his extremely selfish behavior, I will add. Do you see how healthy that guilt is? And if he hasn't already gotten in touch with his guilt, now's his chance.

"Mommy, you forgot about our donuts."

"I didn't forget," you might tell him. "We're not getting them today."
Your child, however, will try to make it your problem.

"But, Mommy," he'll say, as if you're the one dropping the ball, "I *always* get a donut when we come here."

But whose problem is this, anyway—yours or your child's? Your kid will try to make it your problem that he mouthed off

> The "reality" of reality discipline is that it's his problem.

at you and that you're now holding back his donut, but the "reality" of reality discipline is that it's his problem. Remember, you hold the winning hand—those four aces that form your authority.

"Today we're not."

"But why?"

"Mommy doesn't feel like getting you your donut."

Your child will hold on like a bulldog going for the jugular vein. "But why?" he'll ask again.

"Do you really want to know why?"

"Uh-huh."

You now have his full attention and, along with it, reality discipline's teachable moment.

"Because you said something that hurt Mommy." And then you can talk to him about how it's okay to be angry, but it's not okay to talk to Mommy that way.

When it's time for that teachable moment, take the discipline in stride. Don't overreact, reminding your child of everything he's ever done wrong or that you've simply had it and that you've decided to take a stand. But also don't accept excuses from your kid. If you let him off the hook, it only makes your weakness weaker.

And part of our mission as parents is to make sure we stay off the hook and our kids stay on.

I guarantee that you'll often feel like overlooking your child's offense as you face the pressures of single parenthood. But which is more important—that your son likes you, or that he learns to respect you? It's much better for your child to feel the consequences of his actions and see that you're serious—what I call "taking the little buzzard by the beak"—than to try to get on his good side. Besides, if the consequence doesn't carry much weight, he's more likely to try the behavior again.

> Part of our mission as parents is to make sure we stay off the hook and our kids stay on.

As parents, we tend to want to soften the blow and go easy on our children—especially if they have been hurt by life. But for reality discipline to have an effect, you need to hit your children psychologically where it hurts.

USE ACTIONS, NOT WORDS.

As you've probably gathered by now, reality discipline is based on action, not words. If your child is being disrespectful, the words you choose to use mean relatively little unless they are backed up by swift, decisive, and even somewhat unpredictable movement on your part.

Create a short list of things that are important to your child. For your sixteen-year-old son, it might be the keys to your car. For your ten-year-old son, it might be playing on his Little League baseball team. For your five-year-old daughter it might be watching her favorite princess movie. Then, when it comes time to implement reality discipline, you'll know which rug to pull out from under the little buzzards!

It's not easy to stick with reality discipline, especially if you're swayed by guilt. Sometimes, after you've settled down and you're no longer angry, you might start second-guessing yourself.

Maybe I was too hard on him, you think. *Maybe I shouldn't have done what I did, holding him back from that football game with his friends to mow the lawn like he was supposed to.*

Because you must make those judicious calls yourself, without referring to the wisdom of a spouse for backup, you need to anticipate those thoughts. So look at the big picture *before* you dispense your discipline (even more reason to take a breath and a psychological time-out before coming up with the just response). Ask yourself, *What is fair and reasonable in this situation?* An edict such as "No more dessert for life!" for failing to empty the bathroom wastebasket probably falls closer to cruel and unusual punishment than fair and reasonable reality discipline. But say to a treat-loving child, "I made your favorite dessert tonight—pineapple upside-down cake. It's too bad you won't get to share it with us this time. Maybe next time you'll remember to empty the wastebasket."

So stick to your guns in your reality discipline—but think long-range enough that you don't shoot yourself in the foot!

GIVE 'EM BREAD AND WATER.

"Dr. Leman," you may say, "all this talk about reality discipline sounds great in theory, but since the divorce, my kids have gone from bad to worse. I don't even know how to make the change to reality discipline with them."

When you start implementing reality discipline around your home for the first time, you can almost expect that things are going to get worse before they get better. I call that the "fish out of water" syndrome, in which your kids begin to act like hooked fish psychologically, thrashing in the air at the change in environment.

> Stick to your guns . . . but don't shoot yourself in the foot!

That type of behavior can especially be expected if your ex didn't respect you prior to the divorce and your children were old enough at the time to latch onto that. If Dad disrespects you, that sends a distinct psychological message to your kids, especially boys.

I understand how Dad treated Mom, they might think, *and he certainly got away with it.*

If such is your situation and your kids have fallen into disrespect as a way of life, you need to act now. Not only is your ex's rule book probably not going to change, but no meeting of the minds is going to happen between you and your ex regarding your authority over your children. If you, Mom, have custody of the kids, the first thing I recommend you do is to put distance between yourself and your ex-husband, as long you don't do it at the expense of losing your resources (parents, siblings, and good friends).

Next, I suggest that you take those disrespectful kids back to what I call the "bread-and-water treatment," in which nothing is a given, even if it's been the routine up to that point. If you're the custodial parent, Boy Scouts is not a given, playing on the after-school soccer team is not a given, and hour upon hour of TV is not a given. In other words, level the balance sheet back to zero and work up from there as you are able and as your kids contribute to the family.

What you're doing is working toward a new deal for the family. You're rethinking how you're going to live your lives now because what was happening prior to the divorce was not working for you. It certainly won't work for your kids, either, if they're going to continue to talk to you the way they have been talking to you, because you're no longer going to tolerate it.

"All of us need a fresh start," you might tell your kids. "And because there are three of us now instead of four, I'm going to need your help here in the new apartment. I can't fix dinner every night after work, so I'm expecting you two to come home and clean the breakfast dishes, take the garbage out, and help with dinner."

If one of them complains about not being able to do his activities, you might say, "Honey, I simply don't have the time or energy to take you to soccer practice. It costs too much money right now. We'll see how this first semester goes, but for right now we're not doing a thing." If he keeps pressing you on it, you have reality discipline's teachable moment, and you can then say, "I won't tolerate being talked to the way you've been talking to me since we've been in our new apartment. To be quite honest, it makes me feel like not doing anything for you."

In other words, your children will see a toughness in you that perhaps they weren't aware of before. You have to draw an emotional and psychological line to protect yourself, to show your children that you mean business, and to dole out discipline where it's needed. Once a kid sees, hears, and feels those consequences, he'll begin thinking, *You know, maybe I ought to behave differently.*

Remember, no matter how things may seem, kids really do want to please their parents. Most parents miss that point, assuming their kids care little what their parents think about them. But my guess is that even now, as a grown twenty-seven-year-old woman or thirty-five-year-old man, you still feel the importance of your parents' affirmation (if your parents were psychologically healthy), which is exactly what your kids want from you.

That kind of action-not-words stance that causes your children to think, *Wow, Mom's not fooling around,* or, *Dad means business* can be the very thing to help bring them around.

Training a Child *Up*, Not *Down*

Often we think that by telling our kids what not to do, we're preventing bad behavior, but we're actually perpetuating it.

"We'll only be there for a few minutes, so don't ask me for any treats!" you tell your four-year-old son as you pull into the grocery store parking lot.

"When I say it's time to go, I mean it!" you tell your daughter as the two of you spread your towels out at the local pool.

"Now act your age while we're inside!" you tell your seven-year-old daughter as you walk up the steps to church.

You may feel that by laying down the law, you've set your child up for success, but what is the real message behind your warning?

I expect you to misbehave.

Scripture says, "Train up a child in the way he should go,"[4] and of all the important words in that passage, one of the key ones is the word *up*. We may believe that by telling our kids how not to get in trouble, we're training them up—but that's training them down!

As a single parent, you may be tempted to keep your kids on a short leash because you have less time and energy to deal with bad behavior. The danger, however, is that under pressure you'll slip into authoritarian parenting, telling your kids up front what not to do, how not to do it, and in no uncertain terms what punishment you'll dole out if your demands aren't met. But we train our children *down* when we put such negative expectations on them.

When I was growing up, I had a buddy, Moonhead, who always called home to tell his parents where he was. The only problem was, he was never where he'd say he was! That's so typical of what a lot of us were like as adolescents—living up to our parents' negative expectations. My question is, how does a kid like that feel? Does he feel good about himself? He may tell himself that he's having a good time, but that's a hard sell, even to himself, because deep down he's not having fun, knowing that he's disobeying and disappointing his parent or parents.

But what a wonderful pattern you set for your kids when you train them *up*, expecting the best of them! When someone expects the best of you—believing that you are the kind of person who is honest, forthright, and compassionate toward others, that sets you in the right direction.

And as a single parent, you have something going for you that dual-parent households don't have. You can be *consistent* in reality discipline. If you set your child's bedtime at 8:30 p.m., then 8:30 p.m. it is. If you decide that your son is going to help wash the dishes this month and that your daughter is going to take out the garbage, there's no other parent telling your kids otherwise (or sneaking around behind your back, helping your child do his chore). If you tell your children that they can't have seconds on dessert, they can't go to their other parent for a second opinion.

> What a wonderful pattern you set for your kids when you train them *up*, expecting the best of them!

You call all the shots, so take charge and call them, keeping in mind loving, consistent discipline, which means you walk that fine line between permissive (letting your kids get away with everything) and authoritarian (letting your kids get away with nothing) parenting styles.

If your children are going back and forth between your household and your ex's, remember that you are only in charge of *your* household. You have no control over your ex's. And that, understandably, can cause confusion in your children's minds.

Look at it this way. If you've ever traveled in a foreign country, you know how confusing the adjustment can be. In some countries, it's considered appropriate to yell at each other when bartering in the market; in others, you wouldn't dream of raising your voice. In some places, traffic lanes and lights at intersections are mere suggestions; in others they make the city run like clockwork. If you've ever tried shopping in a foreign grocery store where the food is different, the money is different, and the units for measuring weight are different, you know that when you're traveling abroad, different places have entirely different rule books.

It's often the same for your children after you've divorced and established two separate households. At your place, they may eat organic vegetables hand washed in filtered mountain spring water and go to bed at nine o'clock sharp. At your ex's place, Dad may encourage the kids to stay up past midnight and let soda pop flow like booze on Mardi Gras.

I understand that life is *very* different over at "his house" or "her house"; you may wish that your children didn't even have to set foot there. But if the court has mandated it, you might as well accept it (why spend energy fighting what you cannot win?) and get used to what happens when your kids come home after a weekend away.

If you're a woman, you know what it's like to have PMS. If you can think of the transitional period when your kids come home from a weekend at your ex's house as similar to your PMS, you'll be well on your way to handling their mood swings with understanding. When you have PMS, you need a little extra grace and perhaps some time to yourself. Well, when your children come home from a weekend away at your ex's, they often need that same grace, too. The fact is, the patterns and rhythms at your home and at your ex's home are probably going to differ somewhat. Therefore, some of the unruly behavior your child exhibits when he comes home from a weekend at the noncustodial parent's house is to be expected.

But notice that I said your child's change in behavior is to be *expected* and *given grace*—not that it is to be *excused*. At times he's probably going to be angry and belligerent because during that transition between your ex's place and your place he's bumping up against the reality that Mom and Dad are not together anymore, and that they're not ever going to be together. After your child's unstructured time with his noncustodial parent, living on cold pizza, gallons of pop, and popcorn-and-movie nights, it might take one to three days for him to reenter civilized life in your house.

"Three days!" you may say. "But in nine more days he has to go back there. Then we start the whole thing all over again!"

That's true. But I'd take nine days as the custodial parent over three as the noncustodial parent any day.

Your child may claim that living on cold pizza is "the good life," or that "Dad doesn't make me do *that!*" when you assign him the task of cleaning the bathroom. But avoid the temptation to be the favorite parent, because by giving in to that competition you're only undermining what's best for your child. If you want to win at that, here's the formula: Serve ice cream three meals per day, set no bedtime, and do all the chores yourself! All you'll end up with is an exhausted child with no sense of responsibility and a bad tummy ache!

Although Dad may have more money and give the kids a roller-coaster ride of a weekend, remember that the lessons that will really make a difference in your children's lives are the cost-free, value-driven ones. Over time your children will learn the difference between your home and your ex's home—and eventually they will see the wisdom in your approach.

Robbie did. "It wasn't until I had my own son that I realized just how much my dad did for us because he didn't always 'do everything' for us. When I went to my mom's, she would take us lots of places and buy us lots of new toys. We had a blast. My dad was on a very limited income. He couldn't spend much money on us, but what he spent was far more significant. My dad spent his time. He was always there doing things with my brother and me. And that's the way I want to be with my own son."

So concentrate on maintaining consistency with reality discipline in your own home. If you're also able to come to some conclusions with your ex about establishing consistency in what is expected of your kids between the households, so much the better. You'll be doing them an *enormous* favor as they travel between the different cultures, even if for all intents and purposes it is essentially a business arrangement in your kids' best interests.

If you communicate well with your ex following the divorce, you should talk about the kids frequently. Chat at least once a week about what's coming up and discuss any issues regarding the kids. That way, if you defer to each other and make joint decisions, your kids won't be playing one of you against the other. For example, if you give an allowance to your kids, there has to be agreement between you and your ex about who is giving how much to which child, so the allowance isn't being sabotaged by the parent who makes twice as much as the other. Also, keep an open-phone policy so that your ex is always free to call you or you are always free to call your ex to talk about what's best for the kids.

When your children see that you and your ex are on the same page regarding their well-being, it builds their self-esteem, and not only is it reassuring for them, frankly it's good for everyone involved in the divorce.

It all comes down to this: If you try to give your kids everything, you'll end up giving them nothing. If you try to do everything for them, you'll end up teaching them nothing. And if you let them get away with everything, you will be choosing to raise selfish children who won't be able to see outside their own perspective to do the world any good.

That's blunt, but it's absolutely true.

The key is reality discipline—and maintaining it consistently in your home.

Remember, you hold all the aces! You may stand only five feet three inches tall and feel like you have all the commanding presence of an elf. But by administering discipline with loving consistency, standing in healthy authority over your child—who may be the high school basketball team's star center at six feet tall—you help him profoundly.

You equip him for life because you've shown him what love is like, and you've set healthy limits.

◈ ◈ ◈

KEY Qs . . .

- Do you tend to err on the side of the permissive parent (letting your kid get away with everything) or the authoritarian parent (not letting your kid get away with anything)? Why?

- In what ways could the principle of reality discipline make a difference in your home? Explain.

- How can you train your child *up*, not down? Think through a couple of practical ways, and then try them out this week.

KEY 5

KNOW WHAT TO SAY AND DO WHEN KIDS ASK...

Your children will always ask questions.
At times, they'll be terribly complex,
and you won't be sure how to respond.
This section gives specific advice
for those who are divorced, widowed,
or never married.
So read the part that applies to you.
(It's okay to sneak a peek at the others, too.)

CHAPTER 13

"Will You Stop Loving Me, Too?"

(And Other Issues for Divorced Parents and Their Children)

Natalie will never forget the day her five-year-old son, Nathan, asked the question she dreaded the most since she had stood with her husband—now her ex-husband—in court.

"Mommy," little Nathan asked, "if you stopped loving Daddy, will you stop loving me, too?"

Natalie was so startled that she almost stomped on the brakes to stop the car. Instead, she swallowed hard and decided to make an impromptu exit off the L.A. freeway.

Glancing in the rearview mirror and seeing the concern in his brown eyes, she knew she needed to address this issue right away. And she guessed there was more behind this supposedly simple question than what appeared on the surface.

She did the right thing. That was one question she needed to answer face-to-face (as she did, parked on a side street in L.A., and again later that night over an ice cream cone at home).

It's uncanny how the toughest questions can come out of our kids' mouths at the most difficult of times. Driving on the L.A. freeway is a challenge to start with, not to mention adding onto that the task of responding in an age-appropriate and psychologically appropriate way to such a complex question.

Nathan's question, "Will you stop loving me, too?" was being asked on two levels. Nathan wanted assurance that his mommy loved him now and would always love him. But he also needed to understand, even more, why his parents no longer loved each other and couldn't get along.

They'd fought constantly before and after the divorce, and it had shaken little Nathan's world.

He'd seen with his own eyes that his mommy and daddy weren't on the best of terms. So if his parents couldn't love each other, how could they love him? If he did something wrong, would his mom send him packing . . . just like she'd sent his dad away?

Chip may have been a terrible husband who had become a horrible ex (and he was, no doubt about it), but you see, in Nathan's eyes, Chip was still *his daddy*. And the court had ruled that he could be a part of Nathan's life on weekends, whether Natalie wanted it that way or not.

Once Natalie identified the fears and questions at the root of Nathan's question, she realized that the way she related to her ex had to change—for her son's sake.

Ex Marks the Spot

If you're like most single parents, you live with regular reminders of your ex's absence. Like every time you show up as the only parent alone for your child's basketball games. And every time you drop off the kids from school at your ex's house. You're reminded every time the child-support check arrives in the mail—and certainly when it doesn't. At times, those reminders may trigger other memories, too. Such as your ex-wife's habit of neglecting the family budget and then overspending, so you're still trying to recover financially. Or your ex-husband's unfaithfulness that rocked your self-confidence to its very foundation.

It's no wonder that you feel angry sometimes. Those feelings of anger can quickly become bitterness. And bitterness can progress to revenge.

If you were to think about the source of your most intense feelings, most likely you'd find that "ex marks the spot," and the spot is full of pain, anger, and regret. Given all that you've been through, you may feel like sending your ex on a long walk down a short gangplank (with no rescue boat in sight).

Instead, let me offer an even better solution—one from which you and your children can emerge healthy and well-adjusted. One in which you can move forward not in bitterness but in love.

Forgive . . . and *Remember*

During the Civil War, one of President Abraham Lincoln's aides approached him and said, "You have got an enemy, and somehow you must get rid of him. Slay him!"

"If I turn my enemy into a friend," Lincoln reportedly responded, "have I not slain my enemy?"[1]

If you are divorced, perhaps your heart for relating to your ex is similar to that of Lincoln's aide—wipe him out of the picture! That's certainly what was on Natalie's mind before her son's "big question" on the freeway, and it may be on your mind, too. After all, your ex has done his or her share of damage, and especially when unfaithfulness and abuse are part of the picture, the damage is *very* great. So by swinging the hammer of revenge, you're only getting even, you figure.

> By wielding the hammer of revenge, you end up setting your children against yourself.

But think about it through a different light. Your kids are always watching. When you have getting even with your ex on your mind, your words and behavior encourage your kids to even up the score between their warring parents. That means you'll find them taking your ex's side as a counterbalance—the exact opposite of what you hope to accomplish!

By wielding the hammer of revenge (as tempting as it sounds and as satisfying as it might make you feel in the short term) you end up setting your children against yourself.

There's something else to think about, too. As long as you choose revenge, you'll forever be ruled by your past, which means everything toxic about your ex will always be present in your heart, mind, and life. And it won't be your ex who's punished by it. You and your children will be the ones who pay dearly for your desire to bring about justice. For your children's sake, if nothing else, you need to choose a different path.

"But Dr. Leman," some of you are saying, "do you understand what my ex has done to our family? How can I feel any peace about that?"

Many of you have suffered horribly as a result of your ex. Forgiveness may be the last thing on your mind. But before you get ready to push me off the gangplank along with your ex for even bringing up the subject, let me clarify what I mean.

When people talk about forgiveness, they often recite the phrase "forgive and forget," as if forgetting somehow follows naturally on the heels of forgiving. But I always say, "forgive and *remember*" because life shows that when you initially forgive someone, those deep wounds that you thought had healed may reopen again in a day or a month or a year or ten years—and sometimes they're even more painful than before. And if that happens, you may be left wondering whether you really forgave the person at all. But if you push the nagging pain out of your mind, telling yourself that you already forgave the person, then you cut short the deeper, ongoing process of forgiveness that you began when you first said, "I forgive you."

What is real forgiveness, and why is it important? It's the key to raising well-adjusted kids in spite of your divorce. But before you can experience and extend forgiveness, you need to be clear about what forgiveness is *not*.

FORGIVENESS IS NOT EASY.

When life has kicked you squarely in the teeth, forgiveness is anything but easy. In fact, it can be one of the most difficult things you'll ever do. Although some people seem to have an easier time forgiving than others, it's never easy to relinquish control. Let's face it. The impulse to get even is instinctive. Consequently, many people who believe in the power and necessity of forgiveness begin feeling guilty because they can't seem to release their feelings of anger.

When you're struggling through the process of forgiving your ex, it's healthy to recognize the steps you've made and to remember where you once were: "Boy, was I ever ready to write him off! But now that I've thought it through and can forgive him, it feels good that I've gone beyond my feelings and embraced a mature choice."

The best choices you make as a single parent are almost always the most difficult ones. Forgiveness is challenging, but stay true to its course. If you do, you will no longer be controlled by your past, and you'll be *acting*, rather than *reacting*, as you interact with your ex.

ONCE YOU FORGIVE SOMEONE, YOU MAY NOT FEEL GOOD INSIDE.
Many of us are led to believe that once you embrace those three words—
I forgive you—your decision will be marked by warm fuzzies toward that
person. But forgiveness simply doesn't work that way.

If there has been significant hurt, you can forgive someone . . . but
still not want to hang out with them. You can forgive past abuse, but
that doesn't mean you blow off what happened (*Hey, it wasn't that bad, I
guess*) or excuse the other person's behavior in any way. You can choose
not to have anything to do with that person for the rest of your life. Or
you may at least maintain a cautious distance. In severe situations, it
may not be healthy for you or your chil-
dren to *ever* see your ex again, even though
you have forgiven him, releasing yourself
of the burden of anger, bitterness, and
desire for revenge.

> Many counselors will
> tell you to "follow your
> feelings," but that advice is
> about as useful (and as
> psychologically stinky)
> as a soggy Pampers
> on a hot day.

Many counselors will tell you to "follow your feelings," but that advice is about
as useful (and as psychologically stinky)
as a soggy Pampers on a hot day. Your
ability to forgive someone should not
depend on your emotions because forgiveness is an act of the will that
sometimes goes *against* your emotions. You don't forgive someone
because you "feel" like it; you forgive because you *don't* feel good
toward that person.

That's why you often need to forgive someone again and again, each
time your pain surfaces. But it doesn't mean you have to be buddies with
that person—or see each other at all.

FORGIVENESS IS NOT A ONE TIME EVENT.
Open a packet of oatmeal into a bowl, add boiling water, and you'll have
an instant breakfast. Stir a teaspoon of instant coffee into the hot water
in your travel mug, and you'll have your morning cup of java as you run
out the door. But as simple as it may sound, you can't simply recite the
words *I forgive you* and expect instant forgiveness.

Forgiveness is a little like eating a double-cheese pepperoni pizza.

You can eat that pizza at 7:30 in the evening, look at the cardboard box flopped open on the kitchen table, and say to yourself, *Polished that off.* But three hours later, that pizza will come back to revisit you. You might use mouthwash and brush your teeth a couple times in an effort to get rid of the taste, but nothing works. You're still reminded of that pizza going down at 7:30.

Likewise, hurt has a way of coming back, and at times—especially when the hurt is deep—you need to forgive someone again and again. You need to acknowledge your pain as it surfaces, in essence saying about the person who caused that hurt, "In spite of all that you've done to me, I will not retaliate." The truth is, if the pain is deep, you *can't* forgive and forget, because you will feel the effects return long after the incident occurred. Instead, you forgive and *act* as if you've forgotten, waiting for your emotions to follow your actions. Waiting for your healing to come.

What are you hanging on to?

Imagine that you have the flu. Your stomach is churning, and your body wants to throw up. Yet you lie on the bed, motionless, because you hate the very thought of going into the bathroom and vomiting. In fact, you lie there for hours, maintaining that nauseated equilibrium. But what happens when you finally do throw up? Your body feels so much better, doesn't it?

Hanging on to your bitterness at your ex is a bit like lying on that bed, refusing to move, even though your body's natural response is to get rid of the sickness inside. As difficult as forgiving your ex may be, when you refuse to forgive, life grows more difficult in the areas of mental health, physical health, and relational health between you and your children. If you find yourself holding resolutely to your bitterness, ask yourself these questions:

- *Am I getting sympathy from friends or family who feel sorry for me because I've been through tough circumstances?*
- *What is the purpose of hanging on to my grudge or my pain? What purpose does it serve in my life?*

Natalie, for example, realized that she was holding on to difficult memories from the divorce simply because doing so gave her extra sympathy from friends and family:

"You've been through *so* much."

"He's such a jerk!"

"That really was a terrible time."

That attention had become her way of receiving the care she was so starved for, the emotional care that she hadn't received since she'd walked down the aisle to marry Chip. The only problem was that hanging on to the list of wrongs Chip had done also maintained her status quo of bitterness, and the emotional toll was debilitating to both her and Nathan.

Moving on in your life means trading in your pain and weakness for strength, bit by bit, as you heal.

Take the High Road!

Take a moment to think about the times your ex has wronged you. Have you got a few in mind? (Or a few hundred?)

Good.

Now I'm going to ask you to do something. It won't be easy. In fact, it may be the most difficult thing you've ever done. But it's necessary so that both you and your children can move on.

I want you to lay down your sledgehammer of revenge.

And don't just lay it down, but place it far enough away that you can't pick it up again to clobber your ex, even if you're tempted (and deservedly so!).

Instead, extend an olive branch of peace toward your ex.

Now you know I'm nuts, right?

"How in the world can I extend an olive branch to him after all that he's done?" you ask.

When Jesus was asked how many times we are to forgive others, he replied, "I do not say to you, up to seven times, but up to seventy times seven."[2] Seventy times seven comes out to 490—that's a lot of times to forgive someone. If you're like me (without the help of Miss Wilson, I probably never would have made it through high school math), you can't even count that high.

Your ex may have lied to you, neglected to live up to his promises, and acted more selfishly than your three-year-old son—and we're not even close to double digits in counting his wrongs! You've felt justified in swinging that sledgehammer around your head a few times. "Revenge," the saying goes, "tastes sweet."

But whoever came up with that saying neglected to finish it. What it should really say is, "Revenge tastes sweet . . . but ultimately it will leave you sick with regret as your kids witness your anger over the years and incorporate it into their own lives."

And that's why you need to extend an olive branch of forgiveness to your ex. You're a *parent*, and as a parent, you are called to lay down your life, time after time after time, for your kids. This is one very important occasion in which you must do so again. You must learn to work in harmony with your ex, for your kids' sake.

You must take the high road. It isn't the easiest road; traveling it requires more energy than the low road. But it's the road that will lead you where you want to go so that you can move ahead in peace and freedom.

How, then, can you take the high road?

DON'T BAD-MOUTH.

If you tear down your ex in front of your children, saying things such as, "That's just like your dad to forget where he's supposed to be," or, "Your mom never knew how to handle money," your kids will psychologically fight to hold onto their hopes for that other parent. They'll prop up that parent with their childhood dreams, and believe me, that fabricated parent won't look anything like the real thing. Your children will psychologically dress up your ex to resemble more of a god than the imperfect human that he or she is. And in the process, you'll weaken your own relationship with your children. Rather than your intended effect—convincing your kids that your ex is a creep—your children will believe the exact opposite: that you don't really know the other parent the way they do.

> If you don't have something nice to say about your ex in the presence of your children, don't say anything at all.

Therefore, if you don't have something nice to say about your ex in the presence of your children, don't say anything at all. As hard as it may be, speak positively about your ex and to your ex, especially in the presence of your kids.

If you need to vent about all the things your ex has done wrong or is doing wrong, choose someone unbiased and not related to you. And make sure you do it out of your children's hearing.

DISAGREE IN PRIVATE.

If you're going to disagree with your ex—and chances are that you will, at least at times—agree to disagree behind closed doors, not in front of the kids. I say this because one thing that will damage your kids (and I do mean damage) is for you to air your conflicts openly in front of them. Anybody who says that it's good for a child to see his parents have conflict is wrong in this case. It's one thing to see your parents disagreeing amiably over where to go for dinner, but it's another thing entirely to see your parents screaming about how much they hate each other and wish the other person were dead. There's not a child in the world who wants to see his parents go at each other like that.

If you disagree, do so out of earshot of your child. And while it's okay to agree to disagree, always try to work toward a compromise that is best for your son or daughter.

AVOID TRIANGLES.

It's Saturday morning of Dad's weekend for the kids, and he has made it clear all week that he wants to take the boys fishing at his favorite lake.

"You need to have them there at the lake at 9:00 a.m. I'll bring the poles and bait; you just make sure you have the boys there on time."

You're there at 8:40 a.m., and a cold mist is drifting over the lake.

Nine o'clock comes . . . and goes. You wonder if you've missed him, so you drive around the lake one more time.

No, you're in the right place.

You continue waiting.

Ten o'clock comes . . . and goes.

"Where's Daddy?" one of your boys asks, tears in his eyes, his lower lip quivering.

That's the question that's been running through your mind for the last hour. You haven't stopped with just asking the question, however. You've also been answering it, playing judge and jury. *It's just the sort of thing he would do, isn't it?* you tell yourself. Memories of your anniversary, which he forgot two years ago, return. You'd like to bait your own hook with your ex, the *worm*, on it.

Your kids are looking to you to do something—and boy, you'd sure like to. But rather than lash out at your ex, the best thing to do is to avoid the triangle between you, him, and your kids. Direct the channels of communication toward the proper place. In that situation, I'd recommend you have one of the boys call his father.

"I don't know where Dad is, honey," you could say. "But you have his number with you. Why don't you give him a call?" And then either hand over your cell phone or find the nearest pay phone.

Rather than *you* phoning your ex-husband and giving him an earful for the lake incident (in keeping with the infamous missed anniversary, in keeping with his forgetful nature that always puts his own interests first, etc.) by suggesting that the boys call him, you help focus on the present situation and keep the lid on past conflicts.

NEVER ASK WHY.

This section is especially for you single moms. If you and your ex find yourself in a power struggle and you ask your former husband the question *why* in response to a suggestion he's made—no matter how off the wall it may be—you may as well be accusing him of stupidity.

A man interprets the question *Why?* as an offensive maneuver, as if you're squaring off against him, and that causes him to immediately put up his defenses. If he comes up with an idea for how the children should be disciplined, for example, and it is completely off the wall, rather than asking *why* or *what*, say something like, "Tell me more about that."

Men are funny creatures (I should know, since I am one). They don't like to be directly questioned, and conversely, when asked for more information, most of them will indeed tell you more about their ideas.

Or you could say to your ex, "I may not know what I'm talking about, but it seems to me that . . . " and then say whatever it is you want to. Even when he says something that's completely wacko, don't yell and scream. Just say, "That's interesting," rather than, "That's the stupidest thing I've ever heard of! How could you say such a thing?"

If you know your ex's rough spots, do your best not to rub salt into the wound. Instead, defuse conflict by using open-ended statements.

DON'T PRY.

For some single parents, communicating with their kids following a weekend at the ex's can resemble more of an interrogation than a welcome-home conversation.

"How late did he let you stay up?"

"Did he have beer in the fridge?"

"Was *she* there?"

Unfortunately, many single parents enlist their kids as carrier pigeons, carrying messages back and forth about the ex-spouse, gaining intelligence data on "enemy territory."

"You tell your father that's the last time I'll let him get away with that!"

"Your mother was always like that. You let her know I said that!"

Your curiosity is natural, but restrain yourself. Grilling your children with questions following a weekend at your ex's place puts them on the defensive and shuts down communication.

> Curiosity is natural, but restrain yourself.

Instead, let your kids open up to you as they are ready. If something wrong is happening, and you have a good relationship with your children, they'll let you know what's going on.

Above all, assure your kids that you will love them—always.

All about Custody

As frustrating as it may be, a judge today is not going to take away the custodial rights of a mother or father in a custody battle unless there is significant reason to do so. And a judge's "significant reason" is almost certainly different from your "significant reason."

"But," you may protest, "he's living with another woman over there!"

I've got news for you. No judge is going to turn your child solely over to you simply because your ex-husband has a girlfriend. You may not like it, it may violate your moral code, but legally it simply isn't going to make a difference.

"But I don't want *that* woman over at my husband's apartment. Especially when my kids are there!"

I agree with you wholeheartedly. If your ex-husband chooses to have a girlfriend over, it is unhealthy for the kids. However, as the judge will remind you, he's your *ex*-husband, and like it or not, they're *his* kids as well.

In general, custody battles are pointless. So in most cases, I recommend you save yourself the aggravation. Your ex will walk into the courtroom on his very best behavior, dressed as he hasn't dressed since the two of you were dating. Standing there in his sport coat and tie, he'll say, "Well, Your Honor, on occasion I've had a girlfriend over." He may even lie! "But she doesn't spend the night. We just watch TV."

No one wins in a custody battle mired in power struggles—except your attorney, who is charging you the hundred dollars per hour that you can barely afford.

There is, of course, one critical exception to my advice about not entering a custody battle, and that is if you know there has been physical violence or abuse to your children. In such circumstances, it is obviously your moral and legal responsibility to defend your kids.

Most of the time, however, custody battles are simply reruns of the power struggles you had before you and your ex separated, with your children on the front lines of your war.

Today's courts are often so PC-oriented that they are hard-pressed to make judgments. If the court has mandated that your husband can come and take the kids for two weeks every summer, you either have to submit to that higher authority, even if you don't feel good about it, or you have to launch a legal battle to keep it from happening.

It all comes down to this reality: You, after all, married this person, and you had sex together and produced children. Those were your choices. As a result, you and your children are now in this situation. If you spend all your time and energy trying to change the situation by doing battle with the law of the land, you may end up like the famous Don Quixote—crazy and charging windmills, and eventually ending up on his backside. How much good will that really do you and your children?

You may not agree with what the courts decide about the "sharing" of your children, but the facts are not likely to change. What you can change, however, is your response to the decision. In order to keep your kids' lives as consistent as possible, put down your sledgehammer of revenge. Pick up that olive branch of harmony. Instead of seeing how much you can muscle away from your ex, do your best to come up with a plan that makes the best of joint custody—namely, what's best for the kids.

> You may not agree with what the courts decide about the "sharing" of your children, but the facts are not likely to change.

GRANT IN FANTASY WHAT YOU CAN'T IN REALITY.
Since the odds are good that neither one of you will receive full custody of the kids, you can always grant in fantasy what you can't in reality when you're talking about the custody arrangements. This sounds strange, but it works to defuse a lot of "ex bombs."

In other words, when your ex declares, "I want my kids!" acknowledge the importance of your ex's relationship with the kids. You might reply, "I want you to be with the kids. That's important."

By saying something like that, you've just affirmed your ex's desire to be with the kids. Then, when you're discussing shared custody, share the power with your ex. A businessman told me once, "Kevin, you've got to let your people win. You can't always win just because you're the boss. You have to let them win, too." So you might say something such as, "If you want access to the children, you tell me when, and they're yours. You want them every other weekend? You got 'em. You want to take them skiing for Christmas break? You got 'em."

Of course, you also have to be realistic about what's best for the children.

"You're a salesman traveling four nights a week," you might say to your ex. "Are the kids going to be raised by your mother? Is that what you're telling me? Or would you rather have them be with me?"

When it comes to power struggles, defuse the bomb. Reach for the olive branch of peace and harmony, and come to a compromise that's best for your children—granting in fantasy what you can't in reality, giving your ex power, but in all cases, being realistic about what's best for the children.

Things That Can Help Provide a Stable Environment for Your Kids

Children will always have questions. At times, those questions will seem endless. But as your children begin to feel secure in the fact that you love them and are looking out for their best interests, they will begin to relax. They will begin to trust again.

Here are some things you can do to provide the most stable environment possible for your kids.

MAINTAIN BOUNDARIES WITH THE "IN-N-OUT" EX.

I mentioned In-N-Out Burger briefly once before, in chapter 9, but I return to it again on this point.

If you've never eaten a burger from the In-N-Out Burger restaurant, you don't know what you're missing. The restaurants use only fresh ingredients—no frozen burger bricks and no burgers baking under heat lamps. And they don't even slap those suckers on the grill until you order them. You won't find a heat lamp, microwave, or freezer on the premises. Their milkshakes are made from real ice cream; their french fries are made from whole potatoes, hand cut right there in the restaurant; and they even bake their own buns. Next to a home-grilled burger, In-N-Out burgers are the best in the world. I know because I've eaten many— at a time, I might add!

Those In-N-Out burgers were the furthest thing from my mind during one airport layover, when a guy walked by me wearing an In-N-Out Burger T-shirt. All I had to do was look at that T-shirt, and it started me salivating right there in the airport terminal, where often the only thing I have to eat is a leftover bag of peanuts from the previous flight.

Visions of those burgers must have been going to my head, because suddenly I said out loud, "Hey, you're making me hungry!"

In hindsight, I'll admit that's a pretty odd first liner to a guy who didn't know me. He looked at me as if to say, *What is wrong with you, buddy?* before he realized with a smile that I was talking about his shirt.

While In-N-Out burgers are great, an in-n-out parent is bad for your child. The in-n-out parent drops by on a whim, without calling. You may be in the middle of fixing dinner, and that in-n-out ex will stop by as if you were fixing it for him, even though you haven't seen or talked with him in eight and a half months. Apparently he hasn't quite gotten a handle on one of the more basic points of divorce: that he's no longer free to drop by anytime he pleases.

Instinctively, you know that an in-n-out ex isn't good for your child. He's there when he wants to be, in and out of your family's life according to how he feels. He's not there, however, when your son has his 104-degree temperature and has to be taken to the doctor, or when you have to scramble to get someone to drive the carpool because your car died along the freeway. After he leaves your home, you kick yourself. *Why didn't I just shoo him out? Why did I even let him in when I knew he'd be disrespectful, verbally abusive, or even violent?*

If your ex is toxic, no amount of exposure to that relationship is healthy for your kid. The question is, do you want to give your child a little poison or a lot?

I recommend that you do all you can to keep that ex from waltzing in and out of your children's lives. If he makes a guest appearance every other year, that will do

> Do you want to give your child a little poison or a lot?

more harm to your children than if you cut him out of their lives and raise them yourself. It's a controversial approach, I know, but I recommend you not let that parent have contact with your children, if at all possible.

Sometimes, I realize, this is out of your control because of a court's ruling. In such cases, you have to follow the law of the land. However, all is not lost. You can still do damage control by keeping a watchful eye out and doing what you can to protect your child physically and emotionally.

Above all, remember that you can't control the other parent—only yourself.

Does that mean saying *no* to your in-n-out ex when he shows up? *Yes*, as much as you may feel he has a right to see the kids! If the judge gave you legal custody of the children, you are their protector—the *parentis*, as it's called in Latin—and that means making difficult choices at times.

> Make visitation constructive and be flexible with your boundaries—but maintain that the threshold of your home is *your* home.

Make sure you set boundaries with that in-n-out ex, because if you don't, he or she will continue to barge through the door as if it's still home. I'm not saying you shouldn't give your ex access if he chooses to make some major changes in his life toward a more consistent relationship with your children. But if you do give him access, do so within certain guidelines. Tell him that he needs to call first and arrange a time if he's going to come over. Make visitation constructive and be flexible with your boundaries—but maintain that the threshold of your home is *your* home.

GIVE YOUR KIDS GUILT-FREE ACCESS TO YOUR EX.

At first glance this point may seem contradictory to the previous one. But this point is not for those of you who have toxic or in-n-out exes.

Yet you may still bristle at the thought. *Give my child guilt-free access to him? Are you kidding? I love my kid!*

"Dr. Leman," you may say, "do you know how my ex-husband lives? His fridge looks like the grocery store beer aisle, and he always has that woman over at his house. He's certainly not living a very moral life."

Still, as long as your children are safe and your ex desires a consistent relationship with them, I maintain that one thing they need is the freedom to pursue a relationship with their other parent, your ex-spouse. This comes as naturally to your children as breathing, so you shouldn't make them feel guilty about wanting to spend a weekend or even the entire summer with your ex. Remember, your kids didn't sign the divorce papers along with you, and they probably dream about seeing the two of you get back together.

Some parents will go about this access to their ex halfheartedly, spitting in their children's soup. In other words, they load on the guilt for the kids desiring to have a relationship with the other parent. They occasionally say such manipulative things as, "Sure, that's fine if you visit your father for the weekend. I'll just stay here at home . . . *alone.*"

But what kind of a confusing, mixed message is that for your children? That's the same as handing a child a piping hot bowl of his favorite soup, then spitting in it as you place it before him. Oh, your negative attitude may be subtle, but your child will pick up on it. If you make your child feel guilty for her desire to spend time with her father, she'll resent you for it, and the more you push her away from her other parent, the more she will resist you and perhaps even rebel.

> Your negative attitude may be subtle, but your child will pick up on it.

"But if my kid is around my ex regularly, won't he have a bad influence on him?" you may ask. Especially if you've already had the experience of your sweet child morphing into Attila the Hun upon returning home from a visit to your ex. As we discussed earlier, adjusting to the differing rules of two households is tricky for a child. So give him grace—but don't allow excuses.

Over time, your kids will learn that there is a tremendous difference between Dad's house and Mom's house, and that the values and ideas expressed in those two households are as different as night and day. Remember, you're taking the long-term view with your child. The view that looks ten to twenty years down the road to the day when your child realizes the difference between the way you raised him and the way his other parent raised him (or neglected to raise him). Whose way do you think he will choose for his own kids?

Right now your ex may be doing well financially; he may be able to give the kids a lot of material things, while you meagerly get by. However, if you are being a faithful parent, a real mom, honest in all things, etc., in time the kids are going to see the beauty that lies in the way you've chosen to live your life.

And they'll look back and want to live life the same way.

BE HONEST IN YOUR ANSWERS.

"Daddy, why don't you love Mommy anymore?"

"Did you ever love her?"

What do you say, age appropriately, when a child asks such questions?

Because each child is an individual, only you can know—by careful study of each of your children—what kind of information is appropriate and when. In other words, your good judgment will have to reign. There is no easy fix or easy solution to these questions.

Here are what some single parents have said to their children at different stages:

- "To tell you the truth, honey, I don't think Daddy and I ever loved each other. Neither of us knew what real love was then. And that's why I want you to understand it, so you don't make the same mistakes we did."
- "Sometimes people 'fall in love,' but for the wrong reasons. True love isn't something you fall wildly into. It's something steady . . . that you stay in forever."
- "There was a side of Daddy's personality that Mommy didn't ever see until after we were married. That made it impossible for us to stay married."
- "I know you know part of this because you experienced it. Your mommy was not able to love me or you the way that a mommy should. So for your safety, Daddy had to make a change. I won't allow you to be hurt like that ever again. I love you, and you will always be safe with me."

There are as many answers as there are situations and children. Keep in mind, above all, "telling the truth in love." "Telling the truth" means you're always honest. "In love" means that you know your child well enough to know how much information and what kind of information she can handle at different developmental stages of her life.

DON'T BE A KNOW-IT-ALL.

If you and your ex are newly separated, you can be sure your kids will be wrestling with tough questions—those you probably don't like to face yourself.

"Why does Mommy want to be with him and not you, Daddy?"

"Where are we going to live?"

"Mommy, do you still love Daddy?"

As much as you may want to dodge these questions, take them as a compliment if your child brings them up, because his initiation shows trust. You may want to gloss over the fact that you simply don't know what the future holds. You may be tempted to say, "Don't worry, it will all work out." But in doing so you're trad-ing temporary relief for long-term confu-sion. As you begin setting your life in order, putting first things first, in many cases you may not have the *slightest* clue what lies ahead.

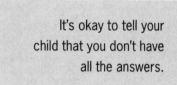

It's okay to tell your child that you don't have all the answers.

It's okay to tell your children that you don't have all the answers. That you don't know whether you and your ex will get back together or whether you'll move back to your old neighborhood. A proper response should simply be, "I don't know." This is a season when more may be unknown than known. Rather than falling into the trap of giving your children false hope simply because you want to comfort them, your *hon-est* answer can provide stability in an unstable time.

Then follow up your answer with reassurance that no matter what happens and no matter what curveballs life throws your way, you will always be there for your children—to talk, to love, to listen, to help them through the difficult times together.

"Are you going to be together with Daddy?" your child may very well ask.

"Honey," you could say, "I don't know. I honestly don't know. Many things would have to change for that to happen."

If your ex is *not* toxic to the family, you might add, "But I do know that your daddy loves you. *I* sure love you. And we're going to continue as a family, even though it's going to be different. Quite frankly, there's part of me that's scared. I really don't know what's coming down the line, and I'm sure that's scary for you, too. We've had to move from our house to this apartment, and we don't have all the things that we used to before the divorce."

> You know what? We're in this together.

Then add that reassurance: "But you know what? We're in this together, and I *do* know this: I love you beyond description, and I'll always be there for you."

With that, you're giving your child a "psychological blankie." An unconditional guarantee. You're saying that no matter what lies ahead, you and your children love each other and will support each other.

I'm not saying that life without a daddy or mommy is going to be a piece of cake, because that's certainly not true. I'm also not saying, "Oh, you'll get used to it," or, "It's not going to be any different," because it's going to be *very* different. The psychological blankie isn't for suffocating the psyche. It's for helping reassure your children that even though things may be frightening right now, you're still there with them, committed to them, come what may.

RECONCILE S-L-O-W-L-Y.

Significant damage takes significant healing. That's true whether you've been in a car accident or whether you're recovering from the pain of a divorce. In either case, charging ahead can compound your injury.

Some of you may be thinking about reconciling with your ex. If you are, do so *slowly*. Don't settle for quick fixes, and don't force steps toward reconciliation because that won't work. Single parents can get into trouble by dashing ahead with great hopes for reconciliation—and instead crashing into a brick wall of deeper hurt. Make sure your steps are slow and mutually agreed upon; doing so will save both of you added heartache.

BUILD BRIDGES, NOT WALLS.

The tendency for many single parents is to wall their children off from everybody else: their ex, their ex's parents, even their own family members, if they disagreed with the divorce.

But one of the ways you can help your children is by building bridges into the lives of those extended family members, including your ex's parents. After all, they've been involved in the lives of your children for how many years? Three? Nine? Twelve? If you build bridges, you may eventually have three or four sets of grandparents at your child's college graduation, but that's healthier than cutting your ex's parents out of the picture if those grandparents provide healthy relationships for your kids. It used to be that parents and grandparents had lots of kids. Today, kids have lots of parents and grandparents.

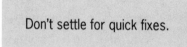

Don't settle for quick fixes.

Just because you get a divorce doesn't mean that the grandparents—on either side—should be removed from your children's lives. There should be an adult conversation between you and your ex in which you both admit, "We didn't do the marriage well, and if we do the divorce like we did the marriage, our kids are going to pay for it. Let's agree that we can live different lives; we don't have to think the same way. But let's come together on this: We are going to do what's best for the kids." As part of that plan, get your own parents on the same page with you regarding extending the olive branch to your ex. Ask them to please not bad-mouth your ex in front of your kids, and explain why.

By involving those grandparents in the lives of your children, you'll be helping build your children's self-esteem.

PRAY FOR YOUR EX.

Right now praying for the person who has hurt you so deeply may be one of the last things on your mind. But I'm asking you to simply consider it.

In Scripture, Jesus told us to pray for our enemies, and that includes your ex. Jesus never promised it would be easy. In fact, praying for your enemies is one of the most difficult things you, as a human being, can ever do. That's because revenge is so second nature for the majority of us.

So when you feel like picking up the phone to call your attorney about another infraction by your ex, try something else instead. Open a dialogue with God. You can be as blunt as you need to be. Go ahead and yell a little. God doesn't mind. He knows you well, and he'll still listen.

He also promises that he's not going to give you more than you can bear. And to make good on that promise, he gives you the help of family, friends, a community of faith, and community resources to make it through the day—not to mention the presence of his Holy Spirit, living inside those who believe in Jesus.

How do you know if you have reached a healthier place inside?

> Go ahead and yell a little. God doesn't mind.

When you can honestly ask God for your ex's best. When you've put down the sledgehammer and picked up the olive branch for good.

If you're at that place, wonderful! If not, realize that all change takes time. Letting go can be particularly difficult for some of us.

You may not be ready to pray for your ex. But at least open a dialogue with God. Tell him how you feel right now about your ex. Include the details. For instance, tell him that, given the choice, you'd prefer to use your wedding photos as fire starters at your daughter's next Brownies' campout. Then ask God to change your heart and to work in your ex's heart.

Prayer has punch. It opens you to the work of God's grace. As you pray for your ex (as hard as that may be right now), your own life may change as well.

Reaching out to "the enemy" is not easy. I know. There have been people in my own life that I would have liked to strangle with my bare hands rather than go before God with my hands folded in prayer. But I pray about those feelings nevertheless.

God listens . . . and responds.

❊ ❊ ❊

KEY Qs . . .

- How would you describe your relationship with your ex right now?

- What particular areas could improve in your communication with your ex? your treatment of your ex? the way you talk about your ex around your children?

- Think about each of your children. How can you "tell the truth in love" to each child about your divorce?

CHAPTER 14

"Are You Going to Die and Leave Me Alone?"

(And Other Issues for Widows, Widowers, and Their Children)

You of all folks know that life can throw you tremendous curveballs. Who would have thought, a year ago, two years ago, five years ago, ten years ago, as you were walking down the aisle to wedded bliss, that you'd be walking down another aisle in a funeral home, attending the funeral of your spouse? that the years you dreamed of having together and raising your kids would all of a sudden be cut short?

Sarah, Avriel, and Felicia can relate. Here are their stories. Maybe portions of theirs are like yours.

SARAH'S STORY

"Mommy, are you going to die?"

Four-year-old Daniel looked up at his mom, Sarah, with tears in his eyes. He was clutching his "blankie"—the baby blanket that he had tossed aside six months earlier, saying he was a big boy now and didn't need it.

But that had been before Sarah's husband—Daniel's daddy—had died. Who could have known, four months earlier, that a regular physical exam would reveal that Anthony had a brain tumor? Within six weeks, Anthony had lost his ability to speak. And young Daniel had watched his daddy die slowly, wasting away day after day.

Sarah choked back tears herself. What could she tell Daniel? Life is uncertain. People die. Yet right now Daniel needed the assurance that she would never leave him, even if the daddy he loved had died and left their family.

AVRIEL'S STORY

Avriel's wife, Becki, had just given birth to their second child. He still remembered her getting into their van early one October morning six weeks later. She had laughed and told him, "Don't worry, honey. I'll be back with groceries in about twenty minutes. After all, I know *you* can't feed the baby!" It was her first real outing since Brandon was born. Avriel smiled and waved her off.

Three hours of worry—and the incessant cries of a hungry baby—later, he'd received a call from the police, asking him to come to a nearby hospital. Becki's van had been struck by a hungover driver, just minutes from their home. Becki had been rushed into emergency surgery, and by the time Avriel drove the twenty minutes to the hospital, Becki was dead.

To say Avriel was stunned is a major understatement. Becki had been an incredible mother. Being a mother was her passion, and it showed. How could he ever measure up? How could he raise a newborn, who would never remember his mother, and a three-year-old, who had always been hanging onto her mommy's leg? Especially when he was grieving his wife's death, too? How could he look Jeri, their daughter, in the eye and tell her that the mommy she loved was never coming home again?

FELICIA'S STORY

It had only taken Felicia three months to fall in love with the dark and handsome Rohil. Six months later, they were married, and less than a year later, the twins were on their way. When the twins turned eight, Rohil revealed some devastating news. He had AIDS, and it was advancing rapidly. He admitted that he had tested positive for HIV shortly before he and Felicia had married, but he just couldn't find a way to tell her.

You see, before they met, Rohil had been involved with several "someone else's"—all guys. He had lived a gay lifestyle for the previous five years. When his parents found out about it, they were utterly shocked. They read him the riot act and insisted he "get his act straight." So Rohil did. He met the beautiful Felicia and married her. But it was all an act.

Felicia was devastated to find out that Rohil had had numerous trysts with guys over the ten years they'd been married. To say she felt betrayed is a major understatement. But the pieces began to fit together—his frequent "business trips," his reticence to have sex with her, and the fact that he never wanted her to see him undressed (he was trying to hide the AIDS sores that were already developing on his body).

Felicia was in a quandary. What should she do? The twins loved their daddy, and Rohil was sick. She couldn't just kick him out, as much as she felt like it. There was no one with whom she could share the news, except for Rohil's parents, since they were already aware of his previous lifestyle and had grieved over it. Felicia's own parents were deceased. She was too embarrassed to tell any of her friends, so she retreated from all of her other relationships and stayed at home as much as possible.

> "Did God take Daddy away?"

Nine months later, Rohil died. The twins had known their daddy was sick, and Felicia had tried to prepare them for the fact that he would die. But nobody is ever ready for death.

"Why did Daddy have to die?" they asked. "Did God take Daddy away?"

Felicia wanted to yell, "No, God didn't take your daddy away. He took himself away by all the things that he did."

She wondered how she could explain to her twin boys what had really happened. Especially since they were *boys*. How could she instill in them the concept of what a healthy male should be when their *daddy* had been a homosexual and betrayed their family? And what should she say to anyone who asked how Rohil died? That he got pneumonia, and it was fatal?

Questions flooded Felicia's mind every day, and there seemed no end in sight to her misery. She grew angry and bitter. She knew she had to make a radical move to change her life—and her boys' lives.

When Death Comes Knocking

Nobody expects a loved one to die. And Sarah, Avriel, and Felicia all experienced death in vastly different ways. Could any of them have guessed that it would happen? Certainly not. Could you have guessed?

What can you do and say to children when their mommy or daddy dies? How can you allay their fears that you, too, will die? that they'll then be left alone, with no one to care for them? or that they will die, too—at a young age?

As we talked about earlier, at the core of each human being is the need to belong. To be connected. To be in community.

When death comes knocking and walks through the door of your home, it carries away with it any sense of safety and stability that your child has felt up to that point in time. No matter what age he is—whether a newborn, a four-year-old, an eight-year-old, or a fifteen-year-old—your child will feel the change in your home environment. No one will need to tell him that life is uncertain. The uncertainty is clear in the fact that Mommy or Daddy is missing.

And that's a heavy burden for a child. Especially for an only child, who doesn't have a sibling to share his fears with and who may fear being left alone even more. So when death has gripped your home, what do you do? How do you explain?

Things That Can Help Provide a Stable Environment for Your Kids

Children will always have questions. At times they will seem endless. But as your children begin to feel secure in the fact that you love them, are willing to listen to them—even if you don't have all the answers, which you don't!—and are looking out for their best interests, they will begin to relax. They will begin to trust again.

> Home will never be the same again. You can't expect it to be.

Home will never be the same again. You can't expect it to be. Things will be different. It may sound harsh, but you need to accept that fact and move on. Otherwise you'll get mired down in anger and bitterness, and those attitudes and behaviors will seep into your kids' attitudes and behaviors. You can grieve, yet still move ahead with what you need to do in raising your kids.

Here are some things you can do to provide the most stable environment possible for your kids when they've lost a daddy or mommy.

TELL THE TRUTH IN LOVE . . . BUT YOU DON'T HAVE TO TELL IT ALL AT ONCE.

The best advice I could ever give any parent is: Tell the truth . . . in love. And this holds true for widows and widowers, too.

Lying to your kids or sugarcoating what has happened won't help. The long-range truth is that Daddy or Mommy is not coming back. They will be a part of your life only in memory now. So don't blithely say things like, "It's okay. Everything will be okay." Things will not be "okay"—they will be vastly changed in your home with the loss of your spouse. *But you and your child can be okay.* You can choose to walk together, hand in hand, through this tragedy.

> The best advice I could give to widows or widowers is this: Tell the truth . . . in love.

How can you do that? You can start by always telling the truth—age appropriately, of course. As a parent, you constantly have to make judgment calls about what kind of information is age appropriate and personality appropriate for your particular child. You may have three children, and their psyches will all be different. They will have different questions. A seventeen-year-old will be able to process information that a seven-year-old cannot.

Note also that I didn't just say "Tell the truth." I added two very important words afterward: *in love.* Your goal should always be love: to help your child understand, to calm her fears, and to assure her that she is loved and that you will be by her side. Remember that *you* are the adult, and your child is *a child.*

A two-year-old needs a hug and needs to be told simply, "Mommy is here. I love you, and I will not leave you." He can't understand the complexities of a statement such as, "Mommy is here. I love you, and I will do my best not to ever leave you. But life is uncertain, and I can't guarantee I'll always be here. No one can guarantee that. But I am doing my very best to stay in good shape, have physical checkups, not get in car accidents," etc. However, a ten-year-old, who has already had his dog die and understands what death means, might require more detailed information to allay his fears about you leaving him.

A thirteen-year-old boy may not be ready to process the truth that his daddy died of AIDS. It may be better to "tell the truth in love," which means giving out the age-appropriate information that your child needs at the present time. When he asks about his dad's death, you could say, "Your dad died of a respiratory disorder. He got pneumonia, and his lungs just grew too weak to breathe"—if that's what finally did kill your husband.

However, if a boy is seventeen, putting two and two together, and he's pushing for more specific answers about his dad's death, it's time to share details that you couldn't share with him earlier in his life. He may even ask you directly, "Was Dad gay?" If so, admit it. Say straightforwardly, "Yes, your dad was gay. Let me tell you what happened and how I met your dad. . . ." As Paul Harvey would say, "Now you know the rest of the story."

> How much should you tell your child and when?

It all comes down to this: At times your child needs to know *bits* of the story. Other times your child needs to know *some* of the story. And sometimes your child needs to know *the rest* of the story.

So how much should you tell your child and when? There is no easy, pat answer to that question. But if you keep the following principles in mind as well as the personality of your child, you will know what to say, and when:

- Tell the truth in love.
- All children deserve respect and a truthful answer.
- Answer only the questions your child asks. No more, and no less.

Back to Felicia's story. Her soul was incredibly damaged after her husband's death. She was not only embarrassed about the way he had lived, but about the way he had died, too. So she moved herself and the twins from their small-town home in Ohio to an urban area in another state. She didn't want either of the boys to have to endure any questions about their dad's death, for any information to "leak" to them about their dad and his lifestyle, or for them to feel the embarrassment that she felt, so she hid the truth from them. She cut off contact with all of their friends because she feared that somehow the boys would find out the terrible truth about their dad.

Her plan seemed to work for two years—until the boys started asking more questions. Finally Felicia realized that she had to tell them something. They deserved some answers. So she called Rohil's parents, apologized for being out of touch with them, and explained her dilemma. They had been wonderful grandparents, and the boys missed them, she said. She invited them to come for a visit over the boys' spring break.

> Answer only the questions your child asks. No more, and no less.

Those ten days with her in-laws were incredibly healing. With Felicia's permission, the grandparents shared what they knew of Rohil's story with his teenage sons. They explained how much they loved Rohil, yet how his choices had made them sad.

During that time, tears flowed. Honesty reigned. There were moments of anger, some slammed doors, and stomping feet. And there were some times of laughter. The boys renewed their bond with the grandparents who loved them deeply.

After that spring break, the questions were far from over, Felicia knew. She was still surprised at times by the boys' questions, their flares of anger and bitterness, and by the memories of their father that made them smile.

A year later, Felicia and the boys moved to Maryland—to a new home a mile away from their grandparents, who had always had such a positive influence in their lives.

Today both of the boys are in college. They are some of the most respectful and serious young men I've ever met. One is pursuing a degree to become a medical doctor, the other a psychologist. Because they learned early about the harsh realities of life, they are committed to helping others physically and emotionally. Felicia has great reason to be proud of her sons.

And the change in their lives all came about because Felicia decided to tell the truth in love, age appropriately. To take a risk instead of running away or sugarcoating what happened.

Every child is unique. Every child will ask different questions at different times, as her heart and mind are ready for the answers. That's why it's so important for you to know your child. To know her heart and mind well enough that you are able to step in and calm fears with truthful information that your child can handle at that particular stage.

At times your child's question will be agonizing for you. But make a pact *now*, before the question is asked, that you will *never, ever* tell your kids lies. That you will always *tell the truth . . . in love.* Your kids deserve the truth. Your daughter may need to be told, "Daddy got sick. We thought it was just a regular illness, but it was more serious than we thought. That's why Daddy died."

> Your kids deserve the truth.

Your kids deserve to hear about what happened from your lips, so they're not blindsided by hearsay information from someone else. You owe them that kind of respect.

BE HONEST ABOUT YOUR OWN FEELINGS.

It's been a rough day. You've been reminded nonstop of your spouse's absence. By dinnertime you're emotionally exhausted and teary eyed. When your child asks you what's wrong, don't just say, "Mommy is just tired. I'll be okay." Instead, say, "You know, honey, I'm really missing your daddy right now. I miss him being with us at dinner. Do you ever feel that way?"

Responding in such a way opens up communication with your child. It tells your child, *If Mommy misses Daddy, it's okay for me to miss him. And if Mommy cries, it's okay if I cry sometimes, too.*

So share your feelings—again, age appropriately, in love—with your child. Revealing that you don't always "have it all together" assures your child that he isn't "wrong" or "bad" if he feels sad or angry about what has happened.

TALK ABOUT THE MISSING PARENT.

Often when someone dies, a basic human response is to not talk about it. *If we don't talk about it,* you reason, *it won't hurt as much.*

But your children *need* to talk about their daddy or mommy, who is now absent from their home. That person was a huge part of your children's lives, and he or she has been ripped away. Yet kids may sometimes be reticent to bring up the missing parent, for fear that you will cry. If your children know that you, too, sometimes feel sad and cry, they will feel more comfortable talking about their missing parent.

Sometimes with young children it may also help to read a book that approaches death in a gentle way, such as *Gram's Song* by Karyn Henley. It can help your child voice questions he doesn't quite know how to ask.

The important thing is to talk about the missing parent. "You know, your daddy would have loved to see you rock climb for the first time. He'd be so proud of you for trying it!" Or, "Mommy always loved roses, didn't she? She'd be so happy that we planted some in our garden this year." Talk about your spouse especially at milestones in your child's life. A first ballet class. A first day at kindergarten. A first baseball game. A first sleepover. A first date.

REMEMBER THE MISSING PARENT.

What do you do on your spouse's birthday? at Christmas? on Mother's Day? on Father's Day? How do you handle the day-to-day times when your spouse's absence seems even more poignant?

When Raoul and his wife, Autumn, found out she had a debilitating disease that was slowly attacking her spinal cord and would eventually lead to her death, they planned ahead. Their girls were thirteen and fourteen at the time of their mother's death. But before Autumn died, she picked out a special present for each of the girls' birthdays, through the age of twenty-one. And she wrote them a letter to go along with each gift, explaining why she had picked that certain present and offering a message from her heart for that particular birthday. She assured the girls of her love for them and how proud she was of them.

Autumn also purchased ten Christmas ornaments, wrapped them individually, and dated them, one for each year. She included a note that explained why she had chosen that ornament and again reminded each daughter of her love for them. She even wrote about silly and serious memories she had of other Christmas celebrations with them. And she concluded each note by saying, "I cannot be there with you this year. But

I will always be in your hearts and your memories, as you were always in my heart and memories."

Lisa Beamer never could have guessed that on September 11, 2001, she would become a single parent when the plane her husband, Todd, was traveling on was taken over by terrorists. She never guessed that, minutes later, Todd would become a national hero. At the time she had two young boys and a baby on the way. How could she keep Todd's memory alive with such young children? she wondered. She found that it was the little things that mattered most to her boys.

Playing catch with the glove their daddy had bought them.

Seeing pictures of them with their daddy (appropriately placed on low shelves so the boys could easily see them).

Talking about how much he had loved them and would be proud of them.

> In what practical ways can you remember your spouse?

In what practical ways can you remember your spouse, in everyday events as well as holidays? What things did your children like to do with your spouse? You won't be able to replace those things because you can never replace the person who is missing. But as you remember and honor those times, you'll build an even greater bond of trust with your kids.

Geri Beth lost her husband, Dan, in a boating accident. Her husband and their two sons were always doing adventuresome things together. It was something the boys missed greatly, "since I'm not the adventuresome type," Geri Beth admits. "I knew I wasn't up to doing all the things he used to do with them—boating, skiing, soccer—but there was something that I could do that would mean a lot to them. So I went to the boys one fall day and said, 'Remember when you and Dad used to rake up all the leaves into a big pile and then jump in? I loved watching you. It made me laugh. Dad isn't here this year, but we could still make a leaf pile and jump in. I bet Dad would like to look down from heaven and see that! It would make him laugh, too, to see us having fun.'

"The boys were thrilled. The next day was a Saturday, and we made a "fall fest" day out of it, complete with raking leaves, jumping into the huge pile, hot chocolate, and s'mores that we made under the broiler in our oven. It was simple, but effective. We spent the day remembering Dan, telling stories about what he did with the boys, and just celebrating him. That was four years ago. Although the boys are now in their teens, they still ask to have our fall fest day. That's how important it was—and still is—to them."

> Remembering those you love is a powerful healer.

Never sell yours or your child's memories short. Remembering those you love is a powerful healer.

BE CAREFUL NOT TO PAINT GOD IN A BAD LIGHT.

Well-meaning folks all over the globe are famous for saying things like

- "Jesus took your mommy to heaven."
- "God needed Daddy in heaven."
- "God loved your daddy, so he took him home to heaven."
- "It was time for your mommy to go to heaven."

But what are they really accomplishing? For a child, such responses set up even more questions, such as "Why would Jesus take Daddy when he knows I love Daddy?" and "Is Jesus that mean?"

In a young child's psyche, he's wondering, *Why would I want to follow Jesus if he took my daddy away? Or, Why did God need Daddy? Doesn't he have enough people up there already? Can't he do things himself? Why did he have to take my daddy?*

Or an older child might think, *So God's the great controller of the sky. But he's evidently not very good at it because he messed up when he took my mom. Or, Doesn't he care that we're hurting here? Why did he have to take my dad?*

By glossing over the reality of death with seemingly warm, fuzzy statements about God "needing" that person in heaven, you're not doing your child any favors. Such statements actually paint almighty God in a bad light. After all, who would want to listen to or follow somebody who takes your parent away from you?

What children need instead is to understand the facts. "You know, honey, I miss Daddy, too. Very badly sometimes. Daddy didn't want to leave us when he did. He wanted to live with us for a long time. But there was a man who decided that he was going to drink while he was driving. Because that man chose to do what was wrong, your daddy died. It wasn't right, and it makes me angry, too. But God did not take Daddy away. Someone made a wrong choice, and that's what took Daddy away from us. God has never stopped loving you, me, or Daddy. God helped us through rough times before as a family, when Daddy was alive, and God is still helping us now."

> Who would want to listen to or follow somebody who takes your parent away from you?

Now *that* is a realistic, loving response that gives the child the information that he needs to and longs to know. It sets up a realistic picture of sin and irresponsible choices—showing that they can have a devastating impact on someone else.

In essence, you've used that moment to share more than grief with your child. You've taught him a little more about what it means to live.

Bad things do happen to good people. There is no way to get around it. You need to teach your children that reality and instill in them the concept that God remains in control, but that he has given us the freedom to make choices. Some people choose wisely; some not so wisely. All our choices have an impact on others.

Now there's a teachable moment that your child will remember for a lifetime.

Where's My Daddy/Mommy?

After the death of a parent, every child asks in some way, "Where's Daddy now?" "Is Mommy in heaven?" "Will she come back? "Will I see him again?"

If you are a person of faith, this is an opportunity for you to explain to your child what you believe. But a simple rule applies: Think through what you're going to say—and the implications of it—before you share it with your child. So if you need to, step back from the question and say, "Honey, that's a very good question. Mommy needs to think about it for a few minutes, then we'll sit down and talk about it together."

For example, an appropriate answer for a younger child could be, "Daddy loved Jesus, and he is now with Jesus in heaven."

An older child may need more specifics. If your spouse had a personal relationship with God, talk about heaven—the place where your spouse is now. Even do some research. Look up facts about heaven in the Bible. Let your child know that it is a place of joy, where we will not be disappointed. A place where our desire to love Jesus and be with him will be fulfilled.

If your spouse did not believe in Jesus, you may have a hard task in front of you, as Felicia did. When her boys asked where their daddy was, she had to tell them, "Boys, I don't really know. Your daddy wouldn't talk to me about that. Only God knows what happened in your daddy's heart and mind before he died. But I can tell you what I believe."

It was an opportunity—though a hard one—to share with her boys why she chose to be different. Why she chose to take them to Sunday school all those years when their daddy refused to go with them.

> Think through what you're going to say—and the implications of it—before you share it with your child.

In the process of her talks with the boys, Felicia was able to reassure them of her love and of God's love for them. But she also didn't sidestep the truth—that their daddy had made some wrong choices in life, and those choices had led to his death. She wanted the boys to make different, healthy choices for their lives. And she was determined to help them learn to do just that.

If your spouse did believe in God, you can honestly say, "Daddy is in heaven. He's smiling down on us, watching us as we talk right now. And he loved you very much. If you choose to believe in Jesus, the Bible says that you will go to heaven, too. That means someday you will see Daddy again. And he'll be so happy to see you!"

Yes, bad things happen to good people. Children of any age need to understand that, in an age-appropriate way. But by learning what to reveal and when, you are giving your child a psychological "blankie" of protection.

No matter what lies ahead, your child needs this unconditional guarantee from you: "Things will be different. That's true. But you know what? We're in this together, and I *do* know this: I love you beyond description. I will always be there for you, to support you, no matter what lies ahead."

※ ※ ※

KEY Qs . . .

- Which situation do you identify with the most—Sarah's, Avriel's, or Felicia's? Why?

- What is your child's greatest fear at the moment? How can you help to allay that fear?

- In what practical ways can you "remember" your spouse with your children?

CHAPTER 15

"Who Is My Daddy/Mommy?"

(And Other Issues for Never-Married Parents and Their Children)

"Who's my daddy?"

Lawonna had known the question would come sometime. She'd tried to prepare herself emotionally for it and had even brainstormed what to tell her daughter, Trisha. But now that the question had finally been asked, nothing she could think of to say seemed right.

Her daughter deserved an honest answer, yet how much should she share? Lawonna had made some big mistakes in her life. Deciding to get involved with Jarod was one of them. He'd hung around just long enough to get her pregnant and hear the news. Then he split for another town. She hadn't heard from him since. News on the gossip line from his friends was that he was somewhere in Cincinnati, doing who knew what.

Trisha's dad was a real loser, in Lawonna's opinion. How could she have been so stupid as to let him sway her into having sex? The only thing he had going for him was his good looks—something Trisha shared. Every day Lawonna could see Jarod in Trisha's eyes.

Yes, Lawonna had made mistakes. But she didn't ever want *Trisha* to think that *she* was a mistake. What could she, as her mother, say that would be truthful yet not hurtful?

Karyn's situation was different. At forty years of age, she had decided it was time to become a parent. There was no guy on the horizon—at least no guy she was interested in marrying—so she moved ahead with her plans. After several years of searching and filling out paperwork, she traveled to another state to adopt a newborn. Claire, now six, is the treasure of Karyn's heart.

But yesterday Claire had come home from kindergarten with a big question: "Momma, the kids at school said that I must be adopted, since I don't look like you. And if I'm adopted, you aren't my real mommy. What do they mean? I thought *you* were my real mommy. And who's my daddy?"

Karyn was stunned. Claire had always known that she hadn't come from Karyn's tummy. That another lady who had loved Claire very much had given birth to Claire and then allowed Karyn the gift of adopting her as a baby. Karyn had often talked with Claire about how different their hair and skin was—Karyn was a blonde with pale skin, and Claire had curly black hair and skin the color of cocoa—but how wonderful that was, too. They joked about how God had made two opposite colors of the rainbow come together in one family.

Now, for the first time, Claire was confused about who her real mommy was and was asking about her daddy. What should Karyn tell her, when she knew nothing about Claire's birth father and only very little about her birth mother? She had always thought that if Claire showed a desire to know, they could search together when Claire was older. But six years old just seemed too young for the type of information that might be revealed through such a search. What could and should Karyn say?

> What and how much should I tell? And when?

Both Lawonna and Karyn, although in vastly differing situations, are single parents who faced the same questions: *What and how much should I tell? And when? How much information can my child process?*

The Real Question

There was more going on behind the scenes in Trisha's and Claire's hearts and minds than their mothers even knew. There was another, bigger question behind the questions they asked. A question that these children, at such young ages, couldn't yet process verbally. And that question is, Who am I?

At the core of each of us is that longing to belong, to connect. To be part of a family. To look like someone else. To act like someone else. To be recognized as part of a group. By trying to identify their "real" parents, Trisha and Claire were beginning to try to figure out who they were, at their core.

We all long to know our roots. Who our parents were (or more about who they were). How that affects who we are—our responses, our talents, our gestures, our physical appearance.

When you identify that longing behind the scenes in a child's heart, it is easier to know how to respond to his "Who's my mommy?" and "Who's my daddy?" questions.

Things That Can Help Provide a Stable Environment for Your Kids

When the questions come, how can you respond appropriately? Following are some guidelines that will help. But only *you* know your child's mind and heart. Only you know your particular situation. That means you must filter any information through your own perspective of what is age appropriate and psychologically helpful to your child.

TELL THE TRUTH . . . IN LOVE . . . BUT TELL IT IN PIECES.

The most important thing to remember is, "Tell the truth . . . in love." That means you start by always telling the truth—age appropriately, of course. As a parent, you constantly have to make judgment calls about what kind of information is age appropriate and personality appropriate for your particular child. Even if you have three children, each one has a different personality. Each one has different questions. A seventeen-year-old will be able to process information that a seven-year-old cannot.

Note also that I didn't just say "Tell the truth." I added two very important words afterward: *in love.* Your goal should always be love. To help your child understand, to calm her fears, to assure her that she is loved and that you will be by her side. Remember that *you* are the adult, and your child is *a child.* And because you are her parent, you need to evaluate psychologically what information she can handle—and when.

Part of telling the truth in love means that you answer the questions your child asks, not the questions she doesn't ask. You give enough information to satisfy that question, without introducing other questions into your child's mind. When she is psychologically ready, a new question may pop up, and then you can answer that one. Children will ask questions until they are satisfied. For instance, if your three-year-old asks, "Who's my daddy?" you could say, "Your daddy is a man Mommy knew a long time ago, before you were born." If your child persists, wanting to know more, you could say, "I don't really know anything else about him, honey. Mommy hasn't seen him since you were very little." That may be all the information your child requires at that time.

> Give *only* the information your child asks for at that moment.

However, if that child asked, "Who's my daddy?" and you explained, "Your daddy is a man Mommy knew a long time ago, before you were born. Mommy thought she loved him, but she didn't. When I found out I was pregnant with you, that man left and didn't come back." By giving *too much information* that a three-year-old can't understand, you aren't answering her simple question. You're merely introducing *more* questions—ones that your child is not psychologically ready for, such as, "What do you mean you didn't love him? Does that mean you're not sure you love me? What if you leave me and don't come back, just like that man did to you?"

So give *only* the information your child asks for at that moment. Too much information can be harmful to a child. When your child starts to put together some pieces and wants more, she'll ask her next question, and you can answer that one.

Raina has perhaps the most difficult task of all to answer how her son, Raisa, came into the world. One late summer night, Raina was walking home after a movie night with friends when she was yanked into a dark alley and raped. Afterward, she lived in fear. She couldn't get that night out of her head. She saw shadows of the man in her dreams, but never his face. She remembered the roughness of his hands and what he did to her. She went from being a confident, happy young woman to a fearful woman who double-locked her apartment door and never went out at night.

When Raina found out she was pregnant with Raisa, she agonized.

How could this be? How could a child result from such horror? Although she'd heard that women who were raped couldn't get pregnant, she was. She found herself in front of an abortion clinic door twice but couldn't follow through on it. After feeling the stirrings of life inside her, she decided that it would be wrong to judge the child for what the rapist had done. So she gave birth to Raisa, fully intending to give him up for adoption.

Then when Raisa was born and Raina saw his sweet face, she fell in love. She made the tough choice of becoming a single parent—taking on the responsibility of a child who was hers, even if she didn't know who his father was.

When nine-year-old Raisa asked over dinner, "Who's my father?" she didn't know what to say. She opened and closed her mouth a few times before she finally said simply, "Raisa, I only met him once, and I didn't really know him. I haven't had any contact with him, and I don't know where he is now."

Raina was right to only give that kind of vague information. Any further details could have been horribly destructive to a young boy's growing sense of manhood and justice. There would be time later, when more questions would come up, to reveal more of the story.

No matter what your story is, here's the key: Tell the truth in love, *always*. But only tell it in pieces, as your child is able to handle it.

MAKE SURE YOU UNDERSTAND YOUR CHILD'S QUESTION.

There's a famous anecdote about a child who asks, "Where did I come from?"

His dad takes a big breath and plunges into a huge discussion about sex, including how the sperm and the egg interact.

When the father is all done and is patting himself on the back for doing such a good job, the little boy simply shrugs. "What I really wanted to know, Dad, is where I'm from. My friend Billy is from Albany, New York."

So before you launch into a big discussion, giving information your child may not be ready for, make sure you understand your child's question. First, ask your child to explain a little more. "Honey, you asked me,

'Who's my daddy?' I want to help answer your question. But could you tell me a little more about what you want to know?" If your child doesn't know how to give more information, it may help to repeat back the question to her—perhaps in a different form, such as: "Honey, you just asked, 'Who's my mommy?' Are you asking about the lady who had you in her tummy? Or are you trying to figure out who is your real mommy—me, or the lady who had you in her tummy?"

Get as many facts as you can first so you're answering the question your child *really* asked, not what you *think* she asked.

PUT YOU AND YOUR CHILD ON AN EVEN PLAYING FIELD.
Older children, especially, appreciate being "in the loop" on family business. It makes them feel appreciated, valued, and trusted. So whenever you can, even the playing field between you and your child. For instance, if your older child asks, "Who's my daddy?" you could say, "Your father's name is Rick. Last I heard, he lived in the state of Ohio, but I have not talked with him in over twelve years. So frankly, you and I are both in the dark about him. We know nothing about him now or what he has done in the past twelve years."

> If you trash-talk your "loser," your child may think, *I'm a loser, too.*

If your child gets that wondering look and says, "What was he like then, Mom? When you knew him? Do I look like him? Did he like to play guitar, too?" then it's time to give some specifics about what Rick was like and what attracted you to him—if Rick was a man you dated and knew on a more consistent basis over a period of months or years. If you knew Rick only for a night, there may not be much you can say about him, other than, "When I first saw him, I thought he was very handsome. He had curly hair, the same brown as yours." But sometimes even a small detail will satisfy a child's longing to connect in some way to his birth parent.

One important caution: Do your best to make the few details you do share positive ones, not, "He was a total loser. I'm so glad he's out of my life." Look at it this way: Your child is a result of the bond between you and that "loser" (or however you think of him). That means if you trash-talk your "loser," your child may think, *I'm a loser, too.*

That puts all of your negative feelings toward that "loser" in a different light, doesn't it?

ADMIT YOUR MISTAKES.

Let's face it. None of us is perfect. And if you got pregnant out of marriage, your "mistake" stares you in the face every day. (Although let's clarify: Your action to have sex outside of the bonds of marriage was the mistake; the child that was created should never be thought of as a mistake.) You made a lousy choice. You met a guy who looked great on the outside but had about as much integrity and morals as a pea. You got involved, and your child is the result.

You may wish you could get a do-over for that time in your life, but that's not possible. Do-overs only happen in movies like *Groundhog Day*. So what are you going to do about it now?

You could wallow in your mistake and beat yourself up about it the rest of your life (and in the process make your child feel like a mistake).

> Do-overs only happen in movies like *Groundhog Day*.

Or you could suck it up and admit you're not perfect. You can put one foot in front of the other and do your best to be a responsible parent now.

You can admit your mistakes—age appropriately, of course—to your children. Let's say your eight-year-old son gets caught being a bully on the playground. You could say to him, "Honey, that wasn't a good choice, was it? Did you know that sometimes I don't always make good choices, either? And I've sometimes hurt people and made them sad, too. Do you think we could work together and help each other make better choices?"

If your daughter is sixteen and about to go on her first date the next weekend, you might say, "Chelsea, I know Friday will be an exciting night for you. I can't wait to hear all about it. Remember when I told you that I didn't always make good choices? that there were some things that I wish I would have done differently? Well, when I went on my first date with Thom, I was excited, too. It was the first time I'd ever been out on a date. And that night I really thought I'd fallen in love. . . ." And then you might want to give a few details about what you wish you had done differently. "That night I really liked him, and I didn't want to say no, because I was afraid he wouldn't ask me out again. So he asked if I wanted to make out a little bit . . . and we did. But then the kissing went further than I wanted it to. Before I knew it, we were in the backseat of his car. When it was all over, I wished it had never happened. I love you, and I don't want you to have to feel that way. If this guy really does care about you, he won't ask you to do anything you're not comfortable with. And he certainly won't ask for sex. No date deserves to walk away with a piece of your body. So don't give it up, okay? You're too important, and so's your body."

If your daughter is seventeen or eighteen, you might want to add, "Honey, because of that night, I have *you*. And I wouldn't trade you for anything or anyone. But I don't want you to go through everything that I have, trying to raise a baby all alone. I want you to find someone who loves you enough to wait to have sex with you until you're married, and I want you to have a husband who will stay around to help you raise a baby."

DON'T LET GUILT CONTROL YOUR DECISIONS.
I had just finished speaking to a group of moms about "mother stress" when one of the moms approached me. "My girlfriend had to work and couldn't be here," she explained, "but she wanted me to ask you what she should do. Her six-year-old daughter constantly hits her all the time, and she doesn't know what to do. She feels so guilty because Andrea doesn't have a daddy. Do you think Andrea is just angry because of that, and that's why she's hitting her mom? What should my friend do?"

I want to hit this point strongly: *No mother should take this kind of abusive behavior from her child. And no child should grow up thinking she has the license to treat someone else this way.*

> The guilt cycle has to end right now.

That mother is operating out of a core of guilt, and she's allowing her child to beat on her because of it. The guilt cycle has to end right now. If you continue to say to yourself, *Everything is my fault. I deserve this,* you'll be stuck in the "kick yourself in the teeth" syndrome that is so common, particularly in single moms. (Interestingly enough, men tend to blame others; women tend to blame themselves.)

This mom needs to take control immediately and say, "Andrea, I will not allow you to kick me anymore. It is not appropriate, and it is going to stop." If the child continues to kick, the mother needs to take swift action, using some kind of discipline that will get the message across. Perhaps Andrea's favorite toys are her collection of horses. Mom then needs to pack up those horses and put them away. Even better, move them to a friend's house so Mom, in a weak moment, can't retrieve them. Then Mom should tell Andrea, "Until this behavior stops, you will not see or play with your horses again."

Remember: In all things, you are the parent. You are not trying to be your child's friend. You are trying to raise a healthy, well-balanced child who will contribute in a positive way to the world.

So think long range. What do you want your child to be like? Don't let guilt control you so you let your child get away with murder.

What's a Parent, Really?

There's a big difference, as you know, between a man whose sperm has entered your body and united with one of your eggs and a man who has chosen to be your steady partner in marriage. Both are termed *father* in this world, but which one counts in the long run?

And there's a big difference between a woman who births a child and one who's continually there to rock a child when she's sick, to kiss her on her first day of kindergarten, to coach her on her first speech in school, to empathize when a friend betrays her, and to shop with her for her wedding dress. Both are termed *mother*, but which one counts in the long run to your child?

There will be times when your child needs to know more details about her birth parent or birth parents. If you have established a good relationship with your child—one of trust—you will know when that time comes because she will ask. Then you can once again tell the truth in love . . . in pieces . . . answering the question that your child has asked.

If you have adopted your child from overseas, you may have only a sheet of information and a few pictures to tell you of her history. Records may be closed, as they were in the United States years ago. In the early 1960s, my mother was an OB-GYN nurse, so I used to hear stories about adoptions firsthand. In those days, if you had an *illegitimate* baby (the term used in those days for babies who didn't have a married mother and father), the baby's chart at the hospital would say, "No publish. No show." That meant the baby's name and the single mother's name were not released to the newspaper, and no one was allowed to see the child. Most of the time the mother of the child was not even allowed to see the baby, if she had chosen to give the child up for adoption. (The theory was that it was easier on both mother and child if they didn't see each other.)

Yet today some of those babies from the sixties are pursuing the opening of those records and are being reunited with their birth fathers and birth mothers. Their need to know is finally being satisfied.

Some of the reunion stories are beautiful, like Trent's: "I have longed, my entire life, for a sibling. When I tracked down my birth parents, I found out both of them are dead. But I have a sister! And she lives only two hours from me. In the year since I discovered this information, my sister and I have met and bonded not only as biological siblings, but as friends."

Other stories are tragic, like Dave's. "I always wanted to know why I was so different in my adopted family. My sister was adopted, too, and she seemed to fit right into our family. I always felt like the odd shoe. When my sister and I were in our twenties, we both decided to search for our birth parents. She found hers easily and has developed a wonderful relationship with her birth mom. They even took a vacation together last year. But my story was far different. Although I found both of my birth parents, neither of them wanted anything to do with me. My birth mom told me never to call back and hung up on me. My birth dad cussed me out and said I was lying, that he didn't have a son. I tried for over a year, then gave up. There will be a hole in my soul until the day I die."

Why do I share these stories? Because if you pursue information about a birth parent you don't know, you never know what you will uncover. Nor do you know how your child will be received. That's why so many adoptive parents or single parents decide not to encourage their children to go after more information until those children are older and able to deal with the emotional stresses that may follow.

Today, with "open adoptions" (at least domestic ones), the adoptive parent many times meets and develops a relationship with at least the birth mother of the child they adopt. Some choose to exchange letters, some even invite the birth mom and/or birth dad to parties and special events for the child. Others simply keep the information tucked away so it is available when the child asks.

How much a child wants to know will depend on that child. Some children have a need to know about a missing birth dad. *I just have to know where I came from. If I look like him.* Others have no interest. *Why,* they reason, *should I have an interest in some guy who chose to walk out of my life before he even knew me? He's not a father to me!*

The key for you is to reflect an open, honest attitude when your kids ask these tough questions.

Like Mara did. "I'm thirty-one, and my daughter is thirteen. She's at that age when I started to get into trouble. My parents always tried to tell me what was right to do, but I always chose to go the opposite way. I was a rebel, and I see that same potential in my daughter. And that scares me! At first I thought, *Since I messed up so much, who was I to talk to my kid about not messing up?* Then I realized: *The very fact that I did mess up is* why *I should talk to my daughter about it.* So I took Linnea out to her favorite place for an early dinner, when I knew the place would be quiet. And I told her that I had made some decisions that, in retrospect, weren't very good.

"'When I first got pregnant,' I told her, 'I was really scared. I wondered if life was worth living. But then some people came alongside me—you know, the Warners—and made me feel like I could get through that pregnancy, as tough as it was. And if I got through it, there would be a natural, wonderful reward at the end. Want to know what that reward was? You! You became a part of my life, and I became a part of yours. And, as Helen Reddy said, "It's you and me against the world."

"'What I had thought was my darkest hour actually helped me set my life straight and get back on the path I wanted to walk. That's when I began to trust God to help me do things differently in my life. It took hitting the bottom of life to make me realize how many poor choices I was making.

"'It wasn't an easy time. I had to go back to Grandma and Grandpa and tell them what I'd done. That I'd blown it, and I was sorry. That I needed their help. And you know what? They cried. But then they hugged me, and we cried together. We figured out new rules for me to follow as I lived in their home. I had just finished high school but wasn't able to go to college like I planned. But it has worked out okay. Nobody could love you like I do. But, honey, I want a different kind of life for you. A life of freedom. Where you can go to high school and have healthy relationships. Where you can go to college and pursue your dreams.

> You are your child's psychological blankie.

"'I know you want to know more about your dad. You've said you even want to meet him. I make you this promise. After you finish college, if you decide you want to look for your dad, I'll help you as much as I can. I'll share with you all the information I know, and we can find him together, if he can be found. It won't be easy for me because I don't have good feelings toward him. But if that's what you want, I'll do it. That's how much I love you. But now is not the time.'"

You—the parent who has walked alongside—are your child's psychological blankie. The questions your kids ask will be terribly complex and often surprising. They will go "to infinity and beyond," as Buzz Lightyear said.

One mom I know thought she had covered everything she possibly could with her daughter, Mei, whom she adopted from China. That is, until a schoolmate told Mei, "If you're adopted, then your real mommy and daddy are *dead*. And if your mommy got you from China, then she bought you. Because nobody wants the girls, just the boys, so they sold you to your mommy." Mei (not to mention her mother) was thrown for a loop.

Here's another mom's story. Sandy's past came back to haunt her when she made a visit with her kids back to her hometown for a festival. "Aaron, my fourteen-year-old, came to me and said, 'Mom, is it true? That guy said you used to be a cheerleader, and that you "did rounds" with all the guys on the football team. Does that mean what I think it does?' I was heartsick. That was a part of my past I hoped would never come to light again. I didn't want my kids to ever know about it. Now not only did they find out, but they didn't find out from me. Some guy just sorta threw it out like party-talk info . . . and blew my kids and me out of the water."

You can't protect your child like a pheasant under glass. Nothing in life is entirely secure. People will say mean things. Your kids will find out info you wish they didn't have. But if you have established a trust relationship with your kids, you will have an open forum to talk with them about that issue.

Tom is one of the best single dads I know. He's a "tough guy" in every sense of the words. He's even got a buzz cut, and he's in the Army Reserve. He's the kind of guy you might eye with a little nervousness if you saw him in a back alley. He's a dad who doesn't put up with any funny business from his three teenage daughters. But you've never seen such a tender dad. Together he and his girls cook, clean, laugh, and live life together. They have a trust relationship that can't be beat.

> You can't protect your child like a pheasant under glass.

"I know there will be times when the girls will wish they had a mom," Tom says, "and I can never be that. But I do what matters most to them—reassure them of *my* love, *my* care, and *my* protection."

In the midst of complex questions, that's what your children need the most.

❋ ❋ ❋

KEY Qs ...

- If you could be granted one do-over in life, what would you ask for? Why?

- Think back through your actions toward your children over the last week. Have any of them resulted from a sense of guilt? If so, pinpoint the specifics of why you're feeling guilty.

- In what areas are you acting as a "psychological blankie" for your children? How can you reassure each individual child of your love, care, and protection?

KEY 6

REALIZE IT'S NOT ABOUT YOU, IT'S ABOUT THE KIDS . . . FOR NOW

You can't do it all,
but you can do what matters most.
You may not make *Time* magazine's
Person of the Year,
but by focusing on your children,
you can top the list of
Most Influential Person in their lives.

CHAPTER 16

Ready . . . or Not?

"I think I've found the guy of my dreams."

"She's so different. Nothing at all like my ex."

"It's been five long years of nothing but kid stuff. It's about time I do something for myself. Everyone's been trying to set me up on a date. Maybe, for once, I should give it a shot."

"At the end of the day, I'm so tired. The last thing I'd ever think of is getting myself dressed up to go out on a date. I just don't have the energy to meet anyone and make small talk. Relationships are a lot of work. . . ."

"I've waited so long to get married. And finally, someone like him came along. How could I *not* marry him? I'd be crazy not to. He even likes my kid!"

If you are thinking of dating, remarrying, or marrying for the first time, this is the chapter for you. And you might be surprised at what I have to say.

I want to start by telling you a story. Along the coast of Africa, six nautical miles from the fishing village of Gansbaai lies a channel between the islands of Geyser and Dyer known as Shark Alley. Here, whether you want to or not, your chances may be as good as anywhere in the world that you'll run into that killer of the deep, a great white shark.[1]

For most people, staring eyeball to eyeball with a nineteen-foot-long great white shark is not their idea of a good time. But a few live for the thrill of climbing into cages in the water to get a closer look at the sharks, which are circling them like hungry kids at a candy counter. (You can count me out of any activity based on the premise of me being bait.) Some people simply love to flirt with danger.

Unfortunately, if you're not careful, entering or reentering the waters of dating can be as dangerous as taking a dip in shark-infested seas. When it comes to finding a spouse, for example, a singles' bar is Shark Alley and a great place to turn into bait yourself—without the cage to protect you from the neurotic guys and gals that hang out there. And, sad to say, sometimes church singles' groups aren't much better!

It's easy to look back at your relationship with your ex and rationalize that you were simply mismatched, that if you found the right person everything would work out much differently. If you're telling yourself, *I'll date if I meet the right man,* you may not have learned your lesson. By reentering the dating scene, you run the very real danger of repeating the same mistakes that may have led to your divorce.

If your spouse died, you may still be in a period of grieving that makes your vision of another potential spouse a bit cloudy. Or if you somehow blame yourself for your spouse's death, you may be wondering if you should "find a wife" or "find a husband" because you wish you could make it up to your kids for losing their mommy or daddy.

> Dating is a risky endeavor. Without careful preparations, you might find yourself swimming with the sharks.

If you've never been married, maybe you've lived for years without any hope of fulfilling the dreams you once had. You may have thought you'd never get married. But now you're asking, *Isn't any guy/gal better than no guy/gal at all?*

I'm not saying that dating *can't* be done successfully. It can, and I've seen it happen. I'm simply saying that dating is a risky endeavor. Without careful preparations—and a few precautions—you might find yourself unwittingly swimming with the sharks. And those who will suffer the most will be your children.

Smelly Slippers, Sheep, and Wishboned Kids

My favorite pair of slippers are incredibly shabby. (Let's just say *chic* would never be used as a description for them.) They look as if Rosie, my dog, uses them as chew toys. Several times I've found them tossed into the garbage—and each time I retrieve them.

Why do you insist on wearing such gross, beat-up slippers? you ask.

Ahh . . . because they're *comfortable.*

And there's the rub for us in life. We want to do what is comfortable for us. And when life throws us a curveball, we head even more toward what's comfortable. Even if—like my slippers when I pulled them out of the garbage can for the fourth time—what's comfortable is a little shabby and smelly.

When it comes to dating, many single parents revert to what's comfortable. And that means if you made a mistake in choosing your first spouse (or the person you had children with), you will most likely fall back into the same patterns. What's comfortable will contribute to your mate selection (in other words, you'll go after the same kind of guy/gal, without even realizing it consciously), and your interactions with that person will resemble patterns that you had with your ex. And that can lead to big trouble. It's no wonder that 70 percent of second marriages end in divorce.

> We want to do what's comfortable.

If you've never married before, you may be thinking, *You know, if this person likes my kid, this may be my only chance. I shouldn't let a good thing get away from me. This might be the only chance I ever have to get married.* And so you settle for second best or a hurried relationship that won't last.

When you're considering dating or marriage or remarriage, suddenly you're stepping into territory that could prove dangerous to you and your children. Above all else, as a parent, you are your children's protector, the *parentis* we talked about earlier. Your kids are always looking to you for direction; they are like sheep, and you are their shepherd. And they need your protection.

You see, sheep are funny characters. I've heard that sheep don't like moving water. Interestingly enough, we read in Psalm 23 that the shepherd leads us beside "still waters." Shepherds know their sheep pretty well; they always have their eyes on those pesky, wandering critters. The shepherd, in fact, knows his sheep so well that he lies down in the gate at night to make sure none of the flock wanders, but if one does, he goes out of his way to find the lost sheep.

In the same way, you are your children's protector—physically, emotionally, mentally, and spiritually. And as a single parent, you are the *only* one lying before the entrance to that gate. That means you have even more of a responsibility to your kids than a parent in a dual-parent home. Add to that the fact that your time and energies are more limited because you are only one person.

So I must ask: If your time and energies are focused on dating, who is guarding the entrance to your kids' sheep pen?

After the divorce, Sandra's ex-husband, Brad, moved three states away. During the four years that followed, she essentially raised their two children alone. Sure, Brad would send an occasional child-support check, when he happened to find work. But he didn't even bother to call or write the kids at all, much less attempt a visit. As far as Sandra was concerned, Brad had been wiped off the face of her children's earth.

Then along came Ron.

At first Ron ranked second only to Santa Claus in the kids' eyes, because he took them to the park and bought them ice cream. He took the family out to dinner at their favorite pizza restaurant and gave the kids money to play video games, which Sandra was always hesitant to do on her limited income.

But then things started to change. Sandra started to book babysitters to watch the kids so that she and Ron could go out by themselves. The kids got ticked, because it seemed like their mom was always out—with *him*. Ron became the enemy, moving in on their family territory, stealing their mom's energy and attention.

But when Sandra and Ron continued to date, it became apparent to the kids that Ron was around to stay. So they adjusted, even though they still complained sometimes. Slowly they began to warm up to Ron again. In spite of their desires to see their mom and dad get back together, they figured that it wasn't likely (their fights on the phone were evidence of that). So the kids gave in and began forming an attachment to Ron.

Then, nine months into Sandra and Ron's relationship, Ron suddenly broke it off. He said that he wasn't ready to be involved with a woman who had kids. That he wasn't ready for the responsibility. Sandra was devastated. She felt betrayed by a man all over again.

And the kids? Well, they were angry. They had been what I call "wishboned."

Have you ever played with the wishbone from the Thanksgiving turkey, with two people pulling it in opposite directions until it snaps apart? Let's say your kids have gone through a divorce or the death of one of their parents or have longed to have a daddy or a mommy for the first time ever. They are wondering if the person you're dating could possibly be "the one" who will permanently enter the life of your family. So, even though they're cautious, your kids risk getting to know your date. Perhaps they even like him or her, thinking he might make a great new dad or she'd make a great mom.

Then that person—your date—walks out on you . . . and your kids.

What does that make your kids feel like?

That Thanksgiving wishbone, pulled apart by you and your former date.

Whenever you bring a date into your child's life, you run the risk of harming your child greatly. And the stronger the bond your child forms with your date, the more the risk of harm. All relationships involve the risk of rejection. You, of all people, know that because of your past experiences.

And that's why it's even more important that you don't expose your *children* to that much risk until the risk is lessened—namely, when you and the person you're

> Relationships are never as predictable as you'd like them to be.

dating are engaged. At that point, your children can begin to develop an intimate relationship with your spouse-to-be. That may mean having a longer time between your engagement and your wedding. But if your spouse-to-be is a keeper, then he or she (and you!) should be willing to wait a bit longer, for your children's sake.

Relationships are never as predictable as you'd like them to be.

As you think about your dating prospects, you may feel as if your hopes and dreams for your own life have collapsed. But because you are the sole protector of your children, you must think *first* about them before you consider dating, marriage, or remarriage. The stakes are much higher for them. You're looking for a spouse; they're looking for a *new parent*.

Considering it through that perspective is a bit different, isn't it?

What if, after a year of serious dating, you find that your date has been two-timing you, or that she isn't as serious about the relationship as you are? Or that it simply isn't working out—as much as the two of you *want* to get married? What happens to your kids if they've been hanging their hearts on the possibility of a new dad or a new mom?

They get wishboned again, and they experience another person abandoning them. That takes a serious toll on children, especially on kids in the formative years between the ages of four and seven.

> You're looking for a spouse; they're looking for a *new parent.*

It is crucial that you *think carefully* before entering the dating, marriage, or remarriage arena. And if you decide to do so, you need to take precautions so your children do not get hurt.

Dating Dos and Don'ts

I'm often asked how old I think children of single parents should be before the parent dates. It's a great question, one that I'm happy to answer—provided you're ready for my answer.

But first I have a question for you: Do you want what's best for your family?

"Sure," you reply. "Of course I want what's best for my children."

Then here's my answer: Don't date until your children are grown up. Eighteen years old and out of the house is preferable. Even better would be twenty-one or twenty-two years old, out of college and on their own, living in their own apartment.

What? you might be thinking. You may be ready to give this book a toss across the room. But give me a chance to explain.

What I just said is controversial, I know, but you asked me what I think is best for your *family*—not necessarily what is most satisfying for you. See the difference? And that means I can only answer honestly: If you abstain from dating, you simplify life immensely for yourself and your children.

I'm not saying that dating can't be done *ever*. That you are doomed to life alone, without a spouse, until your death. I'm just saying that by waiting to date until your kids are out of the house, you make things as smooth as possible for your children, paving over as many potholes in the road of life for them as you can. And, frankly, because they live in a single-parent family, they've had more than their share of potholes and bumps anyway.

My answer is also realistic because, as a single parent, you only have twenty-four hours a day, unlike the forty-eight hours a day a dual-parent home has. You have a limited amount of time and energy. So if you spend a significant portion of your time and energy on dating (as dating requires), you'll only be taking time away from your children. And what matters most in the long run?

Your time with your kids!

If you want to raise healthy kids, waiting to date is the *best* thing you can do for them. Is it possible to date now and come out on the other end with healthy kids? Sure. I've heard numerous success stories.

> If you want to raise healthy kids, waiting to date is the *best* thing you can do for them.

But I've also had numerous people in my counseling office with failed relationships—men and women who have been betrayed once again. Children who once again feel abandoned because of a single parent's dating experience gone awry.

If you face facts, you'll see that dating makes family life more difficult. If you want to protect your kids emotionally, and if they are your first priority, the best choice you can make is to simplify an already complex family arrangement.

However, for some of you, you may already be involved in a relationship or on the fringes of it. It may not be easy to step out. If that is the case, and you do choose to date, there is a right way to go about it.

And by that I mean live the single life. In other words, do not move in with the person you're dating, for any reason. Save a sliver of your free time for yourself and maximize time with your children, even at the expense of your new relationship. The most important thing you can do for your children is to be emotionally present for them.

If you are going to date, here are some things you can do to make your new relationship much easier on the kids.

DATE IN CLOSE PROXIMITY FOR AT LEAST TWO YEARS.
I always tell anyone considering dating (whether single parents or otherwise) that they should date at least two years, preferably three, and within close proximity to one another. *Why so long, when we're "all grown up?"* you ask.

It's simple. Any "date" can hide an addiction—whether alcoholism, use of pornography, drugs, or atrocious spending habits—for a short time if you're not in the same location and going through the seasons of life together. When you're dating, your date will be on his best behavior. So make sure you see each other in various situations (particularly ones in which you can see how that person deals with stress). As nice as a two-hour dinner each week in a swanky restaurant may be, it's also necessary to see each other during rush-hour traffic, when you've got work deadlines and you've been up all night, or when you or the kids are sick.

> I'll put it bluntly. If you're going to marry, date *thoroughly!*

I'll put it bluntly. If you're going to marry, date *thoroughly!* I'm not talking about living together, which puts immense pressure on both you and your children. The question you're trying to figure out, without hurting your kids in the process, is: *Are we meant for each other?* Unfortunately, you aren't going to know some things about the person you're dating until you're actually married, which is why I advise single parents who are dating to consider a long engagement.

DON'T BRING YOUR DATE HOME UNTIL YOU'RE ENGAGED.
Four years after the death of her husband, Beth began dating Ben. They dated for nearly a year. During that time he spent a lot of time with her and her kids. They had picnics together, went to movies, even had wrestle fests on Beth's living room floor. Then Ben broke up with her. Her kids were "wishboned" by the experience.

Beth told herself she'd never do that again.

Then eighteen months later she met John, who had just moved to the area. Not only did he work at her company, but he started going to her church. He seemed like a nice guy, but he wasn't anything special, she told herself.

However, as Beth began to get to know John through her church's singles' group, she found herself beginning to like him. The two decided to go out on a first date. But Beth told John she would meet him at the restaurant, rather than him picking her up at her home. This time she chose not to bring John around her children until she knew what the status of their relationship would be. She wanted to be sure that her children weren't hurt again by her dating.

Two years later, Beth and John knew they were serious. When John asked her to marry him, she said yes, on one condition. That he had to go home, meet her kids, and spend a year letting her kids get to know him first before they got married and he moved into their home.

But isn't that a little crazy? you're wondering right now. *How on earth will I know if that guy or gal will like my kids? What if they're a horrible match? And I've already agreed to marry that person? This is all sounding just a little too out there for me.*

On the surface, it seems logical that you'd want your children to get to know your date. After all, you probably wouldn't be dating unless you were at least somewhat serious about the possibility of getting married and that person becoming your children's stepparent. And so you may be inclined to hang out together with your children to give them and your date a chance to get to know one another.

But if you want to make a successful transition from single-parent family to blended family, here's my advice: Don't bring your date home until after you've dated for at least two years in close proximity to one another and you're already engaged. Then I suggest going a step further: Wait another year beyond that before you get married.

The reason I suggest adding a year-long engagement is that troubles will almost certainly surface as your children begin their relationship with your husband- or wife-to-be (and his or her kids, if any). That's not bad, per se. In essence, you'll have a living laboratory as you allow your two families time to mesh during outings together, with the security that you and your fiancé are already committed to getting married. So you're not running your kids through the relational gamut for no reason.

Use that year to see how your kids do together at each other's school events and sports, knowing that it will take awhile for everyone to get along. Watching carefully what goes on should give you a picture of the challenge that lies before you in blending your families. You may find that your kids begin driving a wedge between you and your fiancé—and that's important to recognize and deal with during that one-year engagement. Then, assuming you do marry, I suggest you buy a home that neither one of you has lived in before. Not only will it help you psychologically make the transition from two households to one, new blended household—where no one has first dibs on the turf—it will give your children an equal, fresh start.

Don't rush ahead into marriage, if that's the direction you're heading; ease into it. If you rush, you risk wishboning your children.

DON'T BECOME SEXUALLY INTIMATE OR LIVE TOGETHER.

On this subject, I won't mince words. If you're going to date, keep your pants on.

In any dating relationship, as intimacy grows, the tendency is to move closer together intellectually, emotionally—and physically. You may intend to remain pure and chaste in your dating relationship, but here's a caution: If you and your date have experienced a sexual relationship in the past, it's going to be extremely difficult *not* to become sexually intimate. And sexual intimacy builds a bond that is only meant to be handled within the covenant of marriage.

> Don't let the "tingles" leave you tangled.

There's no question that you are going to have sexual desires. The question to answer before cold showers lose their effectiveness is, What are you going to do about them? Yes, there is a right way to date—don't let the "tingles" leave you tangled. Don't become physically intimate.

You men, in particular, who were accustomed to regular, marital sex may find it downright difficult to wait. So in trying to do the honorable thing by not sleeping together, do you simply hold her hand for three years? How do you draw the line? When you're talking about adults who have already experienced sex, you can wind up with big problems.

Is it impossible, then, for a single person to date well? No. Difficult? Yes.

If you have acted impulsively on your sexual desires in the past, take a moment to think back about those times. Have they gotten you where you want to be? Perhaps that's how you ended up marrying the creep who divorced you. Or maybe you wound up pregnant, and the guy who had promised you forever did the disappearing trick on you instead. Now you're raising a child by yourself.

Looking at your past will often help you secure a better future. So take time to assess where you may have gone wrong in your previous physical relationships.

Certainly you shouldn't live with the person you're dating, which creates a bond that should only be handled within marriage. It also creates incredible tensions, especially if *he* has kids as well. Move in together, and you may as well open the door of the house and throw in a grenade! Besides, the evidence against living together is well documented: "Three out of four children born to unmarried couples see them split up before age sixteen, according to the National Marriage Project, a research group based at Rutgers University." Also, "a cohabiting partner is three times as likely to suffer depression as a married person and twice as likely to exhibit aggressive behavior."[2]

> You may believe you're falling in love, but by falling into bed you're falling into need.

If you choose to date, don't become sexually intimate or live together before marriage. You may believe you're falling in love, but by falling into bed you're falling into need. You're succumbing to your perceived "need" for sex.

FOLLOW YOUR HEART . . . ON WHOM *NOT* TO MARRY.

When it comes to knowing who to marry, you may have heard the saying, "Follow your heart." While that probably isn't good advice for deciding who to marry, it can be great advice in deciding whom *not* to marry.

You see, our hearts can so easily be swept away by the hopes that accompany dating. You may feel the euphoria of infatuation all over again. But remember—the stakes are much higher this time. You probably wouldn't mind being swept off your feet, but if your heart does a backflip, be wary. You can't always trust your emotions when they are experiencing a conflict of interest.

On the other hand, if your intuition is telling you that something may *not* be right with your date, don't silence those voices—consider them. If you're a single mother, assessing your date's inner character may be easier than you think because women are generally more perceptive than men when it comes to sizing up a man's inner character.

But if you're twitterpated and need a little help, ask yourself these questions:

Is your date gentle?

Is your date the kind of person who treats you and your emotions with care?

Is your date warm and kind to others? Watch how he or she gets along with their own parents, especially the opposite-sex parent. Observe how he treats those in your church and his former spouse's family.

Does your date have a temper?

Does she respect men? Does he respect women?

If you schedule an evening together to watch a movie, but in the middle of it the kids have to be tucked in—again—does he storm out of your apartment? I ask because some people are looking for someone to take care of them rather than living up to the responsibility of being a parent. Does he or she see your kids as an obstacle to you? If so, then your kids will get left behind. And the combination of you and your date will be a lethal one all around.

> Some people are looking for someone to take care of them rather than living up to the responsibility of being a parent.

Can you trust your intuitions completely? No. But they're certainly worth listening to.

DON'T LOOK FOR A SUGAR DADDY OR A FILLY.

There's something romantic about a knight in shining armor: the chivalry, the honor of being pursued and having your heart won—not to mention the financial provision he can bring home to your roundtable. But too often that knight in shining armor turns out to be nothing more than an idiot in a tin can. All the monetary help isn't worth the trappings and the expectations that come with it.

Likewise, many single fathers look for a woman with more curves than the Formula One racetrack at Monaco, only to crash and burn. With a decision to hook up with what I call a filly, single fathers can quickly go from the proverbial frying pan into the fire.

The situation can get complicated quickly, because that single father, for example, may already be paying child support and seeing his own kids every other weekend. Now he has a "filly" girlfriend, who needs lots of attention because she's used to getting it, and she has two kids, who also need attention. And a mom and dad. And two brothers and a sister. Suddenly, that single father's life becomes so complicated trying to keep everyone happy that no one is happy. And his limited resources—time, energy, and money—are being stretched between two families.

> Too often that knight in shining armor turns out to be nothing more than an idiot in a tin can.

"But, Dr. Leman," you might ask, "doesn't it make more financial sense for my family for me to marry than to remain alone?"

Even though *income* levels are higher in stepfamilies, "evidence suggests that stepfamilies are no improvement over single-parent families."[3] There's a verse in Proverbs, that age-old book of wisdom in the Bible, that says, "Better to live alone in a tumbledown shack than share a mansion with a nagging spouse."[4] It really is better to have a harmonious household and little money than to live in financial comfort and risk the bumps of a tumultuous family. If you're looking for a spouse simply for financial stability, you're falling into need rather than falling in love. If you end up as the best coupon clipper this side of the Mississippi, and if your big treat is eating peanut butter and jelly sandwiches on paper plates while the kids happily play on the park swings, then so be it. At least you're providing emotional stability and a happy home for you and your kids.

Sell yourself out for a sugar daddy and the financial pressure may be off. Sell yourself out for a filly and you get someone who looks good, at least on the outside. But at what price for you and your children?

GIVE DULL MEN A SECOND GLANCE.

Remember Beth, who fell into one relationship only to be nuked by Ben and then was gun-shy when she met John? "I was always attracted to the lookers," Beth realized. "You know, the guys who make your head turn to follow them. My first husband was that kind of a guy. Ben was, too. John wasn't like that at all. In fact, I wouldn't normally have given him a second look. But seeing how steady and loving and kind he was to everyone slowly grew on me. Although he isn't the most physically attractive guy I've had in my life, he tops my list of what I wanted in a husband-for-a-lifetime kind of guy."

Your date probably isn't a leading actor in Hollywood, and he may not have the body of a stunt double. In fact, he may have had the same boring job for seventeen years. But don't be too quick to say good-bye to Mr. Dull, because he may be exactly the kind of guy you'd want around if you were to receive bad news on your mammogram.

Mr. Flashy is often a real loser, so don't get sucked in by his charms. On the other hand, give Mr. Dull a second glance—the guy who probably isn't the glamorous man you envisioned sweeping you off your feet and whisking you away to Bora Bora. If your date at first seems dull, don't dump him. Give him a second glance as well as a second chance.

If you are divorced, there's a reason why the relationship didn't work. Perhaps you were attracted to someone like your father, who in your case wasn't the best choice for you. Now you may be attracted to Mr. Flashy for all the same reasons that led to your divorce. Which makes Mr. Dull a much better alternative—and someone who may turn out to be your Mr. Right.

DATE SOMEONE WHO WILL EMOTIONALLY ADOPT YOUR CHILDREN.

It's common for parents of blended families to fight over "his children" and "her children," so Pastor Clyde Besson, who went through a divorce himself, recommends that if you're going to remarry, make sure you both "emotionally adopt" each other's children. "Never marry," Besson writes, "until you are able to release your children to the new mate as if they were his or her own (or in other words, until you have that kind of trust in that person), or until you are able to emotionally adopt that person's children."[5]

The same is true when it comes to discipline. "You might as well recognize that in the area of discipline," Besson writes, "you and your mate will disagree in some areas, no matter who you are. Children pick up on the differences, and they'll play one parent against the other. If it's 'your children' and 'my children,' they are more able to divide you. When it's 'our children,' it is much easier to work through any difficulties."[6]

While it does take a special kind of person to emotionally adopt your children, it can be done.

Beth and John are a wonderful example. John's the kind of guy who always wanted to be a dad. For the past four years, since he and Beth married, he's been thrilled to have that chance. The fact that he isn't starting from scratch with babies makes no difference to him. "The kids love him. They trust him, because he does what he says he'll do. And no matter what he's doing, if they want to talk with him or play with him, he stops and does it. He truly has become their father, in every way. In fact, since he's so patient with them—a lot more patient than I am—he's the one who now takes our daughter to her piano lessons. John and I are working hard to develop and keep that 'relationship of a lifetime' for our sake, and our kids' sake."

Wait to Date—or Proceed with Caution!

I'll say it again, flat out. If you can, wait to date until your children have grown and are out of the home. It will simplify the situation for you and your children and will help you focus on the big task you already have—watching out for your children's best interests.

If you are going to date, do so cautiously, because dating can be like plunging into that ocean filled with sharks.[7] If you've made mistakes before in relationships, you are more likely to do so again, so proceed with extreme caution. Get counsel from healthy friends, family members, a counselor, or a pastor.

Above all, don't rush into anything. If that guy or gal you're interested in truly is the right one for you, then he or she will stick around. If not, isn't it better that you know sooner rather than later?

For your sake . . . and your kids'.

❖ ❖ ❖

KEY Qs . . .

- What experiences have you had with dating? How have these experiences impacted your philosophy on dating now?

- What type of qualities would you look for in a marriage partner? Make a list, then evaluate the characteristics. Are they enduring qualities or surface things? Explain.

- What kind of person do you find yourself most attracted to—the flashy type or the dull type? Why?

CHAPTER 17

It's All about Time

No matter how much money everyone else has (or doesn't have), we all have the same amount of time.

Twenty-four hours a day, seven days a week, 365 days a year.

"No kidding," you say. "And that's what I can't deal with. I have the same amount of time as everyone else to get more done!"

But that's precisely the problem! Too many single parents take on the same load as everyone else rather than adjusting their lives to the time that they have. Consequently, they end up twice as loaded down as dual-parent families (who, incidentally, are overloaded, too, and need the same advice I'll be giving you).

"You don't have to tell me that," you say. "I'm already there. Overwhelmed. There's just too much to do."

"Ain't that just the truth?" I say right back. But the key is identifying the things you *must* do, the things you'd like to do, and the things you simply don't need to do.

The tricky part sometimes is identifying which things are which. So do me a favor. Find some paper and a pencil or pen, and draw a large circle. The circle represents your family's activities. Draw a small circle in the center. That's you, the hub of all the activity. Draw and label a spoke (an activity) from the hub (you) out to the edge of the large circle for each activity you're involved in. Go ahead . . .

> There's just too much to do.

Done?

Now take a good look.

Feel a little tired just looking at it?

Then I've accomplished my purpose. Right in front of your eyes is an excellent visual representation of everything you're attempting to do—and a good answer for why you feel the pressure you do on a daily basis.

All activities in that busy circle are, after all, connected to one hub—you. It's all up to you, whether it's driving your daughter to her friend Sarah's house one evening or deciding whether your son can play Little League baseball this season or whether his younger brother can join Cub Scouts. But there are only so many avenues that can run through the single-parent intersection before you end up with a snarled traffic jam of activity—not to mention an exhausted single parent.

Is that how you're feeling right now?

If so, I've got a guaranteed-to-work solution for you.

A Little Vitamin N Goes a Long Way!

The vitamin N I'm talking about is of the *N-O* variety.

Learn to say no. Limit the number of activities that your family is involved in. While I also urge dual-parent families to escape the activity trap, I'm telling you, as a single parent, that you have to avoid it at all costs! You may have to cut some things out of your life, and your kids may not have all the same freedoms as other kids. (But how much "freedom" is it really when your children are going from activity to activity, and *you* are continually running from place to place?)

I always recommend to parents that they allow their kids only one activity (other than school, of course!) per term—and that's a maximum. Depending on your schedule and the number of kids you have, you may want to limit even further the activities your kids are involved in.

> You shouldn't try to be what you're not.

In the book *Putting Family First: Successful Strategies for Claiming Family Life in a Hurry-up World*, authors William Doherty and Barbara Carlson relate the story of a single parent named Dawn, who said, "Simply, our finances and circumstances did not allow for many outside activities, so my sons were limited in their participation in costly sports programs and extracurricular events. We took advantage of many in-school and after-school enrichment programs as they were usually subsidized, time limited, and fostered the growth of self-esteem."

"Dawn's story," write Doherty and Carlson, "speaks to an ironic advantage that single parents have: they cannot compete with two parents in today's rat race of childhood, so they are free not to try."[1]

"Free not to try"! Did you hear that?

I tell that story to illustrate the point that you shouldn't try to be what you're not. If you try to live your life and arrange your schedule like a dual-parent family does, you're likely to end up exhausted and broke. So instead of comparing yourself to your neighbor or fearing that your child will be labeled as "different" because she can't have the same advantages as other kids, know your limits. Don't push yourself! Say no to activities that stretch you and your family thin.

Live *your* life instead of trying to live someone else's.

Say Yes to Family!

Far more important than the number of activities your children are involved in is making the most of the time you have at home as a family.

When it comes down to it, your presence with your children is far more important (even when they complain sometimes) than your presents. And the time spent around your dinner table is far more important than whether or not they played on a soccer team or attended a ballet class.

> Why not pick an activity you can do together as a family?

The point is that what you do *together* is the key. So if your schedule is stretched far enough with doing only *one* extra activity beyond the normal school day, why not pick an activity you can do together as a family?

Even better, use that activity to *serve someone else.*

How can I think about doing that? you might be wondering, when it's tough enough to get my own stuff done?

Doing for others helps to cement with your kids the concept that no matter how strapped your family might be for money or time, you always have something worthwhile to offer to others. And you can do it *together,* as a family. It's not simply one more activity to keep you busy.

It's an activity that bonds you together as a family—something your kids can talk about with each other. It's part of what makes you a family—something your kids can feel ownership in.

So why not bring a few groceries to a hurting family? serve together in a soup kitchen? become a "Saturday morning family" for an inner-city child? offer to babysit for a family with younger children for a night? paint a mural in the church's playroom? These are just a few of the things single parents I know have done with their children to serve others. Sometimes it's been a one-time event; other times it has become a continuing ministry for the entire family.

Working together on behalf of others will draw you and your children together like nothing else—and it will help to strengthen that bond of a lifetime.

Yes, it takes time to think of serving others. But your kids are watching what you do with your time. That, more than anything else, will reveal to your kids your priorities and your life philosophy. And what they see modeled, they will emulate now . . . and down the road.

Choose a Chair!

"When I was a boy," the famous tenor Luciano Pavarotti once said, "my father, a baker, introduced me to the wonders of song. He urged me to work very hard to develop my voice. Arrigo Pola, a professional tenor in my hometown of Modena, Italy, took me as a pupil. I also enrolled in a teachers college. On graduating, I asked my father, 'Shall I be a teacher or a singer?'

> "If you try to sit on two chairs, you will fall between them."
> —Luciano Pavarotti's father

"'Luciano,' my father replied, 'if you try to sit on two chairs, you will fall between them. For life, you must choose one chair.'

"I chose one. It took seven years of study and frustration before I made my first professional appearance. It took another seven to reach the Metropolitan Opera. And now I think whether it's laying bricks, writing a book—whatever we choose—we should give ourselves to it. Commitment, that's the key. Choose one chair."[2]

As long as your children are in your home, you have one chair: to love your children and parent them well. Choosing that one chair beats playing musical chairs with all that life has to offer. Otherwise you'll be endlessly running around in circles, fighting with everybody else for seats, just like children do in their game.

What do kids really need? Do they really need you to do it all? To run wildly from place to place, trying to please all the powers that be? Trying to prove that you're a "good mom" or a "good dad"? Trying to be both Mom and Dad to your child?

Children, at heart, are simple, and they have simple needs.

LOVE
They hunger for your love, your time and attention. You could work hard to give them an expensive toy they'll play with for a few minutes, or you could take the hours you would have worked to pay for that toy and instead play with your kids at a nearby park. Your presence, not your presents, is what matters most.

DISCIPLINE
They also need your discipline, for without boundaries there is no safety. A good parent isn't a "good buddy." He or she is, first and foremost, a *parent*.

POSITIVE REINFORCEMENT
Children need to not only hear that you love them but also see by your actions that they are valued (whether they were planned or not) and that they have a purpose. They need to know that you are committed to working together as a family. They need to be aware of, and part of the goal of, developing a warm, safe, nurturing home environment and developing into individuals who respect, love, and trust each other.

> A good parent isn't a "good buddy."

You may have two years, fourteen years, or eighteen years to reach your goal of raising your child. (It took Luciano Pavarotti fourteen years to reach his goal.) But what you may lack in resources—time and money—you *can* make up through your loving devotion. In fact, you can even raise healthier kids than those in some dual-parent families! Why? Because your keen awareness of your need to focus your single energies will help you streamline your life and stick to the basics.

So don't let anybody convince you that you should be playing musical chairs. Choose your chair, and stick to it. With no guilt and no second-guessing yourself.

Taking the Long View

Paris's Cathedral of Notre Dame wasn't built in a day. It wasn't built in a year, or ten, or even a hundred. Notre Dame as we know it today was begun in 1163 and wasn't finished until around 1345, nearly two centuries later![3]

Beautiful cathedrals aren't thrown together. They are built one brick at a time with patient care, using the best materials. To withstand the test of time, a cathedral takes

- thoughtful direction and intentional planning;
- years of thankless, dirty work; and
- perseverance when the process seems to drag endlessly on.

Yet there are those glorious moments when the sun shines through partially finished stained glass windows, reminding you what all the pieces and all the work has been about. You glimpse, for a minute, the end goal again, and it inspires you to keep going.

Sounds a lot like parenting, doesn't it?

Raising healthy children, like building a cathedral, takes time and attention. Lots of it.

I sometimes joke that if your child is about to enter kindergarten, you only have thirteen years to make a difference in his or her life. I say "*only* thirteen years" tongue in cheek, because as fast as that time will seem to fly by, that really is a long time when you think about the influence you can have on your child.

And that's the view that I'm asking you to take—the long-term view for raising your children. Because that's the key to making single parenting work.

Yes, you will be busy. Yes, you may have little money. At times when you're up on that cathedral scaffolding, it will be easy to lose sight of the finished product (your child) that you're working toward. Sometimes the process will seem anything but beautiful, with cement and mortar slung all over. But over time, as you get your hands dirty laying one brick at a time, your consistency and perseverance *will* make a difference.

As you keep in mind the blueprint for your child—your overall plans for her growth and development—you will dramatically increase your chances for a solid and beautiful cathedral that others will gaze at in beauty and wonder.

There aren't many greater creations than our own children, wouldn't you agree? Yet some of us throw them together as if they were prefabricated. If you're going to build a cathedral, however, your stonework and masonry ought to be made from the highest quality materials and workmanship. So why wouldn't you use the same types of materials when you build your children?

If you do, your children will be rock solid. Their foundations will be strong. Nothing will be able to take away from their healthy self-image and their unshakable value system.

That's the beauty of the long-term view.

❖ ❖ ❖

KEY Qs . . .

- Look back at the picture of the circle, hub, and spokes you drew. (If you didn't do it yet, why not do it now? Refer back to p. 257.) If you could only choose *one* activity for each child, which spokes would have to go? Why?

- If you could choose only *one* activity for your family to do as a group, what would that be? Or, if you're already doing one family activity, why did you choose that activity?

- As you look at the long-term view, is there anything you would change about how you're "doing life" with your children? If so, what? And why?

CHAPTER 18

Your Legacy

It all comes down to one simple question: If you could fast-forward in time, what would you want your children to say is *your* legacy to them?

- That you worked hard to provide for your family?
- That you were there for them—extending them time, grace, love, and consistency?
- That you made the best of a difficult situation?
- That you always had their best interests in mind?
- That you always believed the best of them?
- That because of you, your children have fulfilled their dreams?

Sonya Carson knew. She had it rough as as a single parent. She could easily have given up. Instead she stuck to her plans. She wanted her boys to make something of themselves. She wanted to leave the world a better place because she had lived. And look at the impact she and her son, Dr. Ben S. Carson, have had on innumerable lives!

If Sonya—who had everything working against her—can make single parenting work and raise healthy children, you can, too.

By taking life one step at a time, you can meet life's daily challenges. You can't do it all. Who can? But you can do what matters most. You may not make *Time* magazine's Person of the Year, but by focusing on your children, you can top their list of Most Influential Person of their lives. And isn't that what matters in the long run?

You are the one who will leave an indelible imprint on your child. What will your legacy be?

❖ ❖ ❖

KEY Qs . . .

- If someone asked your children, "What's the most important thing to your dad/mom?" what do you think they would say? (Even better, why not ask your children—in a nonthreatening manner, of course!)

- Compare what your child would say about you with who you want to be as a parent. What differences do you see? What similarities?

- What matters most to you in the long run? What do you want your legacy to be?

Notes

Introduction: You *Can* Do It!

1. Jason Fields, "Current Population Reports," *America's Families and Living Arrangements: 2003*, issued November 2004, http://www.census.gov/prod/2004pubs/p20-553. No longer available.
2. U.S. Bureau of the Census, *Supplement to the Current Population Survey* (March 1998).
3. National Center for Health Statistics (1997).
4. U.S. Bureau of the Census, *Household and Family Characteristics* (March 1998).
5. U.S. Bureau of the Census, *Children with Single Parents—How They Fare* (September 1997).

Chapter 1: You Can't Do It All, but You Can Do What Matters Most

1. "Stressed Out?" an adaptation of the Holmes and Rahe's Life Events Scale for measuring stress levels, Rutgers, http://health.rutgers.edu/stress/stressed_out.asp (accessed January 31, 2005).
2. Patrick Kavanaugh, "About *The Messiah*," from *Spiritual Lives of the Great Composers*, Handel's *Messiah*, http://www.messiahcd.com/Information/about_The_Messiah/about_the_messiah.html (accessed January 27, 2005).
3. Anne Lamott, *Bird by Bird* (New York: Pantheon Books, 1994), 18–19.
4. "Famous Quotes By: Eisenhower, Dwight D.," Born to Motivate, http://www.borntomotivate.com/FamousQuote_DwightDEisenhower.html. No longer available.

Chapter 2: You're More than a *Survivor*

1. Daniel Defoe, *Robinson Crusoe* (New York: Aladdin Paperbacks, 2001), 101.
2. "From Slow Learner to Brilliant Brain Surgeon," American Dreams, http://www.usdreams.com/Carson.html (accessed January 31, 2005).
3. Ben Carson with Cecil Murphey, *Gifted Hands* (Grand Rapids: Zondervan, 1990), 37.
4. Daniel Defoe, *Robinson Crusoe*, 102.
5. Philippians 4:11-12
6. 2 Corinthians 11:24-27
7. Philippians 4:13
8. "From Slow Learner to Brilliant Brain Surgeon."
9. Carson and Murphey, *Gifted Hands*, 38.
10. Ibid., 143.

Chapter 4: Got Guilt?

1. Peg Tyre, Julie Scelfo, and Barbara Kantrowitz, "The Power of No," *Newsweek*, September 13, 2004, 46, 50.
2. The Quotemeister, "Q and A," The American Chesterton Society, http://www.chesterton.org/qmeister2/wrongtoday.htm (accessed January 31, 2005).
3. Ephesians 4:26
4. Romans 7:24
5. See 1 Samuel 13:14 and Acts 13:22.
6. Glenn Van Ekeren, *The Speaker's Sourcebook: Quotes, Stories and Anecdotes for Every Occasion* (Englewood Cliffs, N.J.: Prentice Hall, 1988), 142–43.
7. Edmund Fuller, ed., *Thesaurus of Anecdotes* (New York: Crown, 1942), 196.

Chapter 5: Three Mistakes You Don't Want to Make

1. Dale Ahlquist, "Who Is This Guy and Why Haven't I Heard of Him?" The American Chesterton Society, http://www.chesterton.org/discover/who.html (accessed January 31, 2005).
2. Dale Ahlquist, "Lecture IX: Charles Dickens," The American Chesterton Society, http://www.chesterton.org/discover/lectures/9charlesdickens.html (accessed January 31, 2005).

Chapter 7: Where's Your Support?

1. Matthew 6:28-31, "The Message"

Chapter 8: Pressed for Time and Money?

1. "Aha! Moment: Harry Connick Jr.," *O: The Oprah Magazine*, Oprah.com, http://www.oprah.com/rys/omag/rys_omag_200401_aha.jhtml (accessed January 15, 2005).
2. Go to www.gcu.edu for more information.
3. Visit the MOPS Web site at http://www.mops.org.

Chapter 9: The Opposite-Sex Fix

1. Marilyn Gardner, "Life as a Single Dad: Growing Numbers of Men Are Rearing Their Children Alone," *The Christian Science Monitor*, July 9, 2003.
2. "Fatherhood in facts and figures," *The Christian Science Monitor*, June 11, 2003.

Chapter 10: The ABCs, Inside Out

1. Clyde Colvin Besson, *Picking Up the Pieces* (New York: Ballantine Books, 1982), 134.

Chapter 11: It's the Relationship, Not the Rules

1. Anecdotage.com, http://www.anecdotage.com/index.php?aid=279 (accessed January 31, 2005).
2. Ephesians 4:26

Chapter 12: Love . . . and Limits

1. Clifton Fadiman, ed., *The Little, Brown Book of Anecdotes* (Boston: Little, Brown, 1985), 135.
2. Ephesians 6:1-2
3. Proverbs 3:12
4. Proverbs 22:6, NASB

Chapter 13: "Will You Stop loving Me, Too?"

1. Glenn Van Ekeren, *The Speaker's Sourcebook: Quotes, Stories and Anecdotes for Every Occasion*, 8–9.
2. Matthew 18:21-22, NASB

Chapter 16: Ready . . . or Not?

1. Shark Watch South Africa, http://www.dive.co.za/index.html (accessed January 31, 2005).
2. "Trend to Live Together, Not Marry, Put Kids at Risk," *USA Today*, October 20, 2003.
3. David Popenoe and Barbara DaFoe Whitehead, information brief from *The National Marriage Project's Ten Things to Know Series: The Top Ten Myths of Divorce*, April 2001, http://marraige.rutgers.edu.
4. Proverbs 21:9, "The Message"
5. Clyde Colvin Besson, *Picking Up the Pieces* (New York: Ballantine Books, 1982), 152.
6. Ibid., 153.
7. If you *are* going to date, I suggest you visit my Web site, www.matchwise.com, which will help link you up with someone you might be compatible with. Another dating Web site I recommend is www.eHarmony.com.

Chapter 17: It's All about Time

1. Dr. William J. Doherty and Barbara Z. Carlson, *Putting Family First: Successful Strategies for Reclaiming Family Life in a Hurry-Up World* (New York: Henry Holt, 2002), 117–18.
2. SermonIllustrations.com, http://www.sermonillustrations.com/a-z/c/commitment.htm (accessed January 24, 2005).
3. Ian C. Mills, ed., "Notre Dame Cathedral, Paris," Discover France, http://www.discoverfrance.net/France/Cathedrals/Paris/Notre-Dame.shtml (accessed January 31, 2005).

About Dr. Kevin Leman
Practical Wisdom with a Smile

An internationally known psychologist, founder of matchwise.com, radio and television personality, and speaker, Dr. Kevin Leman has taught and entertained audiences worldwide with his wit and common-sense psychology.

The best-selling and award-winning author has made house calls for numerous radio and television programs, including *The View* with Barbara Walters, *Today*, *Oprah*, CBS's *The Early Show*, *Live with Regis Philbin*, and *LIFE Today* with James Robison. Dr. Leman is a frequent contributor to CNN's *American Morning* and has served as a contributing family psychologist to *Good Morning America*.

Dr. Leman is also the founder and president of Couples of Promise, an organization designed and committed to helping couples remain happily married.

Dr. Leman's professional affiliations include the American Psychological Association, American Federation of Radio and Television Artists, National Register of Health Services Providers in Psychology, and the North American Society of Adlerian Psychology.

Dr. Leman attended North Park College. He received his bachelor's degree in psychology from the University of Arizona, where he later earned his master's and doctorate degrees. Originally from Williamsville, New York, he and his wife, Sande, live in Tucson. They have five children.

For information regarding speaking availability, business consultations, or seminars, please contact:

Dr. Kevin Leman
P.O. Box 35370
Tucson, Arizona 85740
Phone: (520) 797-3830
Fax: (520) 797-3809

Web sites:
www.drleman.com
www.matchwise.com

Resources by Dr. Kevin Leman

BOOK

The Birth Order Book

Sheet Music: Uncovering the Secrets of Sexual Intimacy in Marriage

Running the Rapids: Guiding Teenagers through the Turbulent Waters of
Adolescence

Making Children Mind without Losing Yours

Home Court Advantage

Becoming the Parent God Wants You to Be

Becoming a Couple of Promise

A Chicken's Guide to Talking Turkey with Your Kids about Sex *(and Kathy
Flores Bell)*

First-Time Mom: Getting Off on the Right Foot (from Birth to First Grade)

Keeping Your Family Strong in a World Gone Wrong

Living in a Stepfamily without Getting Stepped On

My Firstborn, There's No One Like You

My Middle Child, There's No One Like You

My Youngest, There's No One Like You

My Only Child, There's No One Like You

My Adopted Child, There's No One Like You

My Grandchild, There's No One Like You

The Perfect Match

Be Your Own Shrink: 4 Ways to a Better You

Say Good-bye to Stress

Sex Begins in the Kitchen: Creating Intimacy to Make Your Marriage Sizzle

Single Parenting That Works: Six keys to raising happy, healthy children
in a single-parent home

The Way of the Shepherd *(and William Pentak)*
What a Difference a Daddy Makes
When Your Best Isn't Good Enough
Pleasers: Why Women Don't Have to Make Everyone Happy to Be Happy

DVD/VIDEO SERIES
Bringing Peace and Harmony to the Blended Family
Making Children Mind without Losing Yours (Christian—parenting edition)
Making Children Mind without Losing Yours (Mainstream—public-school teacher edition)
Making the Most of Marriage
Running the Rapids: Guiding Teenagers through the Turbulent Waters of Adolescence
Single Parenting That Works: Six keys to raising happy, healthy children in a single-parent home

For further information regarding Dr. Leman Resources, call
(800) 770-3830.